JUST
ASK
JERRY

Good Answers to
Tough Canadian
Gardening Questions

Jerry Filipski
Foreword by David Tarrant

LONE
PINE

Lone Pine Publishing

Lone Pine Publishing
10145–81 Avenue
Edmonton, AB T6E 1W9
Canada
Website: www.lonepinepublishing.com

Library and Archives Canada Cataloguing in Publication

Filipski, Gerald, 1951-
    Just ask Jerry : good answers to tough Canadian
gardening questions / Gerald Filipski.

ISBN 978-1-55105-846-7

    1. Gardening--Canada. I. Title.

SB453.3.C2F53 2011   635.0971   C2010-906794-0

Editorial Director: Nancy Foulds
Project Editor: Kathy van Denderen
Editorial Assistance: Jordan Allan, Kelsey Everton
Production Manager: Gene Longson
Layout and Production: Kamila Kwiatkowska
Cover Design: Gerry Dotto
Photos: Marilynn McAra

We acknowledge the financial support of the Government of Canada through the Canada Book Fund (CBF) for our publishing activities.

PC: 1

Contents

Dedication

This book is dedicated to my wife Julie for always being there for me, to my daughter Kathy for the many story ideas and my son Mike for being a best friend. It is also dedicated to my many faithful readers and gardening friends.

Foreword

During my years of hosting *Canadian Gardener* on CBC TV, I was so fortunate to visit home gardens in all provinces of the country plus two territories. It was a great eye-opener that proved that gardeners find a way to garden no matter where they live, finding ways to beat difficult climates and short growing seasons and resulting in some amazingly beautiful gardens.

Over the years I visited Edmonton quite a bit and came to know quite a few of the local gardening personalities, including Jerry Filipski, so it gives me great pleasure to write this short foreword to his new book. What a brilliant idea to write a book based on the many gardening questions and answers he has fielded over his long career writing for the *Edmonton Journal*.

I always thought the best gardening book you could have would be notes you kept about the actual gardening you did in your own garden. A great idea, but few of us actually do it! So for all you gardeners who didn't or don't keep notes, here is a wonderful book full of useful information, based on the knowledge of someone who has actually done and experienced what he is writing about.

Just Ask Jerry is easy to read and the information down to earth. A must-have for your gardening library and a great resource for novice and expert gardeners alike.

David Tarrant

Introduction

The popularity of gardening continues to grow at an astonishing rate. Many people are rediscovering gardening as a means of returning to the basics of life. These basics include growing your own food in an organic and eco-friendly way. The satisfaction of growing your own produce comes from two major factors. First, you know that what you grow contains only what you have put into it. There are no concerns about hidden pesticides, and the health benefits of growing your own produce are self-evident. Second, people are finding that gardening offers relaxation and an instant stress relief; it soothes the mind and spirit and provides a sense of accomplishment. Whether you garden for the benefit of healthy, homegrown fruits and vegetables or for the beauty you can create in a landscape, gardening is a retreat from the high-paced world we live in. Gardening offers a means of recharging and rejuvenating the body, mind and spirit.

Gardening's growing popularity has led to an increase in the need for knowledge in dealing with the myriad problems gardeners face. In the 17 years I have been writing the question-and-answer gardening column for the *Edmonton Journal*,

I have seen the number of questions increase nearly exponentially. This book comes about as a result of my readers and the gardeners I have met during my many talks and public appearances asking for a book that would answer those questions in an easy-to-read reference format. My aim is to equip gardeners of all ages and proficiency levels with the knowledge and inspiration to meet the challenges of gardening. The answers and comments in this book apply to most regions of Canada, with the possible exemption of those living in the very southern and coastal parts of BC and southern Ontario. Those gardeners in higher hardiness zones might also want to consult with their local greenhouses on issues they're not sure of. I hope this book will help those who have never gardened before and that veteran gardeners will still find the hints and tips helpful.

The format of this book is simple. It offers real questions from real people, and the answers are presented in a down-to-earth manner. For all of those who have asked for this book, I thank you, and, as I end so many of my answers, I hope this helps.

Getting Started

Tools and Equipment

Using the right tool for the right job is something my father taught me when I was a youngster. Gardening tools are an investment that, if cared for properly, can last a lifetime. I still use my grandfather's rake and shovel, and they are among the most prized tools in my collection.

Many gardeners collect gardening tools and gadgets with a passion that would make diehard philatelists and numismatists blush. Garden tool-manufacturers and retailers know this dedication to collecting and take full advantage of this addiction. Next time you are in a garden centre, take a look at the many tool displays and how they are laid out so as to catch the eye. A new weeder that is meant to eliminate back strain and almost does the job itself, a new watering wand that precisely measures the volume of water hitting your plants or a rake that folds in the middle to pick up leaves are just a few of the items to hit the market every year. They are meant to entice you into being the first one on the block to have the new toy.

But buying gardening tools does not have to be a daunting task nor does it have to be a budget breaker. The reality is that you need very few items in your garden tool array to get the job done right. These are the basics.

You'll need a **spade** for digging planting holes, turning the soil over in fall and adding compost or organic matter to beds. This tool is probably the most versatile tool in the repertoire. The spade should have a good quality handle. Opting for the cheaper alternative often results in broken handles and frayed tempers. The new generation spades with fibreglass handles are a great choice because they can take a lot of abuse and strain. I recall digging out many a stump and breaking more spade handles than I really needed to had I chosen a better quality spade.

Some newer spades even have widened lips at the back of the shovel, making it easier to plant your foot to push the spade into the ground. Some gardeners prefer a short handle with a "D" grip at the top. Others, like myself, prefer a long handle. I find that the longer handle goes a long way in avoiding back strain. I also like the added leverage a long handle offers.

Spades are now made from carbon or stainless steel. Stainless steel spades cost more, but the blade will stay smoother longer than the carbon variety. A thin layer of rust will usually form on a carbon steel spade if left unused for a time, and dirt tends to stick more to these types of spades. Stainless steel spades shed soil more readily, but they do tend to wear down a little more quickly. To me, the added cost for stainless steel is simply not worth it. A little cleaning and a light application of lightweight oil to the carbon steel spade will have it lasting a long time.

Some people may ask why I recommend a spade rather than a shovel. When I sharpen my spade, I like that I can easily dig into even the hardest of soils. I find that shovels with a rounded or flat blade require more effort to cut through the soil.

Both a **garden rake** and a **leaf rake** are necessary tools to have. The garden rake is useful for levelling soils or preparing seedbeds such as when seeding a new lawn or raking in the vegetable garden. I like to use both sides of my garden rake. The tines can gather up lumps and stones, clearing the planting area of rocks or large pieces of debris that might impede the growth of tiny seedlings. Once I have cleared the planting area, I turn the rake over and use the flat side of the rake to level the bed. This method removes any deep grooves and holes in the soil. The butt of the handle of the rake can also be used to create planting rows. I set a string attached to two sticks into the soil to mark the planting row. I then draw the handle of the rake lightly along the string to create a planting pocket in the soil.

There is a wide variety of choices when it comes to leaf rakes. The tines can be made of bamboo, plastic or metal. Leaf rakes can also be spring-tined, which is useful for removing thatch or dried grass from lawns as well as for raking leaves. Over the years, I have found my preference is for the plastic type. I find they have just the right amount of spring in the tines when raking leaves or other debris. Most plastic leaf rakes have a wide working area with many tines, and the wider profile does cut down on the amount of time spent raking. A profile that is too wide, however, adds drag to the effort and makes it harder to rake larger volumes of leaves.

New versions of leaf rakes now on the market fold in half, allowing you to "grab" the leaves and place them into a bag. I find that the old method of bending down and grabbing the leaves with your hands still works the best. I have also tried several of the ergonomic rakes that are purported to ease back strain. I found them awkward to use, and while my back might have hurt less, other parts of my body ached from the awkward angles I had to use to do the raking.

A good quality **hoe** is a necessity on any gardener's tool list. Hoes have many uses in the garden. They work well in flowerbeds and vegetable gardens at keeping weeds at bay between the rows, and they are a must for cultivating the soil. Cultivation is important in breaking up soil compaction and allowing air and water to penetrate. In many gardens, especially small ones, the rows can be tight and awkward to get between. A long-handled hoe gets into these spots and eliminates the weeds with little effort.

Hoes come in a wide variety of shapes and sizes. Choosing a hoe is very much about personal preference and what you want to use the tool for. If you prefer to stand while weeding, or if the spaces between the rows are too small to walk between, then a long-handled hoe is the way to go. If you prefer to kneel while weeding, a short-handled type will serve you best.

Over the years, the working end of a hoe has seen an evolution from the standard D-shape hoe. Some of the ones on the market today include triangular, open loop, heart-shaped, offset and even circle faces, among others. The hoe has more variations than most other garden tools, and this variation is what makes choosing a hoe more difficult. Which is best? Which is most versatile? Which one will I like to use? There is no easy answer. I can only relay what I like.

I have two favourites. One is a product called the Winged Weeder. This triangular-shaped hoe slides through the soil with little effort. It does not create large mounds of soil as it moves and yet is effective at both cultivating and aerating the soil. The shape of the hoe keeps it from penetrating the soil too deeply and harming plant roots but still cuts off the weeds as it moves along. I have both the long-handled and short-handled versions. My second favourite is an old tool I inherited from my grandfather. It is technically called a cultivator but also acts as a hoe. The design has three curved tines that terminate in a spade-like end that can be sharpened. In many ways it looks like the farm implement cultivator that is pulled behind a tractor. This tool is excellent for breaking up compacted soil and cultivating the soil in between garden rows.

When choosing a hoe, consider what it will be used for, and remember the old adage, "if it sounds too good to be true, it probably is." Good old-fashioned "elbow grease" will still be needed to get the job done no matter what the claims of the manufacturer.

My **hand trowel** is likely my most-used garden tool. The hand trowel, or hand shovel as it is sometimes known, is a multifunction tool that is an absolute must in the gardener's toolkit. I use mine for:

- digging holes for planting bedding plants or separating their roots

- measuring the space between plants when planting to ensure even spacing between plants— I simply lay the trowel on the ground and measure from tip to handle as I go along or use the distance from the tip of the blade to the top of the blade

- moving potting soil from the bag into containers

- moving or splitting perennials

- removing large weeds

- digging planting holes for bulbs

- mixing compost, manure or fertilizers into potting mixes

Look for a hand trowel that has a good feel in your hand. If it feels too large or too small, your hand may tire from holding it for long periods. I prefer a hand trowel with a rubber grip that offers some cushioning and also makes it easier to hang onto in wet conditions. I also prefer the blade to be unpainted. The paint tends to flake off and the resulting exposed metal rusts quickly. Stainless steel is a good choice, though a bit pricier. One of my favourites is a cast aluminum blade that is very easy to sharpen. I like to keep the blade on my hand trowels very sharp because it readily cuts through harder soils.

Pruners or secateurs are another must-have gardening tool. There is debate among the gardening fraternity as to what type of pruner is best. The two types are anvil and bypass. The anvil pruner has a blade that hits on an "anvil," which is usually a flat piece of metal with a rubber cushion on top. The bypass pruner works more like a pair of scissors, with the two blades sliding over each other. I have both types, and I use them for different purposes. I use the anvil type for pruning heavier branches and stems; it doesn't crush the stems as easily as the bypass type can. However, the bypass type is best for cutting thin branches and for cutting flowers because it makes a clean cut on thinner stems.

Another favourite of mine is the ratcheting type of pruner. This pruner uses a levered, ratchet action, making cuts in increments. With this action it is easy to cut through branches up to 2 cm thick. For thicker branches, a pair of lopping type pruners is a must. Loppers can handle branches up to 5 cm thick depending on the hardness of the wood and size of the lopper. Again, the loppers come in either bypass or anvil, and I truly prefer the anvil type because the bypass type tends to separate and bind when cutting thicker branches.

As with any tool, you get what you pay for. Cheaper pruners are certainly available, but they will often rust quickly, will not maintain a sharp edge and can break. Choose a pruner that feels good in your hand. Remember that pruning is a repetitive action

and can tire out the hand quickly. A pruner that fits well in your hand reduces strain.

Another pruner/lopper tool that I do not use frequently but has saved me a lot of money is an extension pruner. This tool is basically a pruner mounted on a pole that can extend 4.5 m in length. I prune my taller trees with this tool, and the cost-saving comes from not having to pay an arborist or tree service to do the job. Many extension pruners also have a pruning saw attached to the top. This saw allows you to cut through the thicker branches that the pruner cannot. While this tool is not a must-have, it is certainly cost-efficient if you have or plan to have trees in your yard that will need to be pruned.

All of these pruning tools, unlike some other gardening tools, should not be used for purposes other than for what they are intended, namely, pruning stems and branches or cutting flowers, as the blades can easily lose their sharp edge. Keeping them sharp is vital: dull pruners can crush the branches or stems being cut. This damage remains on the tree and can be an entry point for disease. Sharp pruners reduce hand strain and get the job done quicker.

A good **pruning saw** is an excellent tool to have on hand. It cuts thick branches and stems that the pruners cannot, and it gets into tight spots that loppers cannot. As with the extension pruners, a pruning saw is not something that you will use on a daily basis or even monthly, but in any garden that has shrubs and trees, pruning is an essential part of maintenance. Among the variety of pruning saws on the market, some fold up like a pocketknife, others are retractable or still others simply have a curved blade. As with any garden tool, look for one that feels good in your hand. I prefer a saw that cuts on the pulling stroke. In tight spaces, I do the best cuts with a saw that cuts as I pull it toward me. My pruning saw has a curved blade, and I am always amazed at how the curve and the cut on the down stroke allows the saw to quickly cut through thick branches. This tool is not easily sharpened by yourself. When dull, take the saw to a professional sharpener.

Another tool that you may not use on a daily or even monthly basis, but that can prove to be invaluable, is a **garden cart** or **wheelbarrow**. During spring, I use my wheelbarrow daily to move bags of potting soil, bedding plants for planting or new shrubs and trees. I also use it to move large boulders, loads of soil, tree stumps, mulch and compost, heavy containers with and without plants, gravel, logs, sod, harvested vegetables, pruned limbs and branches, leaves, material for the compost

pile, concrete, sand, bricks, pavers and even my kids. Seriously though, a wheelbarrow or garden cart can be a lifesaver in the right job, and it can be used for so many purposes. Storing these carts can be a challenge for those who are space restricted, but if you can find a way to keep one, you will never regret it.

Wheelbarrows have come a long way from the original heavy metal tubs mounted on a wood frame with a metal wheel. Today, pneumatic tires are the standard, and the metal tubs are being replaced with heavy-duty plastic ones. The plastic tubs are much lighter and every bit as durable as the metal ones. The heavy wooden frames have been replaced by tubular metal ones that are also very lightweight. If you don't have room to store a full-sized wheelbarrow, many small plastic garden carts are on the market now. These carts are ideal for small jobs or small yards. They are durable, and although their hauling capacity is less than a heavy-duty wheelbarrow, they can do most jobs.

A tool that you will use almost on a daily basis is a **garden hose**. Taking the time to choose a good quality garden hose can go a long way toward avoiding years of frustration from kinks, lack of flexibility, leaks and other problems. Warranties can run from a year to a lifetime, and in this case, you get what you pay for. The hose is one garden accessory where paying extra at the start can actually save money in the long run.

Of the many types of garden hoses on the market, the cheaper ones are made of 100 percent PVC. They don't last very long and are very stiff. This type was the first hose I owned, and my patience with it lasted only one season. The clincher came when trying to water in my trees in fall. The cool fall air stiffened the PVC to the point that the hose acted like a giant python. When the hose began throwing death-grip coils around my head, with me running out of energy in this fight for survival, I knew it was time for a new hose.

The next step up in quality is a blend of PVC and rubber that makes the hoses more durable and flexible. In the past, 100 percent rubber hoses were the best quality, but the new blends of PVC and rubber, or even 100 percent polyester, offer longevity and superior strength.

Check the number of plies or layers used in making the hose. The cheaper hoses will consist only of an inner liner and a covering. Better quality hoses will have at least two plies of synthetic mesh wrapped around the inner liner to add strength. The best quality hoses offer eight plies of strength. The couplings are also important. Plastic couplings will simply not last. Galvanized steel is better, but brass is best. Weight is not

a consideration any longer. The lightest hoses are often the strongest today.

My favourite hose is the Flexogen made by Gilmour. I have had mine for over 20 years, and it has never leaked or kinked. Gilmour still makes fine quality garden hoses. The Flexogen hose comes with a lifetime warranty, is made of polyester and has an eight-ply construction reinforced with two tire cords. It is also burst resistant to 500 psi, which makes it well suited for watering on even the hottest days of summer. The features I like the best is that it retains its flexibility in even the coldest weather and is lightweight. The flexibility goes a long way to avoiding the "python syndrome."

You may want to consider adding quick-release connectors to your hose. These products eliminate the need for constantly having to screw the hose couplings on and off the water source or even when attaching watering devices. The different brands of connectors are all made of plastic, but of course, some are better than others. The less expensive varieties have been known to crack or break, and often they are not as easy to connect or disconnect. My favourites are connectors made by Gardena. This brand is very good quality, and my connectors have never cracked or broken over the years. If the connector starts to leak a bit, simply change the O-ring seal for a few pennies and your connector will be as good as new.

You should also decide how you will store your hose when not in use. There are many types of hose hangers and carts on the market. If you plan on leaving the hose in one spot, then wall type hangers will work well. They come in the plain model that is simply a metal or plastic hanger that attaches to a wall or fence over which the hose is draped for storage. More elaborate hose storage units come with an electric motor for winding the hose with no effort. If you have several outdoor water bibs and need to move the hose from one to the other, then a hose cart is the way to go. Choose a cart that is lightweight and yet sturdy enough to support a hose full of water. A metal cart is far superior to a plastic one. My plastic hose cart gave up the ghost after only two years. The next one I buy will be metal.

Along with the hose, a **handheld watering device** is a necessity. Unless you have an irrigation system, a **sprinkler** for watering lawns and gardens is a great tool as well. When choosing a handheld watering device, consider what you will be using it for. I recommend having two types. The first is a hose-end spray nozzle that has multiple settings on it. These nozzles can be used for a multitude of tasks. I like my nozzle to have a gentle shower setting

for general watering needs, a sharp stream for washing some insects, such as spider mites, off plant leaves and a setting for misting plant leaves or watering delicate seeds or seedlings. Some nozzles on the market have many more settings than these basic ones I have described, but I rarely use those settings.

I also use a long-handled watering wand with a showerhead-like attachment at the end. It is excellent for delivering a gentle stream of water to plants at the soil level. This type of watering keeps the soil from splattering and compacting, which can happen if the water is delivered from a greater height. It also can keep the water off the leaves of plants. In some cases, with diseases such as with verticillium wilt, applying water to the leaves can actually spread the disease or create conditions that encourage the disease infecting the plant. Applying water with a high mineral content to the leaves can result in mineral deposits forming on the leaves. Watering wands are also invaluable for watering hanging baskets or containers on raised plant stands.

A lawn and garden sprinkler is another good weapon to have in the gardening arsenal. I happen to collect lawn and garden sprinklers, not by choice but because I am constantly searching for the perfect sprinkler. My lovely wife can confirm the

15

presence of this quirk: she knows that when I enter the watering section of a garden centre, she must otherwise occupy herself because I will be there for a time.

I refuse to invest in a sprinkler or irrigation system. My thinking is that I can easily move the hose to water the areas I need to, and the cost of a hose and sprinkler is far less than an installed irrigation system. You see, I am inherently a penny pincher when it comes to gardening, and yet I am practical as well. I believe that I can water my lawn and/or garden far more efficiently than any irrigation system can.

The focus then turns to what type of sprinkler to use. I have used nearly every type of sprinkler on the market, and my favourite is the impulse sprinkler. I'm a quantitative kind of guy and like to have scientific proof that I've made the correct choice. To check this, I ran a simple scientific test of sprinklers. I tested an impulse type, an oscillating one and a single-stream 360-degree sprinkler. The single stream was of the same type that you might find in a lawn irrigation system, but the one I tested was connected to a hose. I placed empty soup cans at various points around my lawn to collect water, then I tested each sprinker. The impulse sprinkler did a superior job of distributing the water evenly over the entire test area. The oscillating sprinkler tended to

distribute more water in the middle and at the two low points of its run, and the single-stream sprinkler did not do a good job in the area between the end of the spray and the sprinkler itself.

A must-have tool for me has always been a **handheld weed puller**. This simple device has a forked tip at the end of a long shaft and a handle. The shaft can be curved or may have a piece of metal attached with a rounded shape. The premise is to insert the forked end of the weed puller into the roots of a weed and then pull down on the handle, thus popping the weed out of the soil. This tool works remarkably well and is an excellent green alternative to using herbicides. I have always found weeding to be therapeutic. The therapy comes from removing weeds that detract from the beauty of nature and the landscape you have created, and the simple activity can be very calming.

The new generation of weed pullers have a long handle that saves a lot of back strain by allowing you to pull weeds while standing. These pullers have a device at the working end that is pushed into the ground around the weed. Most of these pullers then grasp the weed and pull it out of the ground as you pull up on the handle. As with all tools, choose a weed puller that is of good quality. Early in my gardening days, I recall purchasing many a tool for $1.49, only to use it once and have it disintegrate in my hand.

Another device I find invaluable is an **edging tool**. It consists of a half-moon-shaped piece of metal with a honed edge attached to either a long or short wooden handle. I prefer the short-handled type because it is more versatile. The intended use of an edger is, of course, edging. The tool is excellent at keeping a tidy edge of lawn where it meets a sidewalk or other hardscape. I also find it useful for removing sod. I seem to be constantly cutting new beds in the lawn as I run out of room in existing beds. The problem is that plant breeders keep introducing new and exciting varieties of plants, and how can I plant those new plants unless I have the space in beds?

I use the edging tool to cut out the shape of the bed and then use it to cut the sod away from the soil. It acts like a knife going through the grass roots horizontally. After the cut, it is a simple matter of either rolling up the sod or removing it in pieces. It is important that the cutting edge be very sharp when cutting or edging sod to decrease the drag.

If you have a lawn, a **lawnmower** will be a necessary purchase. There are three choices in mowers. The first is the standard gas-powered mower, the second is an electric mower

and the third is a reel mower. In today's eco-friendly garden, electric or reel mowers are the best choice. Electric mowers have come a long way in the past few years. They are more powerful, and many are now rechargeable, which eliminates the need for the annoyingly long and obtrusive electric cord. If you prefer an increased workout in addition to being eco-friendly, then the push reel mower is the mower of choice. Of all three mowers, this mower is the best choice for the health of the lawn. The scissor-like cutting action cuts the grass precisely and cleanly with no ragged edges, which often occurs with gas and electric mowers.

Although technically not a tool, **gardening gloves** are a necessity for any gardener. Not only do they keep your hands from getting deeply soiled, but they also offer protection from cuts, blisters and sharp twigs, branches and thorns. While garden gloves are very much about personal preference, there are some things to consider when choosing a pair.

My biggest issue with gloves is flexibility. I certainly like to have my hands protected, but I do not want a pair of gloves that tire out my hands because they are too stiff or too thick. I also like to feel what I am doing, such as pulling weeds or thinning new sprouts. For these reasons, I have two kinds of gloves. One pair, which has leather palms, is used

17

when pruning roses, for example, or for other heavy-duty chores where my hands need extra protection. For other jobs, I use the new generation of gloves that have a textured rubber palm and a breathable cotton, knitted liner and back. The cotton allows heat and perspiration to escape, leaving my hands cooler and keeping my fingers away from direct contact with the latex. The rubber offers a great grip, in addition to being cut-, puncture- and abrasion-resistant. These gloves have become my favourite garden gloves, and they are extremely durable as well as comfortable. Atlas Fit is my personal preference, and they come in a variety of sizes for men, women and even children.

Any gardener who plans on doing weeding or planting will need **knee protection** when kneeling to work. There are two ways to go. One is to use some type of a kneeler; the other is to use kneepads. The decision is again very much a personal choice. I have used both and tend to lean toward the kneeler. I just find it easier on my knees than kneepads and also use it to sit on for certain gardening tasks. My favourite kneeler is a simple piece of carpet remnant, though you can buy many different types of kneelers that are designed specifically for gardening. Some are simple pieces of foam while others can include handles that make getting up and down easier.

Kneepads annoy me when I walk about from job to job. I like to wear shorts in the garden, and the straps of the kneepads irritate the backs of my knees as well. Some gardeners swear by kneepads, however, and would find my carpet remnant insufficient protection for their knees. By all means, protect your knees no matter what form of protection you choose. If you spend a lot of time on your knees when gardening, you can cause some serious orthopedic issues if your knees are left unprotected.

When it comes to eco-friendly gardening, one of the best tools to have is a **rainwater collection system**. Water is a precious resource that is too often taken for granted. For centuries, gardeners have collected rainwater to water gardens and lawns without giving much thought to the matter. Today, with the increasing focus on the conservation of our water resources, collecting rainwater re-emerges as not only an economically viable watering alternative but also an environmentally essential one.

Global concern continues to rise as supplies of freshwater, once thought to be limitless, are showing signs of being taxed. Lawn and garden watering make up 40 percent of average water usage during the summer-months. A 75-gallon barrel of rainwater can save an estimated 1300 gallons of tap water during summer when water demand is highest.

Collecting rainwater is something every gardener can do and do so economically. The benefits for the gardener lie in saving money on utility bills and helping to preserve an important natural resource. The benefit for the plants is that they receive water that does not have chlorine or other chemicals added to it as does tap water. Rainwater is a soft water, as opposed to the mineral and salt-laden tap water of many cities. Any experienced gardener will attest that you can water all you want with tap water and never have better-looking plants than those watered with rainwater.

The chlorine and other additives in tap water can damage the naturally occurring and beneficial bacteria in soil. These bacteria are essential to good, healthy plant growth. The other consideration that most gardeners overlook is the temperature of the water itself. Tap water arrives at the plants in a cold state. Anyone who has run through a sprinkler in summer to cool off will know that tap water is very cold indeed. This cold water temperature can shock plants and can even slow down their growth.

Plastic barrels are the best choice to collect rainwater—they will not rust and are basically maintenance free. A dark-coloured barrel, which will not allow light to penetrate to the interior, will reduce the growth of algae in the container. A lid will keep debris and insects out. The barrels themselves are available from a variety of sources. Look through your Yellow Pages for plastic manufacturers or plastic extruders for sources of barrels. You may be able to find used barrels as well. Check for ads in your local newspaper. Do not use barrels that have stored caustic chemicals or other non-organic liquids. Water barrels are also available at many garden centres. Some newer ones on the market are very aesthetically pleasing. Some are finished to resemble stone, have screens to keep out mosquitoes, debris and vermin, and come equipped with spigots. They would look attractive in any setting, but their price makes them prohibitive for some gardeners.

Building your own rainwater collection system is not difficult nor should it be expensive. Barrels with removable lids work the best. The lid seals the barrel once it is full and preserves the rainwater until you are ready to use it. Select a convenient downspout from your roof's eavestrough system and place the barrel close to it. Ensure that the barrel rests on a level surface to avoid any danger of the barrel tipping once full. You may need to cut the downspout to the correct length for the rain to enter the barrel. The downspout should rest just above the top of the barrel. Attach some fine mesh to the top of the barrel. The mesh should be fine enough to keep mosquitoes and debris out but still allow the water in. The rainwater can be accessed in one of two ways. First, you can use the age-old method of simply dipping a bucket into the barrel and hauling out the water. Second, you can attach a tap at the bottom of the barrel— simply drill a hole just large enough for the threads on an outdoor tap, screw the tap into place and caulk it tight. If you decide to increase your storage capacity, you can always add more barrels in tandem later.

If you choose to go with the tap, you will first want to raise the barrel off the ground to a height of 90 cm–1.2 m to allow the water to flow out with a little pressure thanks to gravity. You can now either fill your watering can easily with the tap or attach a garden hose or even soaker hose for watering larger areas.

Manufacturers are offering more and more commercially made rain barrels. Some come with the screens and spigots already installed. Mine is such a barrel. It also came with a 1.2 m length of hose already attached to the spigot. At the end of the hose is a valve for turning the flow on and off. The cost has come down over the past few years on these barrels, and a good quality one can be purchased for $70 to $80.

There are some amazing facts when considering how much rain can be

saved from the downspouts of an average house. You can calculate the area of roof that drains into a downspout easily by multiplying the width times the length of the roof. If your roof measures, for example, 40' × 25' (12 × 7.5 m), the area would be 1000 sq ft. For every inch of rain that falls on a 1000 sq ft catchment area, after taking into account friction, evaporation and spillage, you could capture 468 gallons of water.

Maintaining Your Tools

Keeping your gardening tools and equipment in good condition serves a twofold purpose. First, by not allowing the tools to rust or deteriorate, you don't incur the cost of having to replace them before their time. Second, tools that are clean and sharp work far better than ones that are not.

Get into the habit of cleaning your tools after each use so they're always ready to use the next time. After each use, I wash off any dirt and dry the tool to reduce the chance of it rusting. My tools hang along my garden shed wall and are readily visible, thus saving me time when I am in a hurry to find a particular tool. When I hang the tool up at the end of the day, I always take the time to check that it is still sharp.

Pruners, spades, cultivators, hoes and loppers are just a few of the tools that need to be sharp to work best.

Sharpening your gardening tools can be done using a variety of methods. One of the easiest is to use a tool designed specifically for such a task. My favourite sharpening tool is the Accusharp Gardensharp. Just a few strokes with this tool give you a razor-sharp edge. I bought mine on eBay.

Another tried-and-true sharpening method is to use a small file. When sharpening pruners or loppers, sharpen only the cutting blade—the side with the shiny, thin edge. The correct cutting angle for these tools is 20 degrees, so when sharpening with a file, try to maintain that angle. Clamping the tool in a vice will help to avoid a wavy blade caused by the blade moving during the sharpening process. Sharpeners on the market are designed specifically for pruners or loppers. The added cost of buying these sharpeners is unnecessary—the Gardensharp or a file will do the job nicely. Spades, hoes and cultivators do not need a honed cutting edge as do the pruners and loppers. The edge on these tools needs to be thicker, strong and sharp.

You can sharpen your lawnmower blades easily using these step-by-step instructions:

1. For a gas mower with a rotary blade, disconnect the spark plug (consult the owner's manual). For an electric mower, unplug the cord from the power source.

2. Use a wrench to remove the blade from the mower deck.

3. Scrape off any rust, dirt and grass build-up with a wire brush.

4. Use a file or grinding wheel to sharpen the blade on the cutting edges. File or grind away the rough spots until the surface is not pitted and is smooth. Follow the angle that is there.

5. Check the blade for balance. This step is important because an unbalanced blade can create safety issues by causing severe vibration. Balance the blade on its centre. If it tips to one side, remove a little more metal on the side opposite until the blade balances evenly.

A reel mower usually comes with a sharpening kit. If not, you can find such a kit in many hardware stores.

Soil and Amendments

Soil is the foundation of any good garden and yard. Many gardeners invest a great deal of time and money into the aesthetics of their garden and yet settle for a soil base that lacks organic matter, is heavy in clay or is substandard in other ways.

They cannot understand why their plants do not perform well. Soil is the single most important factor when planning a new landscape, renovating an existing one or improving the quality of a garden or bed. Good quality topsoil can be the difference between a lush, eye-appealing bed and one in which the plants never achieve their true potential.

A critical component of soil is its organic content. If you are bringing in topsoil for a new project or modifying an existing one, the organic content of the soil should be the first priority. Take the time to go out to the source of the soil and examine the product carefully. Look for soil that is dark and has an earthy smell to it. It should be free of stones. Ask the supplier if it is weed free.

As with so many things in life, you get what you pay for. I have made the same mistakes many of us have when choosing soil. In my first home landscape plan, I went to a nearby excavation and talked the contractor into delivering some of the topsoil they had stripped off during the construction of a new development. I managed to get the soil for the cost of a case of beer. The result of that saving was that the soil contained more weeds than even the most avid horticulturist could possibly identify. An added "bonus" was the horsetail weed that the soil contained, which was unfazed by any herbicide and spread with reckless abandon. It proved to be my nemesis for many years and forced me to spend more time on my knees pulling this scourge than I ever could have imagined. The moral of the story is to exercise due diligence when choosing or amending a soil.

Sand, silt and clay are the three basic soil types, but most soils are a combination of the three. All soil types will benefit from the addition of organic matter, and that really is the bottom line. I am frequently asked what is the best additive to use for soils. Factors to consider when choosing a soil amendment are:

- how long you expect the amendment to last in the soil
- the soil texture
- the pH of the amendment and of the soil

Compost and manure are the best choices for improving the organic content of soils because they are less likely to change the acidity of the soil than other amendments such as peat moss.

An age-old debate has centred on the pros and cons of compost and manure. Part of the problem is that manures differ in their NPK

(nitrogen-phosphorus-potassium) breakdown. The same can hold true for compost, which depends on what materials are put into the composter. Let's begin by having a look at the NPK analysis of various manures. I can hear that laughter out there! "Martha, Filipski is now going to tell us which poop is the best!" This scientific stuff comes from Rodale's *All-New Encyclopedia of Organic Gardening: An Illustrated Guide to Organic Gardening* by Sunset Publishing and the *Rodale Guide to Composting*. The manure NPK list:

chicken: 1.1/0.8/0.5

cow: 0.25/0.15/0.25

horse: 0.7/0.3/0.6

steer: 0.7/0.3/0.6

rabbit: 2.4/1.4/0.6

sheep: 0.7/0.3/0.9

Note that the nutrient values of manures vary greatly and also depend on the age of the animals contributing to the manure and what they are fed.

In the 2006 issue of *Harrowsmith*, the analysis of compost NPK came in as follows: N=0.5–3.5, P=0.5–3.0, K=1.0–5.0. The ranges you see result from the variations in what was put in the compost to start with. So, if we look solely at the numbers, it would appear overall that compost is a better nutritive soil amendment. However, organic additives such as these have their own intangibles when it comes to comparing them. The microbes in each organic additive can tip the balance when it comes to which is better. Some people would have you believe that manures are richer in microbes, while others say that compost is the clear winner.

But there is no clear winner. I think both additives are just as good for building up the organic matter in your soil. Both can help over time with a soil that is loaded with clay. My choice has always been compost, just because I have easy access to it in my own compost pile. I like that I can know and control what goes into it. I have had some weed issues with a few manures that were probably not composted long enough to destroy the weed seeds, but those episodes are few and far between.

I no longer use peat moss as an additive because it can change the acid levels of the soil. If you are interested in acidifying the soil for acid-loving plants, peat moss is a great choice. A new player on the scene is a product called sea soil. This organic additive is made by composting fish by-products and forest fines (bark and other organics). Sea soil has no foul odour and has a weed-free status.

So, after all this rambling, what is the bottom line? The answer is simple. Make up your own mind on organic amendments. You can always do a little science by running your own experiment. You will need eight containers: one for each of the six manures, one for compost and one for sea soil. Use the same potting mix for all containers. Mix the potting soil with the additive and use the same type of plants in each container. Monitor the growth and size of the plants. By fall you might (or might not) have the answer.

Many people ask if there is a magical solution to subsoil problems such as clay. There is a magical solution. It is called organic matter. The problem is that it takes years of effort, and you must constantly add these amendments for them to be effective on the subsoil.

Drainage is another issue when it comes to soil. We tend to think of soil as being solid, but the truth is that soil is composed of many small air spaces, liquids and solids. At the correct levels of moisture, approximately 50 percent of the air spaces will be filled with water. After watering or rain, the soil may be saturated with water filling most of those spaces. In soil that does not drain well, these spaces will remain filled with water for longer periods of time and in some extreme cases may never drain away completely. With the poor drainage, plants will suffer because the roots are deprived of oxygen. Commonly, the problem of poor drainage relates to the clay content in the soil, but other problems such as buried waste from construction, stones or rocks may be the culprits.

Grade—the slope of the yard—is another important factor when it comes to soil drainage. Drainage grades may change over time as the soil settles. Grading problems will manifest themselves in a variety of ways. Often the poor condition of the plants will be the first sign of a problem. If you suspect drainage is an issue, check the moisture content of the soil in the suspect area. If the soil feels wet and not moist, or if there are standing pools of water, it may be time to call in a pro to check out the problem. Many gardeners have tried re-grading on their own with disastrous results. Grading or re-grading is a job best left to the professionals.

Soil Acidity or Alkalinity

Often, problems with plants persist no matter what a gardener does. The addition of fertilizers, organic matter or other amendments just doesn't seem to have any effect. The problem can stem from the soil itself. The pH level of a soil is the measure of the acidity or alkalinity of the soil on a scale of 0 to 14, with 0 being the most acidic and 14 being the most alkaline. A 7 on this scale is considered to be neutral. While many plants prefer a neutral soil ranging from 6.2 to 7 on the scale, other plants prefer more acidic conditions. Plants such as evergreens and blueberries, for example, prefer soils that are in the 4.5–5 range or slightly higher.

Testing the soil with a simple home-testing kit is one way to find out what the problem is. These kits are available in most garden centres and, while they are not 100 percent accurate, they can give a good indication if the problems with your plants might be the result of soil pH. If you want to have completely accurate soil testing, you will need to contact a soil-testing laboratory in your area. Look in the Yellow Pages under "Laboratories."

Soil pH can both directly and indirectly affect plants. The direct effect is as previously mentioned, namely, the soil can be either too acidic or too alkaline. The indirect effect of soil pH shows up in the following ways:

- the availability of elements essential to plant growth and vigour

- the activity and numbers of microorganisms that are essential for good soil conditions

- the actual condition of the soil itself

Doing the research on your plants and knowing the pH they prefer will go a long way toward ensuring their health.

Three compost bins made of wood boards.

Compost

I would be remiss if I didn't spend some time talking about my favourite soil amendment, compost. To a gardener, the term "black gold" does not refer to crude oil. Black gold in gardening can only mean one thing, and that is compost. Compost is arguably the most important tool in the gardener's arsenal. Compost can make clay soil viable. It can enhance and enrich any soil and even act as a mulch that not only helps conserve moisture but also adds nutrients every time you water. The added bonus with compost is that it is all natural, and it improves the soil and helps eliminate garbage going to the landfill. Compost is an eco-friendly material that can provide nutrients and essential elements to plants without resorting to synthetic chemicals.

Composting is simple to do and is economical. To start, all you need is an inexpensive composter, which can be bought at any garden centre or hardware store. Scepter makes a composter out of recycled plastic that works very well. I have one myself, and I like the sliding door at the bottom for easy removal of completed compost and the easy-open door on the top for adding compostable material. Or you can build a composter yourself. Many plans are available. Doing an online search for composting or composters will yield a return of many websites that have free plans for building your own composting system.

It is easy to remember how to compost if you use the green and brown principle. Green materials are high in nitrogen and are easy to break down. Examples include lettuce leaves, carrot peelings, apple cores, grass clippings, weeds, etc. Brown materials are high in carbon content and break down more slowly unless mixed with green materials. Brown materials include sawdust, shredded branches and twigs, dried leaves, soil, manure, etc. A list of compostable and non-compostable materials, according to the City of Edmonton website on composting (www.edmonton.ca/for_residents/garbage_recycling/compostable-materials.aspx), includes the following compostables:

- yard and garden waste (grass clippings, fallen leaves, flower and vegetable waste, small twigs, straw, hay, peat moss)
- kitchen waste (fruit, vegetable peelings, tea bags, coffee grounds)

Non-compostables include the following:

- meat, fish or bones
- fatty or oily foods
- cheese and dairy products (these attract animals, create odours and take longer to break down)
- pet litter (kitty litter, dog feces)

- weeds with seed heads or persistent roots (e.g., quack grass)
- diseased plants

To start the process of composting, layer brown material at the bottom of your composter or pile. Apply a layer of finished compost, soil or well-rotted manure next; this will provide the organisms that are necessary to start the composting process. Alternate layers of green and brown material, adding another layer of soil, manure or compost every so often as you fill your composter. The composting material needs to be moist—it should have the same moisture content as a wrung-out sponge. Turn the composting material every one to two weeks to move the outside material into the centre and to add air to the mix. While you turn the material, check for wetness. If it feels dry, add water. Too much water will cause aerobic bacteria to die and the anaerobic type will take over, often resulting in a foul odour. If this problem happens, turn the pile more frequently to help it dry out.

As the microorganisms consume the organic matter, heat is produced. It is not unusual for a compost pile to reach temperatures of 40–45° C. Depending on what you add to the pile, you could have compost in two months from start to finish. The composting process stops or is drastically reduced in winter. Save your household "greens" in a garbage can or barrel (with a lid) over winter, allowing them to freeze outside, then add them to your composter or pile in spring. There is nothing like compost to make that "green" or eco-friendly garden work at its best.

To review, here are the environmental benefits of producing your own compost. First, you reduce the amount of garbage going to the landfill. Second, the organic matter that you are recycling by composting reintroduces the material into your little piece of the biosphere. Finally, compost is a far better source of natural nutrients than any synthetic fertilizer and is safer for the environment. The nutrients that compost adds to the soil are released over a long period of time. (Many synthetic fertilizers offer a blast of nutrients and then fade quickly.) The slow-release system of compost is of great benefit to plants as the nutrients are available over a longer period of time. Compost also makes an excellent mulch. It serves two functions in this application. Not only does it help conserve moisture, but it also adds nutrients as it breaks down.

Vermicomposting

For condo and apartment dwellers who have always wanted to compost but never thought they could, or for homeowners with little free space for larger composters,

vermicomposting is the answer. Just what is vermicomposting? Red worms are put into a plastic or wood bin with moist shredded newspaper, peat moss, brown leaves or straw. Food scraps such as apple cores, vegetable peelings and coffee grounds are buried in the bedding. The worms eat the scraps and release a substance called vermicompost, which is a great compost that can be used to enrich the soil of your house plants, container gardens and flower beds.

Vermicomposting is usually done indoors and is a great way to compost in a limited space. It is also a great way for backyard composters to continue composting indoors through winter. There is no need to worry about having worms in your home. The worms will not roam, as they are more than happy to stay in their container munching away on yesterday's refuse. The worms used in vermicomposting are not the regular earthworms you find in the garden. They are red worms or red wrigglers. These worms are voracious eaters. According to many composting experts, a pound of red worms will consume a half-pound of kitchen waste a day. As they eat, they will deposit black worm castings, or vermicompost, and no, it does not have an unpleasant odour to it.

The best types of containers to use are plastic storage bins with tight-fitting lids, though you can use foam cooler chests or a wooden box. The container will need to have air holes on the side or in the top. The depth of the container should not be more than 30–45 cm (12"–18"), and you will need to have a square foot of surface area for every pound of waste you add. So, a 2' × 2' box will allow 4 pounds of waste a week.

Bedding for your worms is very important. Bedding can include shredded newspaper (of course, never my gardening column because you all save those, right?), cardboard, potting soil without any additives, fall leaves or a combination of these. Fill the bin nearly to the top with this bedding and then sprinkle it with water until it is as wet as a wrung-out sponge. The bedding material should form a ball and stick together when squeezed in your hand.

Here is what to feed or not to feed your vermicomposter:

Feed

- vegetable scraps
- grains
- fruit rinds and peels
- breads
- tea bags
- coffee grounds and filters

Don't Feed

- cheese
- meats

- fish
- oily foods
- butter
- animal products

Feed your worms by burying the waste in the bedding. To keep away fruit flies and odour, cover the top layer of waste with a few inches of bedding. If you cut your waste into smaller pieces, it will disappear faster. Worms do not like citrus waste so it is best to keep it out of the vermicompost.

After three to six months, the worms will have not only consumed all your waste but also the bedding—this is the time to harvest the compost. There are two methods for harvesting, but the one I prefer is the side-to-side method. Move all the worms and compost to one side and fill the other side with fresh bedding. For the next six weeks, add waste only to the fresh bedding side. All your worm friends will migrate into the new bedding, allowing you to harvest the vermicompost they have left behind.

You can use the harvested compost in your gardening applications. Mix it with potting soil (one part compost to three parts potting soil) and use it to topdress your pots and containers. Sprinkle 2.5 cm of compost on top of the existing soil every one to two months. You can even use the compost as part of your seed starter mix or add a sprinkle of compost along the bottom of the seed row or into the hole when transplanting seedlings. You wil be amazed at the difference in your plants when using the compost.

There are relatively few problems when using this method of composting, and any problems that might occur are minor. Fruit flies are a common complaint when vermicomposting. These tiny flies are a nuisance more than anything else. They are not dangerous and do not bite. By keeping the waste you add covered by at least a few inches of bedding, you will keep the fruit fly problem at bay. Alternatively, you can simply freeze the waste before adding it to the composter. Odour is the other concern, and it can easily be corrected by keeping the waste covered with the bedding as just described. Adding too much waste to the composter can result in some odour, but this problem can easily be rectified by removing some of the excess.

Mulching

In dry summers, soil moisture conservation is of prime importance, and with water utility rates on the rise and the increasing concern about protecting water resources, mulch is becoming much more than an aesthetic touch for a neat garden—

it has become a necessity for every gardener. Mulching is a technique that has been used for centuries and involves laying a substance on the top of the soil to protect the plants from heat, cold and drought. It is also effective at keeping fruits and vegetables clean, as well as reducing weeds in and around desirable plants. Organic mulches can also add nutrients to the soil as they break down.

According to Dr. Mary Ann Rose and Dr. Elton Smith at Ohio State University, a study done in 1969 by Weyerhauser Co. showed that a 5 cm layer of mulch

- reduced soil moisture loss by 21 percent
- reduced soil temperature in the upper 10 cm of topsoil by 12° C
- delayed soil temperature from reaching freezing by two days as compared to unmulched soil

A wide variety of mulches are available to the home gardener, including organic and inorganic mulches. Some examples of organic mulches include shredded tree bark, compost, leaves, grass clippings, shredded newspaper, wood chips, pine needles, sphagnum peat moss, animal manures and straw. Inorganic mulches such as landscape grade plastic, landscape fabrics and rocks are available, but organic mulches offer many more benefits, including better insulation. Organic mulches also replenish soil nutrients.

Bark wood mulch in front of rustic wood pergola and bench.

A 5 cm layer of organic mulch has been found to be the most effective. This depth of mulch provides the optimal conditions for the prevention of weed growth, soil moisture conservation and soil temperature modification. Mulch applied at a depth less than 5 cm will dry out the soil too quickly and is not as effective in weed control. Mulches applied at depths in the 7.5–18 cm range can also cause severe problems. The roots of the plants can actually suffocate owing to a lack of air penetrating the soil. An excessive layer of mulch can also cause waterlogged soil conditions. Excessive mulch applied next to the trunks of trees or stems of plants can lead to rot, disease and pest problems.

The natural breakdown of organic mulches can help condition poor soils. Peat moss, grass, straw, manures, compost and leaves are excellent examples of organic mulches that are useful in adding nutrients. If you choose to use animal manures, take care to use only well-rotted manures. Fresh or "green" manures can burn plant material.

Uncomposted wood chip or bark mulches call for special treatments because of their high carbon to nitrogen ratio. The soil microorganisms can easily decompose these organic mulches. The nitrogen in the soil is used by the microorganisms during this breakdown process, which can lead to a nitrogen deficiency for plants. Apply a nitrogen fertilizer at the time of mulch application to avoid this problem.

Choosing the right mulch is as important as the actual application itself. Most mulches require little maintenance, but some, such as grass clippings, shredded bark, peat moss and straw, can become matted. Peat moss, while an excellent organic mulch and soil conditioner, can become hard over time. This matting and/or hardening can render the mulch impervious to water and air and create more problems than it solves. If you choose such mulches, be prepared to rake the mulch occasionally to keep it from matting, especially in spring. If you have acid-loving plants such as blueberries or azaleas, using a beneficial mulch such as pine needles or peat moss will add a slight acidity to the soil.

Prior to applying mulch for the first time, check the soil for proper drainage. A poorly drained soil with a layer of mulch can create water-logged conditions. You may need to amend the soil to improve the drainage by adding organic matter such as compost to the soil. If weeds are a major concern, a combination of inorganic mulch such as landscape fabric and a bark mulch, for example, can be useful. The landscape fabric allows air and moisture to penetrate but is effective at keeping weeds at bay. The organic mulch on top of the fabric adds aesthetics and insulation.

For vegetable gardens, the mulches of choice should be organic and should break down easily. At the end of the gardening season, you should be able to readily mix the mulch in with the garden soil in preparation for next year's planting. Aesthetic appeal of the mulch in the veggie garden is less important—grass clippings, straw, leaves, manures and compost make excellent vegetable garden mulches. These mulches will not only keep the soil from splashing onto fruits and leaves but also conserve moisture and add nutrients. Maintaining even water levels is important to many vegetables such as tomatoes to prevent problems such as blossom end rot.

Applying mulch is best done after spring planting or in early summer before the heat of summer reaches maximum temperatures. A second application may be needed in fall to prepare certain tender perennials and roses for the winter. Mulching too early in spring may prevent complete evaporation of winter moisture. Many plants in the home landscape will not tolerate having "wet feet" or waterlogged soil in the root zone. When reapplying or adding mulch to a previously mulched area, do not add more than the 5–7.5 cm depth, including the depth of the previous mulch.

Mulching may well be the most important tool the gardeners of today and the future have in their arsenal. Ask yourself, what other gardening tool or technique offers so much:

- protection from summer heat
- solutions to the problems of frost, heaving and cold extremes in winter
- environmentally friendly water conservation
- reduced or eliminated weed problems
- soil nutrient replenishment
- eye-appeal
- inexpensive to use

Organic vs Inorganic Fertilizers

To me, using organic fertilizers such as manures and compost is the most eco-friendly way to garden. However, if you prefer to use a synthetic fertilizer instead of or in tandem with organic additives, there are many effective products on the market. It is never my intention to preach on the virtues of using one method of gardening over another. My position has always been to provide researched information that will allow you to make your own educated decision on which system works best for you. The same is true in the debate of organic vs inorganic fertilizers. Here is a short list of pros and cons for both methods:

Organic Advantages

- less danger of overfertilizing; the nutrients are released slowly over time as the soil organisms break down the organic matter
- helps condition the soil and overall improves its structure
- increases the ability of sandy soils to hold water
- can, over time, help clay soils by changing the soil structure and breaking up the clay component

Organic Disadvantages

- organic fertilizers are not available to the plants immediately; if the plant needs an instant boost of fertilizer, an organic cannot provide it
- owing to the action of certain bacteria, when adding a large amount of organic matter, there is a possibility of temporarily depleting nitrogen in the soil when using organic fertilizers

Inorganic Advantages

- nutrients are available immediately; the plant does not care whether the nutrients come from an organic source or an inorganic source

Inorganic Disadvantages

- can burn roots if applied too heavily
- if it's not a slow-release fertilizer, it can burn leaves and grasses if applied without being watered in
- repeated applications can cause a buildup of salts in the soil
- excessive rain or watering can wash fertilizers below the root level of plants, making the nutrients, especially nitrogen, inaccessible to the plants

According to Statistics Canada, Alberta and Saskatchewan led the way when it came to the number of households using chemical fertilizers on their lawns or gardens in 2005: 45 percent of households used these fertilizers. The lowest use came from Québec at 15 percent of households. The national average was approximately 32 percent. When it came to the highest number of households that watered their lawns, Alberta led the way again at 64 percent. PEI was lowest at 18 percent, and the Canadian average was 54 percent. These figures are a cause for concern in urban areas certainly, but even more so when it comes to communities with lake properties. These concerns result from problems associated with lake property owners fertilizing their lawns and subsequently watering

them, causing the fertilizer to leach into the lake.

In 2009, Manitoba became the first province in Canada to restrict homeowner use of lawn fertilizers containing phosphorus, in this case more than 1 percent phosphorus. The province hopes that the restriction will result in a 1 percent reduction to the amount of phosphorus that ends up in Lake Winnipeg. The lake has a problem each year with algal blooms that are fed by the phosphorus. On January 1, 2010, Alberta banned the sale of weed and feed products. When the government first announced this ban would be coming, homeowners bought every bag they could find in order to stockpile the products. The issue with these combination fertilizer products is the amount of weed killer in the formulation. According to Alberta Environment Minister Rob Renner, "By eliminating products that encourage mass application we will reduce the amount of chemical run-off in our waterways," adding that more than 10 times the required amount of pesticide can be applied to lawns when weed and feed is used.

The concerns over the use of lawn fertilizers in lake areas are spurring owners of second homes into action. A friend informed me that the Summer Village of Itaska Beach on Pigeon Lake in Alberta had made a bold move to ban fertilizer use.

I found it interesting that we may finally be seeing the light when it comes to fertilizer use affecting our lakes and streams. In Itaska Beach, effective January 16, 2008, the council passed a bylaw that "bans all fertilizer use in the Summer Village of Itaska." The council announced that they recognized that "fertilizers are a possible source of the problem with the water quality at Pigeon Lake." The council is also encouraging other municipalities around the lake to pass similar bylaws.

We will discuss fertilizer use for lawns and other plant applications in following chapters specific to each plant or application type.

Questions and Answers

Q. The lawn surrounding our seven-year-old home is built on extremely hard soil. Short of tearing it up, how can we loosen the soil? The yard slopes quite a bit, so fertilizer just washes away.

A. There is no easy solution to your problem. It will take a lot of time and effort and still may not yield the results you desire. I wanted you to know this before you read on.

The first thing you will need to do is to aerate the lawn. Deep core aeration is the best method for your situation. Have the company you hire to do the aeration make at least two passes. Make the first pass in an east-west direction and the other in a north-south direction. Normally, after such aeration, you would leave the plugs in place to break down, but since these plugs will contain the problem soil you describe, it is best to remove the plugs completely by raking them up and tossing them into the trash. The next step is to bring in good quality topsoil and lay it down on top of the existing sod. Rake the soil to a depth of around 5 cm. You will need to repeat this procedure every spring until you see signs of recovery from your lawn.

The slope you mention may compound the problem if you can't fertilize. It may also be the reason the lawn looks poor. Water does not have a chance to penetrate deeply before it runs off in a steeply sloped situation. The best time to try to fertilize is when you lay down the top-dressing, as the fertilizer will tend to stick to the top-dressing rather than to the bare lawn.

In all honesty, I think this may be a hopeless cause. You may need to just tear out the lawn, regrade, if possible, and replace the poor soil with good quality loam.

Q. We are about to remove 11 spruce trees from our yard. They were originally planted too close together, and they are very old. As you know, the soil that we will be left with is very acidic and dry. Can you tell me how to bump up this area for planting? Also, what trees or shrubs would do well in this soil? We are looking for greenery that will grow very quickly—the old trees provided a great deal of privacy for our yard.

A. I would remove some of the old soil. Ideally, taking out a depth of 2.5 cm of soil is best. Replace any soil you remove with either a good quality loam and/or compost. The more organic matter you can add now, the better it will be. I assume you are going to have the roots removed as well? If so, the stump removal process will help "till" the soil, and it is a great time to introduce the organic matter.

As for replacement trees, try Swedish columnar aspens or tower poplars. They grow quite quickly to around 4.3 m high and 1.4 m wide. They are quite tolerant of most soil conditions, and their columnar shape means you can plant them fairly close together to make a screen.

Q. I have a major problem with the clay soil in my shrub beds. Weeding the beds is very difficult and time consuming because the weeds stick to the soil as if they were epoxied in place. Tilling the beds by shovel leaves lumps between 5 cm and 13 cm in cross section. The beds are extensive and measure about 500 sq ft (46 sq m). Most of the plants are cedars, junipers and spireas and are growing well. The soil

is unsuitable for more herbaceous material, which is what I would like to add. What amendments do you recommend?

A. Topsoil is called the "A" level. Below the "A" level is the "B" level, which is clay, and it has far less organic matter than the "A" level. Below the "B" level is the "C" level, which has more clay and even less organic matter. Although we have a good layer of topsoil, this layer is scraped off during construction of housing developments and is stockpiled. After construction when the topsoil is replaced, it may have been mixed with some clay from the "B" level or even the "C" and then returned to the site, making it poorer in quality than it was originally.

This situation is not only true for new construction areas but also in many older, more established areas as well. Another problem is that sometimes builders only return a thin layer of topsoil, maybe 10 cm, instead of the thick the layer found originally on the site, and no matter what you plant, the roots will be in clay. If you have control over the amount of topsoil being placed around your new construction, try to get at least 20 cm of topsoil in your beds.

If you are in an established home, you will need to add amendments to improve the quality of your soil. It is easier said than done. Adding organic matter such as compost or rotted manure is the best way to improve the clay problem. In a bed of the size you describe, it also means adding large quantities of the organic matter to make an impact. Three to four bags of compost will not make a difference. How much should you add? A good start would be 7.5–10 cm of organic matter.

It is your choice on how to incorporate this matter into your soil. You can rent a tiller and till it in to a depth of 35 cm. The problems with doing this are that first, you will need to make sure the soil and clay levels are dry. Using a tiller on wet clay will only exacerbate the problem by compacting the clay even further. Second, tilling into clay is a bumpy adventure to say the least, but it can be done.

The alternative is even more labour intensive but is an age-old solution to the problem. It is called double-digging. With this method, you start with a 30 cm wide strip and remove the topsoil from this strip by placing the soil into a wheelbarrow or container. Next, add 5–7.5 cm of organic matter to the subsoil and work it in with your spade into the existing clay. The next step is to dig another 30 cm wide strip right next to the first one, but instead of putting the topsoil into a container, put the topsoil on top of the organic matter in the previous trench. You continue

along using this method until the whole bed is done. I know this is arduous work, but it really works, and it can be done a trench or two at a time.

You will need to keep adding compost or manure to your topsoil every year as well as the original addition of organic matter. Adding 5 cm of organic matter to every bed each year is an excellent idea for anyone with poorer soil conditions. This addition will not have to be incorporated as intensively into the clay layer.

Another alternative is to work coarse sand—and I stress the word "coarse"—into the clay layer. It is critical to use a sand, such as a builder's sand, because if you use fine sand, it will incorporate itself into the clay, and you will end up with a concrete-like layer that will be impermeable to water. The idea is to add enough coarse sand to end up with a 1-to-1 ratio of coarse sand to clay. Again, this calls for a large amount of sand to be added and is also labour intensive. There is no easy solution to poor soil conditions, unfortunately.

My final suggestion is to use raised beds. By constructing a bed that is raised 15 cm, you will have the height of your bed plus the height of the existing topsoil to work in. Sometimes this is the least labour-intensive solution. All you need are some landscaping ties to build the bed and then enough new topsoil to fill the bed.

Q. We had a new house built and there is 15 cm of topsoil on top of hard clay. The clay is so hard we can't even get a garden fork into it. What can we do to break it down?

A. The problem you describe is called hardpan. This layer of clay or compacted soil below the topsoil depth is concrete-like and hard to work. There are other factors, but in your case, the compaction problem with clay soils can be caused by two factors. First, it may be simply a matter of clay soils being worked while wet. The resulting compaction can create a severe hardpan condition.

The second cause may be a chemical problem caused by sodium. The movement of water and air through soil depends on the soil being somewhat porous. That in turn depends on the individual soil components, clay minerals and organic matter that stay clumped together. Sodium destroys this "soil structure" by causing individual soil particles to repel each other. The particles move into the spaces of the soil and hinder water transport. One of the symptoms of high sodium include puddling of water at the soil surface.

One recommendation is to add gypsum to the soil. Gypsum,

according to some experts, has the ability to penetrate the fine clay particles in heavy or hardpan-type soils and loosen the soil structure. Over time, this process creates air and moisture spaces that eventually loosen and break up the soil structure. There are differing opinions on the effectiveness of gypsum as a soil amendment. I spoke to Dr. Les Fuller in the Renewable Resources Department of the University of Alberta about this problem. Dr. Fuller said that, "if the problem is simply a compaction problem, the gypsum may not be totally effective." Dr. Fuller went on to say that the best thing to do would be to have a soil sample taken and analyzed for the Sodium Absorption Ratio (SAR).

Dr. Fuller's and my advice is add organic matter to the soil to condition the clay. It's not easy and may not solve the problem with one application. You are looking at regular applications of organic matter over several years. The best way to apply the organic matter is to work it directly into the clay with a rototiller. You may need to hire a heavy-duty tiller to do this job.

Adding compost or other organic matter into the tilled clay over several years will eventually show an improvement in the soil structure. Another option is to have the existing topsoil moved to one side, till the clay, add the compost, retill and then replace the topsoil.

Q. It's been over 40 years and our soil must be very tired. We have done nothing more than water and sometimes fertilize our perennials and shrubs. I would like to revitalize the soil. Neither the perennials nor the shrubs are growing or flowering much anymore. My husband agrees that something needs to be done, but he does not agree with my plan to dig peat moss, well-rotted manure and compost into the ground. He does not want the soil to spill over onto the grass and brick walkways. Is there another way to revitalize the soil?

Many perennials need to be divided, and we can redo the beds and replant them. What do you recommend we do with the shrubs? Should we dig around them?

A. It definitely sounds like time to help your poor, tired soil. Forty years for any soil is a long time to go without organic amendments. The proof of its need for help can be seen in your perennials and shrubs, which are no longer performing well.

It's pretty tough to improve the soil without adding organic matter. If you are both in agreement on improving the soil, then there is no easy alternative other than adding organic matter. If I understand your husband's concern, he does not want to add amendments to the soil which

thereby raise its level and have it spill over onto lawn or walks that abut the soil. The concern over spillover can be handled in several ways. First, you can add your amendments and then dig a trench between the walk and/or lawn and the bed. Push the soil from the trench up into the bed. You will end up with a taller bed and the trench will trap any soil that wants to spill. If you keep pulling the soil up into the bed, when you weed it will not be a large problem. For a time, your soil in the bed will stand above the previous level, but that is an aesthetically pleasing look for many people. If you don't like this look, the soil will compact over time back to its original level or a level you choose.

The second alternative is to install an edging, something as simple as cedar shakes or shingles cut to the height you want and tapped into place with a mallet. You can also use a plastic landscaper's edging with a rounded edge or even recycled plastic edging strips that are a little more decorative and are hammered into place with no digging involved. The edging will keep the soil contained and off the lawn and walks.

The final alternative is to remove the top 20 cm of existing soil and put it aside. Then dig out and remove the bottom 20 cm of soil. Replace the soil you saved and add organic matter to bring it back to its previous level.

You should be adding compost and well-rotted manure. I prefer compost as an organic additive. Peat moss, in large amounts, can turn the soil acidic. If your soil does not drain well and tends to compact easily, consider adding a small amount of sand to the compost. Coarse garden sand is best. Add it at a rate of a small spadeful to 3 cu. ft. of organic matter. When adding the organic matter or other amendments, you will need to work it into the existing soil very well. You can rent small handheld tillers for this purpose. They are great for working the soil in and around shrubs.

Digging up and dividing existing perennials is a great idea. It will not only allow you to work with the soil without any obstacles, but the division will also help renew the plants' vigour. As for the shrubs, I would dig all around their roots and remove much of the soil from around the rootball, but leave the shrub sitting where it is. Do not dig below the rootball, only along the top and sides of it. Try not to disturb any of the roots. Add new soil/compost around the rootball of the plant and tamp the soil in place.

To keep this job from becoming large, add organic matter every year to your beds. Every spring, work in some fresh compost before you begin planting, or make it part of your spring maintenance routine.

Q. What is the best way to start a new garden plot? I have placed black plastic down to kill the grass as per your suggestion in a previous column. Can I add soil on top of landscape cloth, or should we dig the grass up, and if we did, how deep down do we go?

A. The plastic is a great way to kill the grass without chemicals. I would not place landscape fabric on top after the grass has died, though. I would recommend removing the dead sod, which will help to improve the drainage. If the existing soil is of good quality, then you may only need to add organic matter such as compost to the bed. If the soil is of poor quality, then removing it and adding new topsoil is the best way to go. It is your choice on how to add the new soil or organic matter into your bed. You can rent a tiller and till it in to a depth of 35 cm.

If you have a lot of clay below the topsoil, tilling into clay will be a rough ride, but it can be done.

Q. Can you please tell me if wood ashes are beneficial to a garden? We have a wood-burning stove and have been adding the ashes to our garden, but I really would like to know if they are harmful or beneficial to the soil.

A. According to Purdue University, "Wood ash does have fertilizer value, the amount varying somewhat with the species of wood being used.

Generally, wood ash contains less than 10 percent potash, 1 percent phosphate and trace amounts of micronutrients such as iron, manganese, boron, copper and zinc. Trace amounts of heavy metals such as lead, cadmium, nickel and chromium also may be present."

Wood ash also contains at least 25 percent calcium carbonate. This ingredient can rapidly increase soil pH, increasing the alkalinity of the soil. If your soil is already slightly alkaline, you can cause problems by increasing the pH even more. If your soil is acidic, you can actually help improve the pH through the addition of wood ash.

I recommend having your soil tested. If your soil is neutral or slightly alkaline, you should find another way to dispose of your ashes. If it is slightly acidic, you can safely apply 20 lbs/100 sq ft annually.

Q. I am thinking about getting some mushroom compost from a farm outside the city. Is mushroom compost good? Or is it full of salts and weed seeds? How much should I add to the soil, or can I use it as a mulch? How does mushroom compost compare to our regular city compost?

A. Mushroom compost is an excellent means of adding organic matter to your garden. I recall reading a very interesting report that was originally published in 1997 by the Ontario Ministry of Agriculture, Horticultural Research Institute of Ontario. The experiment found that sphagnum peat- or composted pine bark-based planting media that had been amended by the addition of spent mushroom compost were both excellent growing media for the test plants. They also found that the initially higher than desirable levels of salts in the compost-amended media were quickly leached "within one week of planting" and were not harmful to the test plants. You can read about this study at www.mushroom-sms.com/SMS_Container_Growing.pdf.

Now, having said this, there can be variability in some mushroom composts or manures depending on their sources. The nutrient and salt content can depend on the type of manure used. Some growers use chicken manure while others prefer horse manure.

Applying 10–15 cm of the compost to your garden or bed and mixing it thoroughly will work best. You can use the compost as a mulch as well. By using it as a mulch each time you water the nutrients will be released into your soil. I like to do both. I apply a thinner layer of compost and mix it in and then use some as a mulch to a depth of 8–13 cm. As for how it compares to the city compost, it would depend on the nutrient content of the mushroom compost you are using.

Q. I have been saving my lawn clippings and putting some of them into my composter. I'm wondering if I can take some of them and just dig them directly into the flower beds without composting?

A. Yes, you can. In fact, the grass clippings are one of my favourite things to use when mulching tomatoes. In fall, after I pull up the tomatoes, I just dig the lawn clippings directly into the bed. The clippings will add good organic matter to the beds as well as help to condition the soil. Grass clippings contain about 4 percent nitrogen, 0.5–1 percent phosphorus, 2–3 percent potassium and smaller amounts of other essential plant nutrients; basically a 4-1-3 fertilizer.

Q. We have a home office and generate quite a lot of computer paper. After I put the paper through my paper shredder, can I add it to my composter or put in on the paths in my veggie garden?

A. It depends on whether the ink you are using is soy-based or not. If it is, you can compost it or use it in the paths. If it is not, it may not be safe to use.

Q. My concern is what happens to pesticides during the composting process. Is it something to be concerned about? What are your opinions on this subject?

A. I did some research on this question and found some interesting information. Ohio State University, Department of Horticulture and Crop Science says, "One concern with composting is the fate of lawn care pesticides. Grass clippings and leaves treated with these products should not be used as a mulch immediately after application and mowing, but should be composted. The most widely used pesticides degrade rapidly during composting or become strongly bound to organic matter in the compost. Their degradation is accelerated by the high temperatures and moist conditions that occur in a compost pile." There is an excellent paper on this topic online at www.ciwmb.ca.gov/Publications/Organics/44200015.doc.

The general belief by most experts is that *most* turf and garden pesticides that are currently permitted and applied at label rates will be broken down and degraded more quickly in a compost pile than they will be in most other environments. The key here is to thoroughly compost the material containing the pesticides. I would avoid composting materials that have been exposed to pesticides. To me, it is not worth the risk—but that is only my opinion.

Q. I have a question about earthworms that we find while digging in the garden. Are they the same kind of worms that are used in composting and turning kitchen waste into worm castings? Can I just pick these worms out and put them into my compost pile?

A. They are not the same kind of worm. The worms needed for composting are red worms. You can find more information about worm composting and where to buy the worms on the City of Edmonton website at www.edmonton.ca/for_ residents/garbage_recycling/worm-composting.aspx.

Q. I just finished building a compost unit and have started putting material in from garden clean-up. My wife thinks that putting material in over the winter would be a waste of time, as it would only freeze. Please advise if adding kitchen material, etc., to the pile is advantageous over our winter.

A. I always tread lightly when answering questions that involve husband-and-wife disagreements. I'm grateful that in this case the answer is that both parties are right. The compost pile will do little composting as it gets colder, and once the pile freezes, no composting will occur. However, you should still be adding kitchen scraps, etc., all winter long because they will be broken down once spring arrives. Many gardeners clean out their compost pile/bin in the fall to make room for all the material that will be added over the winter but will not be broken down immediately.

Q. I would like to add some wood chips as a soil amendment to my soil. I have heard that they help with the clay problem. What is your opinion on this?

A. Wood chips can make a good soil amendment as long as you are not using cedar chips. Cedar takes a long time to break down and contains growth inhibitors that could affect other plants growing in the amended soil. When using wood chips as an amendment, you will need to add nitrogen to the soil. If additional nitrogen is not added, then the microorganisms responsible for the decomposition will "steal" the nitrogen from the soil, thus depleting the nitrogen levels available to other plants.

The formula for adding nitrogen is as follows for a 100 sq ft area:

Year 1: add 1 lb ammonium sulphate for each 1" layer of wood chips

Year 2: add ½ lb ammonium sulphate for each 1" layer of wood chips

Year 3: add ¼ lb ammonium sulphate for each 1" layer of wood chips

Year 4: add ⅛ lb ammonium sulphate for each 1" layer of wood chips

Q. The veins on the leaves of my petunias are green and the rest is yellow. I added some blood meal to the soil. Will that help? What can I do to avoid this problem? What do you think about mushroom compost? How much should be applied to the soil?

A. The chlorosis (yellowing) you describe could be caused by an iron deficiency. Petunias are prone to this type of chlorosis. It can be caused by a few different things. First, your soil may have a pH that is too high. The ideal soil pH for growing petunias should be in the 5.6–6.0 range. You can do a quick test of your soil with a do-it-yourself soil-testing kit available in garden centres. A pH that is too high will inhibit uptake of iron. If your soil pH is too high, incorporate some peat moss into the soil to lower the pH. A second cause may be the lack of fertilizer. A well-balanced fertilizer such as 20-20-20 with micronutrients is the best to use. Fertilize the plants regularly (weekly) with the well-balanced fertilizer. The blood meal will help supply extra iron as well.

Mushroom compost is an excellent choice. It adds many nutrients and micronutrients. Apply it at a rate of 1 cubic yard to 100 sq ft of garden. That will give you a depth of 5 cm of compost, which is ideal.

Q. I have made large containers for growing vegetables mainly because we have a serious weed problem. Is it wise to fill these with composted soil from a recycle plant to grow vegetables?

A. The City of Edmonton Composting Facility has some information available online at: www.edmonton. ca/Environment/WasteManagement/ CompostingWasteFacts.pdf.

On this information fact sheet the city has a list of uses for the compost. Among the uses listed are:

- home use (in soil blends)
- gardens and flowerbeds
- lawns and topdressing
- mulch
- agriculture
- general field soil supplement
- reduced chemical fertilizer

It would appear that the compost is safe for vegetables. Check with wherever you are getting your composted soil from.

Q. I bought my house two years ago and moved in when it was winter. Last spring, I planted many perennial flower seeds hoping for my yard to be in "full bloom" by summer. It never happened. In most areas of my yard, nothing seems to want to grow, weeds included. I have a few perennials that I got from my mom. Most of those have died as well. I think that perhaps the previous owners may have sterilized the soil. Is it possible to rejuvenate that soil without having to buy topsoil (funds are sorely limited)?

A. To me, the telltale sign that there is something amiss with the soil is that even the weeds will not grow in it. You may want to take a soil sample to a soil-testing lab to see if they can determine exactly what is the problem.

If it is a sterilant, there is little you can do other than wait for the chemical to break down on its own. Residual effects from sterilants can last for years. That is why the average home-owner should use extreme caution when applying sterilants. They not only affect your yard for many years but also can leach into neighbours' yards as well.

Is this area next to a sidewalk or driveway? If so, it may contain salt that was used in the winter to remove ice. Salt can be a very effective sterilant.

I have several ideas you can try with your problem. First, get the soil tested so that you will know exactly what the problem is and how to deal with it. Second, free topsoil is available, but you have to look for it. Check out the classifieds and give some excavation companies a call. Quite often they are more than glad to get rid of soil providing you pick it up. Make sure to be diligent about ensuring the soil's quality, though (see p. 22–23). Third,

start watering the area regularly in an effort to start diluting the chemical.

Q. This question may seem silly, but can you tell me when is the best time to add compost or manure to my flower beds? I see other gardeners using synthetic fertilizers throughout the growing season. I have been applying my compost and manure only in spring. Should I be doing more the rest of the growing season?

A. I can tell you what works for me. I add compost and manure every spring to all of my beds, working it into the soil very well. After planting and when the plants have grown a few leaves and are established, I add a layer of compost as a mulch. This layer serves a twofold purpose. First, it helps conserve moisture and helps to keep the weeds down. Second, it provides nutrients to the plants every time I water.

For my containers, I make a compost tea. I add a couple of hand shovelfuls of compost to a five-gallon pail of water and let the tea "steep." Then I drain off the liquid part of the "tea" and use it for watering my containers and other plants. The compost left in the bottom of the pail is added to the garden as organic matter. By using the compost as a mulch and as a tea, you can provide added nutrients to your plants throughout the growing season.

Q. You answered a question recently about lilacs planted with landscape fabric and rock mulch, in which you suggested removing the rock mulch and using an organic mulch such as shredded bark instead. Should the landscape fabric be removed also?

I have a couple of ornamental trees in my yard. Last year, I removed old landscape fabric and rock mulch that was there from the previous owners and replaced it with bark mulch but did not put any landscape fabric underneath the bark mulch. I am wondering if there should be landscape fabric underneath or not.

A. A good quality landscape fabric can be very effective at keeping weeds at bay. However, I have found that over time, many fabrics tend to get clogged with dust, dirt and debris. The debris stops the water from penetrating and also cuts off the air circulation. Both water and air are vital in keeping plants happy. Even the most expensive landscape grade fabrics clog in time. Removing the mulch and using a sharp spray from a hose to clean off the fabric can remedy this problem, but if you have large areas with fabric, this job can be quite time-consuming.

I never use landscape fabric in my beds. I certainly have used it and love it for its weed protection in places such as on the side of the house where decorative plants will not grow.

I use an organic shredded bark mulch with no fabric under it. I like that I can simply move the mulch to plant new plants or move things around easily if I need to.

Even in places such as under a large evergreen, I lay the mulch down on its own with no fabric. Using an organic mulch means that over time it breaks down, but I add more mulch each spring, and it works very well. I love the way it looks, and the added benefit is that many organic mulches such as shredded cedar smell great.

Q. I have a problem with a sandy soil that does not hold moisture very well. In addition to adding more organic material to the soil, is there anything else I can do to help with this problem? I am interested in having a landscape that is very low maintenance; having to water all the time because of the sandy soil is a problem for us.

A. Organic matter is a great solution to condition your sandy soil. It will help retain moisture and will not allow the water to run through the soil freely. One of the most efficient ways of creating a low or no maintenance landscape is through the use of mulches.

In a low-maintenance landscape, preserving moisture is the primary reason for mulching. During times of heat and low water, mulching can make the difference between a plant surviving or dying. It is especially true in an application where regular watering may not be possible, such as in a second home. An added bonus with mulching in a low-maintenance landscape is that the mulch serves a decorative function and even leaves or needles falling on the mulch do not look untidy. They simply look like a part of the mulch. If you want a low-cost mulch, grass clippings can make very effective mulch. I use grass clippings in my vegetable garden, and they are effective at keeping weeds at bay and the moisture in the soil. As the clippings break down, they add valuable organic matter to the soil.

With many attractive mulches on the market, including cedar bark nuggets or shredded cedar bark, mulching can add to the appearance of the landscape and make a plain bed into a point of interest. Organic mulches such as barks, peat moss or compost can add to the organic content of the soil enriching it as they break down as well.

For more on soil and amendments, see also:

p. 61 I have clay soil; how do I make a raised bed?

p. 68 What kind of amendments should I add to the soil to grow carrots?

p. 69 How can I grow vegetables in my heavy clay soil?

p. 90 What can I do with heavily compacted soil?

p. 111 My grass is a sickly green colour; could there be a problem with the soil?

p. 123 Should I fertilize in the fall?

p. 125 What kind of fertilizer should I use?

p. 205 How can I prepare my soil for planting a maple tree?

Vegetable Gardening

More and more gardeners are looking for eco-friendly alternatives and are finding that growing our own vegetables is a great way to reduce our demands on the environment.

By growing your own vegetables, you can reduce the carbon footprint that is involved with the production of the vegetables. If we think about commercially produced and marketed tomatoes, for example, the carbon footprint resulting from the production, transportation and marketing of these tomatoes is much larger than the footprint that results from growing your own. When you add in the fact that homegrown vegetables just taste better and in most cases are less expensive than store-bought produce, home gardens make a world of good sense. Economic factors and environmental concerns are among the main reasons for the increased popularity of vegetable gardening.

There is also a large amount of interest in organically grown produce. In my opinion, the reasons for the interest are twofold. First, consumers are interested in their health and in avoiding foods that may be exposed to pesticides or that are grown with synthetic fertilizers. Second, consumers with an eco-friendly conscience want to avoid foods that have been exposed to chemicals that are harmful not only to humans but also to the environment we live in.

You can grow many vegetables in your own garden.

According to Statistics Canada (2008), nearly 75 percent of Canadians garden in some form or another, and of those, previous studies have shown that one in three grow their own vegetables. More and more gardeners are growing their own vegetables today. There are signs in the gardening industry that indicate this trend is indeed happening. The W. Atlee Burpee Co. has seen the demand for seeds double, according to Tracy Lee, director of horticulture at the seed company. The Garden Writers Association of America, in a survey done in April 2009, noted that 12 percent of respondents who did not have a vegetable garden were planning to add one.

As I tell people who attend my tomato workshops, there is nothing that can beat the taste of homegrown produce, especially tomatoes. If you grow your own tomatoes, you can allow them to ripen on the vine. This ripening gives the tomato its full and best flavour and is a technique that is not used often by commercial growers. Commercially grown tomatoes are picked when still green or semi-ripe to ensure that they do not bruise when shipping. Some of the semi-ripe tomatoes that are picked will have 90 percent of their red, fully ripe colour but are still far from being ripe and full flavoured. The tomatoes that are picked early are then often forced to ripen by using ethylene gas. Small wonder that these tomatoes never have the same taste as those that are allowed to ripen on the vine in the home garden.

Heirloom Seeds

Another area in vegetable gardening that is showing a renewed interest is heirloom seeds. An heirloom variety by definition is a plant that is a cultivar that was commonly grown during earlier periods in human history but which is not used in modern large-scale agriculture. Heirloom plants must be open pollinated. That simply means that they have to be pollinated by bees, other insects, birds or other natural means. Some of these varieties lost favour and were no longer used because of certain characteristics. For example, some tomatoes were prone to cracking, or they may have had imperfections in their appearance such as bumps or an odd shape. These features made them less desirable for sale than hybrid varieties that were bred for their perfect appearance and other desirable traits.

The interesting thing is that many heirloom varieties taste better than the hybrids. Tomatoes such as 'Brandywine' have excellent flavour. The tantalizing flavour more than makes up for this tomato's ugly duckling appearance with its few bumps and lumps. Gardeners are more interested in what their vegetables taste like than what they look like;

thus the renewed interest in heirloom varieties.

There are literally thousands of varieties of heirloom plants. By growing heirloom seeds, you can harvest the seeds each year and plant them again the next year because those seeds will produce the true form of the plant you harvested them from. Saving the seeds also ensures that those varieties will survive and not die out—that is the goal of the organization Seeds of Diversity. Seeds of Diversity is a Canadian charitable organization dedicated to the conservation, documentation and use of public-domain, non-hybrid plants of Canadian significance. Their objectives are to search out, preserve, perpetuate, study and encourage the cultivation of heirloom and endangered varieties of food crops.

Growing heirloom seeds can be an interesting and beneficial hobby. By experimenting with varieties of seeds, you can choose the variety that you like best, and if you save the seeds, you can plant the same favourite variety year after year, thus saving time and money. There are many varieties of heirloom plants that have interesting textures and colours. Striped tomatoes are an example of the uniqueness of heirloom types. 'Striped Roman' is a very unusual, sausage-shaped tomato with red and orangey stripes. This tomato also has excellent flavour. How about a purple carrot named 'Cosmic' that is also an heirloom type? Heirloom seeds can be fun to grow and produce tasty vegetables.

If you are interested in trying heirloom seeds, more and more seed companies are carrying them. You can get more information by going to the Seeds of Diversity website (www.seeds.ca/en.php), and if you want to know where you can buy the seeds, check the same website by clicking on the link "Looking for Seeds?"

There really is no excuse for not being able to enjoy fresh vegetables from your own garden. We will look in more detail at outdoor container vegetable growing in the Container Gardening section (see p. 149), but it needs to be mentioned here that you can grow enough vegetables in one container to have your own salad garden. You can also grow some varieties of veggies indoors.

Indoor Vegetables

It is a sad time when the last vegetables have been harvested in fall. I'm always looking for ways to lengthen the growing season of my veggies. I cover my tomatoes with plastic panels to protect them from the cold nights. By doing so, I manage to squeeze out an extra two to three weeks with the added effort, but the end of the season always comes with a resounding thud. A recent article

I read addressed the issue of growing veggies inside during winter. I have tried growing vegetables indoors in the past with some success. The idea of being able to pick your own tomatoes or other vegetables in the dead of winter has great appeal.

In the past, vegetable seeds were hard to find in retailers during winter, but more and more garden centres now carry them throughout the year. It must be a result of demand, so perhaps there are more indoor vegetable gardeners out there than I know about. Temperature, pollination and lighting are important things to consider when planning your indoor garden. Leafy vegetables such as lettuce and Swiss chard prefer growing in cooler temperatures. A bright room that is not used a lot would make a perfect spot. You can lower the temperature in that room down to 15° C, and the leafy veggies will be happy. I recently grew Swiss chard in a container indoors. I chose a packet of seeds that contained the white, red and yellow types of chard. Not only did the chard grow extremely well indoors, but it also made a very colourful display.

Vegetables such as tomatoes and sweet and hot peppers require warmer daytime and evening temperatures than the leafy vegetables. A south-facing room is desirable, but a west-facing room with supplemental lighting may work as well. The daytime temperatures for these plants should be in the 21–23° C range, and the nighttime temperature should not fall below 15° C.

Lighting is a bit of an issue but one that is easily overcome with artificial lights. Because the sun is so much lower on the horizon during winter, it does not provide enough light to the plants. Vegetables, and especially tomatoes, will need six to eight hours of light per day. A combination of cool-white and warm-white fluorescent lighting works well. The plants will have to be very close to the lights to get the maximum effect. Aim for a 15 cm distance from the lights when placing the plants.

Another factor to consider is where to place the plants: do not place them too close to cold windows. The cold air coming off these windows can adversely affect the plants. I have seen plant leaves freeze when touching a cold window. While placing the plants to get natural light is a benefit, keeping them warm is paramount.

When it comes to a planting medium, choose a good-quality potting mix. The soil-less potting mixes make great choices for growing veggies indoors. Because these soil-less mixes are rather low in nutrients, you will need to fertilize the plants on regular basis. A fertilizer such as Miracle-Gro is an excellent product to use. A great way to fertilize is to water the plants

with a dilute solution of fertilizer. Mix up a solution at ¼ the recommended strength of the fertilizer, and use this solution to water your plants. A good schedule is to alternate plain water and the fertilizer solution. One watering with plain water, the next watering with the fertilizer solution is a good regime. If you would rather go the eco-friendly route, add compost to the soil-less mix instead of fertilizing.

Another key to keeping veggies happy is even moisture. Evenly moist but not wet is the best. There is also a concern with a lack of humidity during winter. Mist your plants on a regular basis. The alternative is to place them on a shallow tray filled with pebbles. Add water to the tray to a depth just below the top of the pebbles, and place the plants in their pots on top of the pebbles to increase the humidity surrounding the plants.

Here is a list of veggies to try indoors:

- bush beans
- cherry tomatoes
- eggplant
- leaf lettuce
- radishes
- small-rooted carrots
- spinach
- Swiss chard
- various hot peppers

Starting from Seed Outdoors

Starting vegetables from seed outdoors can be a rewarding and cost-friendly way to get your vegetable garden growing. Many vegetables can be started from seed simply by planting them in the ground after all danger of frost has passed. Some vegetables can even be planted in early spring because they tolerate colder conditions, and some even tolerate a light frost.

Here is a partial list of vegetables that can be planted in the ground in early spring (approximately six weeks prior to the last killing frost) according to Colorado State University (CSU). After the plant name, you will find the suggested minimum planting temperature according to Alberta Agriculture:

- broccoli (4° C)
- cabbage (4° C)
- lettuce (0° C)
- onions (0° C)
- peas (4° C)
- spinach (0° C)

According to CSU, seeds that can be planted two to four weeks before the average last spring frost include:

- beets (4° C)
- carrots (4° C)
- cauliflower (4° C)
- celery (4° C)
- chard (4° C)
- radishes (4° C)

The CSU list of non-cold-hardy vegetables (plant after the last frost) includes:

- snap beans (15° C)
- sweet corn (10° C)
- tomatoes (10° C)

Finally, CSU lists the plants that need hot weather and should be planted at least one week after the last frost:

- cucumbers (15° C)
- melon (15° C)
- peppers (15° C)
- pumpkin (15° C)

Remember that the suggested planting times are guidelines only. If spring is wet or cold, you may have to modify the planting times accordingly. For plants such as tomatoes, peppers, melons and sweet corn, you can start the seeds indoors. Cucumbers do not transplant well and are best planted outdoors well after the danger of frost has passed.

Starting your own vegetables from seed indoors is not a daunting task. For a planting medium, use a soil-less potting mix. Look for sterilized potting mix that is ready to use with no mixing involved. The pots or containers for starting the seeds can be anything that is suitable. I use the plastic containers you get at supermarkets that are used for bakery goods such as cookies. And, no, that does not mean I eat 400 cookies just to get the containers. I can hear all that snickering out there! Ask friends and relatives to save these containers for you. These containers are ideal because they come with hinged lids that can be kept closed to keep in the humidity or opened if the sun causes too much heat to build up in the container.

Before adding the soil-less mix to the container, it is a good idea to soak the soil first. Put it in a small pail or container and water it very well. Mix it around with your hands and allow the mix to absorb the water. The mixture should be moist but not to the point of having water dripping off if you pick up a ball of it in your hand. Add enough of the mix to the container so that it is within 5 mm of the top of the container. Doing so will allow you to water without having it run over the sides.

Different seeds have different requirements. Take the time to read the seed package to find out how deep the seeds should be planted, how long to germinate and so on. Keep the containers covered until the seeds sprout. If the seeds need sun and light, then the containers should be placed in the sunniest location— south and west windows are the

best. If it is a sunny day and the sun is shining directly on the container, prop open the lid to keep the temperature from getting too high. If the soil-less mix begins to dry out, water carefully so as not to disturb the seeds. Keep the soil evenly moist. The soil should never be allowed to dry out completely.

Once the plants have all sprouted, leave them uncovered. You may need to thin them out. Carefully pull out the unwanted plantlets. Pull out the ones that are growing too close together, leaving the strongest plantlet standing. Once the plantlets have two or three leaves, you can transplant them into individual containers such as peat pots or used milk cartons filled with potting soil. Keep the soil moist but not wet and in full sun until ready to plant outdoors.

In addition to the satisfaction of growing your own plants from seed, you will appreciate the ability to grow the varieties that you choose to grow and not the ones that the greenhouses have decided to grow. For example, growing heirloom varieties of vegetables is easy when you choose to start your own seeds. Finding these same varieties as bedding plants in local greenhouses is almost impossible.

Community Gardens

If space for a vegetable garden is an issue in your yard or if your property is simply not conducive to a garden, there are alternatives. One alternative is to make use of a community garden. Community gardening saw its beginnings in Canada in the form of railway gardens. In 1908, Canadian Pacific Railway provided seeds as an encouragement to station agents to cultivate small gardens on station property. The idea was enthusiastically adopted across the country. As the station agents gained expertise, it was often they who helped to create local horticultural societies and garden clubs.

Today, community gardens can provide a valuable food source for people in need as well as for those looking for pesticide- and chemical-free produce for themselves and their families. A community garden can be started anywhere there is free land available. It is preferred that the property has a water supply as well.

There are many benefits to community gardening other than growing your own vegetables:

- Organic food is available for everyone involved in the garden. Some gardens grow produce exclusively for those in need through donations of produce to local food banks. Other gardens encourage gardeners to contribute to the food bank through the "Plant a Row, Grow a Row" project. Gardeners in this project not only grow their own food but also plant an extra row for harvest and donation to the food bank.

- Community gardening is an excellent recreational activity and is a great way for urban residents to get back to nature. It also enables neighbours to get to know one another and share an understanding of each other.

- Experienced gardeners help teach novices. Gardening proficiency is enhanced through exchange of ideas and group problem solving.

- It promotes safe neighbourhoods. The gardens discourage untoward activity, especially in vacant or undeveloped sites in high-crime areas. It can promote local revitalization. Increased resident involvement leads to a pride of community.

I know one friend who produces enough vegetables in his community garden to feed his whole family, and he is also able to supply bumper crops of veggies to the food bank. When I asked him why the sudden interest in vegetable gardening, he replied that he has found it extremely satisfying to grow his own vegetables, and being able to supply the food bank is important to him and his family.

Vegetable Gardening Basics

It is very easy to start your own vegetable garden. If you have a small spot in your yard that you are not using, all you need is a rototiller to break up the soil and ready it for planting. Try planting root vegetables such as potatoes for the first year or two in your new garden. Potatoes are easy to grow and require little maintenance. They are also nitrogen-fixing plants, which means they can convert nitrogen in the atmosphere into nitrates in the soil that are usable by plants. This nitrogen helps to condition the soil, and after you have grown potatoes, you can move on to growing other veggies.

Root vegetables such as carrots, turnips, beets and parsnips will do very well without a lot of water and attention. Mulching with something as simple as grass clippings will help to conserve moisture as well as keep weeds down. Remember that your vegetable garden does not have to be huge. My first house had two enormous vegetable plots that totalled approximately 1800 sq ft of space. I felt I had to plant it all with veggies, and I spent the rest of that summer tending to the crops with little time left for anything else. Your garden could be as small as you like. A 4' × 4' garden will produce a good crop of veggies by using the square foot gardening system. Several years ago, a book came out entitled *Square Foot Gardening* by Mel Bartholemew. I became a disciple and now offer you, my faithful readers, the opportunity to learn more about this great gardening system.

This method is appropriate for gardeners with space limitations or who want to transform their existing vegetable gardens into more efficient systems. The square foot system is low maintenance and water friendly, meaning that the normal maintenance of weeding, fertilizing and digging have been reduced or eliminated. The system also uses 80 percent less water than a normal garden scenario. Another advantage is that it uses far less space than conventional gardening, specifically 80 percent less space. While I have used the system primarily for vegetable gardening, it can be used for growing annual flowers just as easily.

I know many of you are probably thinking, "Okay, so what is this going to cost me in money, time and effort?" The answer is: very little. All you need is some 1' × 6' or 2' × 6' lumber and a few ingredients to make your own soil-less potting mix, and you are ready to start gardening. The lumber is used to construct raised beds that are 4' × 4' squares. These squares can easily be constructed simply by nailing together the boards, or for extra strength, you can use metal clips that are specially designed for raised beds. You then divide the

4' × 4' beds into 16, 1' × 1' squares by placing thin wood strips at 1' intervals. These strips should run from board to board horizontally and vertically, creating the 16 squares.

Place these measured beds on existing soil, and fill the square foot garden with a mixture of one part each of compost, peat moss and coarse vermiculite. If you are placing the beds over a lawn, you can either dig out the lawn or cover the grass with cardboard to keep the weeds from coming through your bed. You no longer have to worry about having poor soil in your yard or perhaps too much clay. The raised bed solves all those problems because the roots of the plants do not need to grow in your poor soil. They grow in the soil-less mix you provide for them. This feature is a huge advantage.

There are other advantages of a 4' square garden. You can reach into the centre of the square from any side and never tromp all over your freshly cultivated soil. Since the soil doesn't get compacted by people walking all over it, the need to rototill (or double dig if you want to go the high-level aerobic route) is eliminated. With plants grouped together, maintenance and cultivation is easier. With the plants more closely spaced, weeds also have a hard time getting established. The old row system of vegetable gardening uses space very inefficiently and results in the soil getting compacted in the rows from being walked on.

You can plant a different flower, vegetable or herb crop in each square foot. If the seed packet recommends spacing 12" (30 cm) apart, you would plant one plant in the square. If the spacing says every 6" (15 cm), you would seed four per square foot. Spacing 4" (10 cm) apart would require nine seeds per square foot. For example, Bartholemew suggests planting one pepper plant per 1' square. Therefore, if you planted an entire 4' (1.2 m) main block in pepper plants, you would have a total of 16 pepper plants. In another example, Mel suggests planting nine spinach plants in each 1' (30 cm) block. Therefore, if you planted an entire 4' (1.2 m) main block in spinach, you would have 144 spinach plants. You can buy Bartholemew's book (which came out in a new, updated edition in 2009) or get information about this system online at www.squarefootgardening.com.

If you have a second home and are looking for a fast and easy way to grow a vegetable or flower garden, this garden system may be the one for you. It is very simple to install a drip irrigation system into the square foot garden. Having your drip irrigation system on a timer means your garden could be watered efficiently and effectively without you even being there to do the watering. Also, unlike traditional gardening methods, your preparation time is cut in half because you do not have to prepare the soil for planting. If you find your soil-less mix getting a little tired, in this system you just add more compost or peat moss.

Spending time to plan your vegetable garden will reap rewards for years to come. For example, digging a veggie garden in a shady spot is a definite no-no—most vegetables require at least six hours of sunlight per day to perform at their best. The garden should be close to a reliable supply of water as well. With a few exceptions, vegetable plants need water on a regular basis to produce the best and largest produce.

One area I feel strongly about is teaching children where food comes from. I am very interested in how many young people are into gardening. When I first started doing public appearances some 17 years ago, I would get very few young people coming up and asking me gardening questions. Within the last several years, I have noticed far more gardeners in the 20- to 30-year-old age range asking questions and expressing their passion for gardening. It is encouraging to me. For years, I was concerned that the next generation seemed to be losing interest and focus in gardening at a time in the world when we most needed this return to basics.

It is critical that children learn where the food they eat comes from and how it grows and how to help it grow. We need to foster the knowledge that growing our own food is healthy for ourselves and for the earth. As the global concerns about the availability of food continue to grow, educating children on how to garden will become increasingly important. Drawing kids away from their computers and gaming systems and helping them to appreciate nature and gain respect for their planet is yet another positive on how vegetable gardening can benefit us all. I think that realizing that gardening can help the environment in many ways is a strong incentive for younger people to get on board.

There is a quotation from J.C. Loudon that nicely sums up the appeal of vegetable gardening: "For all things produced in a garden, whether of salads or fruits, a poor man will eat better that has one of his own, than a rich man that has none."

Tomatoes

If I had to come clean and admit one obsession in gardening, it would have to be tomatoes. I have had an interest in growing as many varieties of tomatoes as I could over the years. I have decided in this book to reveal some of my tomato-growing secrets that previously were only available to those who took one of my tomato-growing seminars.

Vegetable gardening is seeing a revival with more and more gardeners returning to growing their own food not only because it is economical to do so but also because it is a healthy choice. Tomatoes are one of the most popular vegetables, and while they are relatively easy to grow, there are secrets that can make them grow better and bigger.

Growing tomatoes has been a passion of mine for the past 40 years because to me there is nothing that can compare to the taste of a homegrown tomato. The store-bought varieties just do not have the flavour, juiciness or even aroma of homegrown. Much ado has been made about the "tomatoes on the vine" that many supermarkets carry today. Even these cannot compare to those grown in your own garden. Over my many years of growing tomatoes, I have accumulated a small library of tried-and-true techniques for growing the biggest and best-tasting tomatoes.

The basics for growing tomatoes successfully begins with the following must-haves:

- Sunlight—A minimum of six hours of sunlight per day is an absolute must. While tomatoes may grow in semi-shaded locations, your production will not be optimum nor will the size of the tomatoes. Tomatoes love heat and lots of it. Planting them against a house or fence that faces south is an ideal spot for them.

- Moisture—Tomatoes prefer to be kept evenly moist but not wet, especially when the plants are setting the fruit. Physiological problems such as blossom end rot can develop if the moisture levels are not even. Do not allow tomatoes to dry out completely.

- Soil amendments—Prior to planting every year, add organic matter to the soil. The best material to use is compost or well-rotted manure. Tomatoes love organic matter in the soil, and the more the better.

- Fertilizer—Tomatoes are very heavy feeders and need to be fertilized on a regular basis to optimize their production. Some gardeners like to use Miracle-Gro applied every two weeks. Others like to use a dilute solution of Miracle-Gro (¼ strength) with every watering. If you are interested in growing totally organic tomatoes, one of the best ways to add nutrients is with liquid fish fertilizer or fish emulsion. This product is my personal choice, and I think it gives the best tomatoes. I apply fish fertilizer once a week. Yes, it does smell a bit, and you might attract a few cats (I'm kidding), but it works very well.

The fish emulsion provides the tomatoes with the trace elements they need in addition to a 5-1-1 completely organic fertilizer.

Tomatoes actually prefer to be planted deeper than they were growing prior to transplant. If the tomato plant is 60 cm tall, for example, strip off the lower leaves and plant the tomato up to 30 cm deep in the soil. This deeper planting allows the stem to produce more rootlets at a faster rate because more of the plant stem is exposed to the soil. These rootlets in turn will take up water and nutrients more quickly. Any time a plant can be encouraged to have a larger root system is a good thing. The plant will grow more quickly and be healthier as a result.

Another planting technique that works well is called stem rooting. Tomato plants will form roots anywhere the stem contacts the soil. Many gardeners take advantage of this by planting tomatoes horizontally with only the tops sticking out of the ground. To set out plants in this manner, dig a trench several inches deep and as long as the roots and stem. Lay the plant in the trench, allowing the top two or three sets of leaves to come to the soil surface, and gently firm soil around the roots and stem. Roots will grow quickly in the warm, top inches of soil, getting the plant off to a fast start.

I firmly believe in the use of mulches when growing tomatoes. You can easily increase tomato production and vigour through the use of a mulch because mulches act to maintain the even levels of moisture I mentioned previously. You end up having to water less frequently, but the tomato still has access to the moisture it needs. My favourite type of mulch for tomatoes is grass clippings. I lay them down so they are 2.5 cm deep around the stem but not touching the plant. Grass clippings are inexpensive, easy to apply and last for most of the growing season. They are also good at keeping the weeds at bay and keeping the moisture in. One of the new trends in mulching tomatoes is to use red plastic mulch. This technology claims to increase tomato yield by 20 percent. Red is the part of the light spectrum that is most used by the tomato plant, so the red-coloured mulch adds to the red light being absorbed by the plant.

Of the many varieties of excellent tasting tomatoes, here are some of my tried-and-true favourites:

- 'Brandywine': an heirloom variety that has excellent flavour

- 'Sub-Arctic Maxi': a very early variety; smaller tomatoes but excellent taste

- 'Early Girl': another early variety with slightly larger fruit

- 'Beefsteak': an old favourite that is hard to beat for flavour, size and meatiness

- 'Polish Giant': I grow these for fun; they take up to 100 days to mature but can grow up to 2 lbs in size!

Questions and Answers: The Most Popular Vegetable Topics

Q. I have a question that may sound rather silly, but does it matter if rows in the garden are planted going east/west or north/south?

A. Your question on the direction of the rows is not silly at all. I don't think it makes any difference which direction the rows run, but the most important consideration is to have the taller vegetable plants placed so that they do not shade the lower growing types; if the rows run east and west, then the taller plants should be planted in the north rows, and if the rows run north and south, the tall plants should be on the west side.

Q. I plan to create a vegetable garden 1.5 m by 3 m over a part of our existing lawn. I plan to have a raised bed about 10–13 cm. The reason for the raised bed is because we live on an acreage with clay as our soil. You would be hard pressed to find any real loam on our acreage. These are my questions:

1. Do I dig up the soil underneath before I put the new dirt on? I hope not.

2. Do I spray the grass with anything to minimize grass peeking through the bedding plants? (I don't mind pulling it out as it appears.)

3. We have a fine crop of dandelions, and of course they will also come through. Should I just let them grow through and then deal with them?

I would really like to keep away from any chemicals, if possible. If I sprayed with a chemical, when the roots of the bedding plants get down 10 cm, it could kill them as well. I plan on growing peas, carrots, lettuce, cucumbers and a few tomatoes. Hoping you can point me in the right direction.

A. The base of a raised bed is as important as the bed itself. If the bed is not properly drained, problems can be created. Drainage is crucial.

Any sod at the base of the bed should be removed. Water the sod heavily a few hours before removal, and rent a sod cutter to make the job easier. If you don't have access to a sod cutter, use a flat shovel. My favourite way of removing sod is using a half-moon-shaped edging tool that I sharpen to a razor edge. Then I use the edging tool to outline the area I plan to remove. I then simply kneel in front of the area and

Vegetables growing in raised beds.

slide the edging tool under the sod and just push it along. Every few feet I cut across the grain and remove the piece and toss it aside. I like this method because I can easily control the depth of the cut.

I recommend digging or tilling the clay base to a depth of 15–25 cm. Add organic matter such as compost or well-rotted manure into the clay and mix it in well. Adding coarse sand or pea gravel can also help with heavy clay soils. Always add the sand last so that it will sift down through the soil during tilling. Till the entire bed. When done, it should be about level with the original grade. Ideally, the raised bed should be at least 25–40 cm high—the 10–13 cm you

mentioned will not be deep enough to keep your vegetables happy.

You can cover the area with heavy-grade black landscape plastic for the summer to ensure that any grass or weeds are dead. The heat generated under the plastic will kill the grass and weeds effectively without chemicals.

Q. I've seen raised beds for flowers and vegetables in various gardens. Can you tell me what the advantages are as compared to just planting straight into ground level? Also, how does one go about building a raised bed? What is the base, etc.?

A. There are many advantages to raised beds. They provide better drainage and warm up faster in spring than traditional gardens. The growing season can be started earlier as well. The beds are easier to weed, irrigate, mulch and harvest. Only the garden area under production, not the paths, is watered, fertilized and mulched, which saves both time and money. Since the beds are never walked on, the soil doesn't compact, and better quality vegetables result. Space is saved, so more crops can be raised in a smaller area. An added benefit is that the beds make the garden more attractive. Clay can be a problem in many areas, but a raised bed can bypass the difficulties of having to deal with heavy, clay soil.

Construct the frame with a nontoxic building material such as stone, cinder blocks, bricks, cedar or untreated wood. I avoid pressure-treated lumber and creosote-treated railway ties. Some garden catalogues and centres now offer raised bed frames that snap together and can easily be taken apart. Lee Valley Tools (www.leevalley.com), for example, has clips that can be used to fasten together planks. You can build a raised bed using this clip system in a matter of an hour or so.

I recommend tilling the soil that will be under the bed as it allows more room for root development. The main requirement of the base of the bed is good drainage. It is imperative that the bed be able to drain properly. Fill the bed with a good-quality, lightweight soil mix to which a generous amount of compost has been added.

Q. I am planning to build raised vegetable garden beds this year, but I don't know what material would be best to use. I am a bit concerned about using treated wood for a vegetable garden, but I want something that will last. What material is best?

A. There is concern about the chemicals of pressure-treated lumber leaching into the soil. According to Dr. Allan S. Felsot, environmental toxicologist at Washington State University, "Some leaching of CCA (chromated copper arsenate) indisputably occurs from treated wood, but the next question is its fate once in the soil (or compost). The metal oxides tend to bind to the soil particles, except in highly acid soils (pH of 4.0 or lower) and, therefore, are not easily absorbed by plants. Even if maximum amounts of CCA leach, little chemical actually enters the root and edible parts of plants. Furthermore, the plant itself is likely to show symptoms of toxicity at levels far below those considered toxic to humans."

However, other schools of thought consider the leaching to be a potential problem not only directly to humans but also to the environment. If you have reservations about the use of pressure-treated wood, my advice is to line the inside of the beds with landscape-grade plastic. If you want to avoid the risks totally, use cedar. It's a little more costly and may not last quite as long as the treated wood, but it will do the job for you. Perhaps the best alternative is to use timbers made of recycled wood products and plastic. This "plastic wood" is relatively new on the market and is a safe alternative.

Q. I built a deck using Trex decking boards and have quite a few left over. I was wondering if I can use them for a raised vegetable garden. I have no clue what they are made of.

A. I checked out the Trex website for more information. The site explains very well what the boards are made of: "Trex composite products are made of a unique combination of wood and plastic fibres. Trex gets its plastic and wood fibres from reclaimed or recycled resources including sawdust and used pallets from woodworking operations, and recycled plastic grocery bags from all over the country…Trex products are incredibly safe for the whole family—they don't contain any harmful chemicals…"

From this information, it seems that Trex would be a safe and good product to use for your raised bed. The Trex company is very environmentally conscious. If you want to read about how their plants are "green," you can visit their website at www.trex.com.

Q. We understand the benefits of crop rotation, but the tiny size of our veggie patches coupled with our preference for certain types of peas and beans preclude rotation. Are there nutritional supplements we might add to the soil? For example, we love snow peas and beans and have just enough room for both. What might we use to augment the nutrition in the gardens, depleted through last year's crops?

We have had great success over the years using window boxes for lettuce and spinach. The boxes sit on the railing around our deck, which makes it highly convenient for fresh salads. Out the door to the deck, snip, snip and fresh salad is available. We've found we get two crops from the initial seeding and earth fill, then two more when we replace the earth and re-seed in early summer. We've also found lettuce to be extremely hardy.

Once the seeds germinate, we wait for the green leaves to peak through. When that occurs, we watch the overnight temp carefully and have a few old sheets available for cover if severe temperatures are forecast.

The deck placement also prevents neighbourhood rabbits from feasting on our lettuce, although we notice some songbirds are occasionally attracted for a brief green snack.

A. Your email is a good example of a technique for growing lettuce that works very well for you. I am always extolling the virtues of container vegetable gardening for anyone who has space issues or who just wants to have a handy source of lettuce greens. My dad grew lettuce greens right next to his back door and enjoyed being able to harvest them even on a rainy day. I now grow all of my lettuce in containers close to the house. Convenience is not the only reason. By growing in containers, I free up valuable space in my garden for other vegetables that need the space to perform at their best.

As for your question on soil nutrients, the peas and beans you grow are both legumes. These plants work together with bacteria in the soil to actually improve soil fertility by adding nitrogen. Together the plants and bacteria fix nitrogen from the air, making it available in the soil. That takes care of the nitrogen, but there are other nutrients that may need to be replaced. Compost is the best solution for improving soil fertility. Compost can even help with replacing micronutrients. I would add a generous portion of compost every spring before planting. You can work it into the soil. I also like to use the compost as a mulch on top of the soil. A 5 cm deep layer of compost will produce compost tea for your plants every time you water. This tea will filter down to the roots, providing even more nutrients.

Questions and Answers: Propagation

Q. I've started some tomato and okra seeds in covered trays, and they have sprouted. Do I remove the lid and mist daily, or do I wait to see if every seed is going to come up? Do I keep the dome on them?

A. Heat can build up very quickly in an enclosed container in the sun. If you have the sprouts in full sun, it is best to open the dome to allow it to cool inside. You can simply prop it open with a stick. Once you are certain no further seeds are going to sprout, you should remove the cover.

Transplant the sprouts into individual pots when they have grown 2 full sets of leaves. When you're ready to transplant, water the plants and the ground where they'll be planted. It's best to plant on a cloudy day so the heat of the sun doesn't cause wilting.

Water your new transplants once a day for about a week until they are well established. If the plants start to wilt, cover them or give them shade until they revive.

Q. I am attempting to start some vegetables indoors this year, and never having done so before, I'm not sure about the start dates. When the seed packet states that it can be sown indoors eight weeks before the last frost date and the number of days to germination is 21, does the eight weeks take that into account or do I actually start sowing 11 weeks before the last frost date?

A. The date of seeding takes into account the number of days to germinate. In other words, if the seed packet says to plant eight weeks before the last frost, that means it takes three weeks to germinate and five weeks of growth before the plants are ready to be set out.

Questions and Answers: Potatoes

Q. We put a lot of manure in our vegetable garden, and now our potatoes are very scabby. How can we correct our problem so that we can grow nice potatoes again?

A. Common scab disease in potatoes has been found to be much worse in soils that have been treated with heavy manure applications. Common scab is caused by a soil-borne organism called an actinomycete and probably occurs wherever potatoes are grown. The disease does not affect the eating quality but may affect the appearance of the tuber. Severe scab infections will reduce the yield. Part of the loss is from the extra peeling required when tubers are severely scabbed.

Rotating crops is a good idea with potatoes. Growing potatoes in the same spot year after year encourages scab formation. Do not grow potatoes in a known infected area for four to five years. You can also try growing scab-resistant varieties such as 'Russett Burbank' or 'Netted Gem.'

Q. For the last couple of years, when we peel our potatoes, there are very tiny black dots in the potato flesh under the peel and they go into the potato. To get rid of them we have to cut away part of the potato. If you miss some, there are dark spots on the boiled potatoes. What causes this problem, and how do we treat our potatoes to prevent it?

A. The problem is likely potato flea beetles. According to the

Potato plants.

Government of Alberta Agriculture and Rural Development, "Flea beetle adults overwinter in the soil in and around potato fields. Their survival is increased in elevated areas that are free from flooding. In mid-May to early June (around the time that potatoes emerge and are growing), the 1st generation of adults emerge and begin to feed and mate on potato foliage. Adults jump when disturbed and can fly. Adults can also fly into new potato fields. Eggs are laid in the soil and 1st generation larvae emerge and feed in the soil on tubers from early June to mid July. In Alberta, under typical conditions, only one generation is observed, however, a second generation can occur under warm conditions."

Spraying with an insecticide such as Doktor Doom House and Garden at the time the adults emerge can help control the insects. Culturally, keeping the amount of litter down is an option. Either pick up or rototill in any debris. Some potato growers have reported success using the yellow sticky traps available in garden centres. According to the Government of Alberta, "Flea beetle populations can be reduced through regular crop rotations. Populations will tend to build up if potatoes are grown repeatedly. Separation from other fields and freedom from volunteer potatoes can also help to minimize levels."

Q. What can we use to control wireworm in our potatoes?

A. Wireworms in potatoes can cause varying degrees of damage. The trails they leave as they eat through a potato can make the potato unpalatable. At this time it is very difficult to control the insect with the available insecticides. Agriculture and Agri-Food Canada, in a recent research update, is actively studying low-risk insecticides to control wireworm in potatoes. In the meantime, crop rotation is suggested. Do not plant potatoes in the same spot for two to three years.

Q. My question is about new potatoes. My daughter has an acreage and she let me plant about 50 potato plants in her garden. They were doing very well until her area was hit by a major hailstorm. I have not seen the damage, but she says the garden is destroyed.

Can I leave the potatoes in the ground and hope they will continue to grow, or should I dig them up and use them as baby potatoes? My husband believes they will rot if left in the ground. I don't think new potatoes will keep very long.

A. If there is some stem and even a few leaves left on the plants, they may survive, but if the leaves are shredded and the stems flattened, it would be best to dig up the potatoes because, yes, they would spoil if left in the ground. It is unfortunate, but eating tasty, new baby potatoes makes it a little less traumatic.

Q. I am planning out my vegetable garden and have a question about potatoes. Last year I planted what I think were 'Red Pontiac,' and all the potatoes had scab. I was hoping you might be able to tell me what varieties I should plant so there is no scab.

A. 'Netted Gem,' 'Early Gem' and 'Norland' are potato varieties that are resistant to scab. They are not, however, totally resistant—it is true for all varieties. Cultural practices may help. Rotate your crops regularly. If you have an area that has had scab, do not plant potatoes in the spot for at least three years. Keeping the soil moist but not wet helps as well.

Q. I am going to plant some new varieties of potatoes and I would like to harvest them earlier this year. Last year I got caught by the early snow we got in October and had to harvest my potatoes in very messy conditions. Is there anything I can do to ensure an early harvest?

A. I was reading a Lee Valley Tools garden catalogue and ran across an article on a technique called "potato chitting" (also called "greening potatoes"). It is a method that I had forgotten about until the article jogged my memory. It is an old English technique that is used to get your potatoes off to a growing start.

It makes use of light to encourage the potatoes to begin sending out green shoots. The light stimulates the formation of alkaloids in the spuds. The alkaloids act as a natural protection against bugs and some fungi.

The method is simple. Two to four weeks before planting, lay out the potatoes in a single layer in cool room (13° C) with bright but indirect light. When the resulting sprouts get to be about 38 to 50 mm (1.5 to 2 in), they are ready for planting. There are several advantages to using this method. First, you will be able to tell which potatoes are viable and good for planting. Discard any spuds that don't sprout. According to the Royal Horticultural Society, "Early cultivars will crop earlier and more heavily if chitted. Chitting later varieties results in earlier foliage…and they mature earlier."

Questions and Answers: Carrots

Q. I have a small plot in a community garden. I planted quite a few different veggies last year and some performed better than others. One of my major disappointments was with my carrots. They were very stunted and not very good at all. One of the experienced gardeners who has a plot near mine said it was likely because of the clay in the soil. He said that he adds a lot of compost and manure to his plot and that helps his carrots and other root vegetables he grows.

Do you think that clay is the problem, or is it the variety of carrots that I used ('Red Nantes')? Do you have any tips for me? I love the taste of homegrown carrots and would really like to be able to grow my own.

A. It is definitely true that carrots do not like clay soil. Adding organic matter and working it in well and deeply is a key to having success with growing carrots. You should know that a one-time addition will not solve the problem. You will need to add the organic matter every year before you plant or after you harvest. It does not necessarily have to be compost or manure, although those are among the best soil additives. You can use leaves or even grass clippings. The one thing I do not recommend is peat moss because it tends to increase the acidity in the soil. If you are going to use manure, make sure it is well rotted and not green. Green, or fresh, manure can actually burn plants and their roots.

I also recommend you double dig in the organic matter. With this method, start with a 30 cm wide strip and remove the topsoil from this strip and place it into a wheelbarrow or similar container. Next, add 5–7.5 cm of organic matter to the subsoil and work it into the existing clay with your spade. Next, dig another 30 cm wide strip right next to the first one, but instead of putting the topsoil into the wheelbarrow, put the topsoil on

top of the organic matter in the previous trench. Continue along using this method until the whole bed is done. I know this is arduous work, but do it a trench or two at a time.

The alternative is to plant short-rooted carrot varieties that will not be affected by the clay as much. Two examples of short-rooted carrots are 'Bunny Bite,' with a 4 cm root and ideally suited to growing in the shallowest of containers or in soil with a high clay content, and 'Short 'n' Sweet,' a dwarf variety with 10 cm tapered roots. As its name suggests, the taste is very sweet and the carrot is very tender. There are many other varieties that will work. Just check with your local garden centre.

Q. I have very heavy clay soil in my yard. Although I am trying to add compost to my vegetable garden every year, it is a slow process, and the soil keeps me from growing my favourite vegetable, which is carrots. I don't want to grow short varieties of carrots, and the long varieties never do well in the soil. What can I do?

A. I suggest you install some raised beds. If you can add a bed over your existing garden that is 12" (30 cm) deep, you should be able to grow anything in it. The principle is simple. By adding 12" (30 cm) of soil on top of your existing soil, you now have enough good soil depth to grow even the long varieties of carrots because they will not grow down into the clay.

As for what type of raised bed, you can use landscape ties but look for the ones that are not treated with arsenic. You can also use 2' × 6' or 2' × 12' lumber to make the frame for the raised bed. Some home centres even carry metal clips for making the raised beds. Again when choosing the lumber stay away from the arsenic type. I believe that all lumber is now treated for outdoor use without arsenic, but I am not completely sure.

Q. I have a question about my vegetable garden. This year I planted the same rows of carrots I always do. In the past, they always came up. This year I started with fresh seeds and planted them the same way, but only a few came up. What happened?

A. Your problem could be a result of two causes. First, the weather this spring has wrought havoc with many gardeners who seed outdoors. The extremely cool nights were simply not conducive to good germination. The second cause may be the seeds themselves. Although the package you bought was new for you, it may have been old stock. Seeds that are a year old can lose their ability to germinate properly.

My guess is that the first cause is the most likely one. I have not spoken to a gardener yet this year who has

You can enjoy a variety of vegetables throughout the growing season.

not complained of poor or slow seed germination.

Q. I have a small garden in my backyard. It has never been great but good enough so I can eat fresh during summer. I add peat moss and compost to it every spring. When we built our house, we scraped the clay and had good black dirt added. I have an apple tree fairly close to the garden, and one neighbour has a cedar tree nearby and another has a blue spruce. During summer my soil becomes rock hard, and when I dig, I'm digging up roots. This year my carrots and beets were "mini" when I dug them up. The tree roots must be sucking up the moisture and nutrients I'm adding. I usually rototill in spring and hand dig in the fall. I pull up all the roots I can. What can I do about this problem? I have no place to move my garden location.

A. My guess is that the spruce is the likely culprit, but it does sound as if other roots may be contributing to the problem. My suggestion is to raise the garden up. In other words, use raised beds.

Q. Last year my carrots had a very strong taste and an almost woody texture. Is it a result of something I did or didn't do? Do you have any tips to keep this from happening again?

A. Your question sent me off on one of my research forays. I had always wondered why some carrots developed that strong taste you speak of but never really knew why. According to the Alberta Agriculture and Food website, one possible answer may be that during prolonged hot weather, carrots can develop that strong taste and a coarseness in the roots. Last summer did have its share of hot weather, so that may be part of the reason. The other possibility, according to the University of Minnesota, is that carrots can develop the taste as well as become pithy if they are allowed to remain in the ground for too long.

There is a rather fine line that carrot gardeners walk here. Leaving the carrots in the ground longer increases their sweetness, but leaving them in too long can affect their taste and texture. In your case, the snow was also a concern. I will be honest here and tell you that I, too, have been caught by an early snowfall with my carrots still in the ground, but I am willing to risk it to get that sweet taste.

Questions and Answers: Peas

Q. I have rototilled my pea stalks into my garden for the last five years. Every year, the pea stalks have been covered with powdery mildew. Is this practice okay, or does it contribute to a build up of mildew in the soil? This year I planted the peas in a different part of my yard, away from my garden plot, and there is still powdery mildew on them. The mildew does not occur until the end of the season when I have harvested most of the peas. Also, some of my other plants have powdery mildew. It has been my practice to rototill everything back into the soil (I don't compost).

A. Most varieties of peas are notorious for getting powdery mildew, and there are mildew spores everywhere. They are in the air, in the soil and of course on plants. You should not till in the infected stems. You should put them into garbage bags, making sure the bags are tied tightly, and throw out them out with your trash. You can control the mildew by using garden sulphur spray. Cultural methods to help control this problem include the following:

- plant in well-drained soil

- space your plants for good air circulation, often a problem with peas as they are grown too closely together

- do not handle or work with the plants when the foliage is wet

- water well during dry spells, and do not water on the plant itself but apply water to the base instead; soaker hoses work well

Questions and Answers: Tomatoes

Q. My tomatoes are growing nicely and are almost ready to harvest, but they all seem to have developed cracks on the top of the fruit near the stem. What causes this problem and can I prevent it?

A. My tomatoes are doing the same thing. I grew them in containers, which makes maintaining even moisture more difficult. This problem often happens when the tomatoes experience rapid growth during periods of hot weather such as we experienced this year. There is no cure other than ensuring even moisture. Mulching will help.

Q. I have a problem with tomatoes. It was diagnosed as septoria leaf spot, which I was told is a fungus, and it ruined our tomatoes last year as well. The tomatoes grow against the house and have a southern exposure. We replace a good part of the soil and add compost each year; the site is the only place we have to grow tomatoes. Can you tell me if the spores of the fungus remain in the soil and, if so, is there any way to eliminate them? I was told to use Bordeaux mixture on the infected plants, but they still look pretty unhealthy. The tomatoes have almost all ripened so I have stopped the treatment and will destroy the plants soon. The variety we have is Early Girl, and the yield was poor. I would appreciate any suggestions and advice for next year that you can give me.

A. Septoria leaf spot is a fungal disease of the stems and foliage. It does not affect the fruit directly. The symptoms are small, roughly circular spots scattered over the leaf. These spots enlarge to become 1.5–3 mm in diameter with dark margins and tan centres. Small, dark fruiting bodies that look like pimples develop in the middle of the spots. It is in these bodies that the spores are produced. Older leaves near the ground usually show symptoms first. Rainy weather or even water deposited when watering plants can cause the disease to progress rapidly. Do not water the leaves when watering the plants—apply water only to the base of the plant. When leaves are heavily infected, they drop prematurely.

The disease overwinters in the soil on tomato plant debris or on weeds. Remove all plant debris from the area. Do not plant tomatoes in the same spot for at least four years. Bordeaux mixture (copper sulphate and lime with water) is a good choice for treatment. Read the product label before application to determine how long the waiting period is between treatment and harvest.

Q. My problem is that both my tomatoes and my zucchini plants have developed black spots at the ends of the fruit. They have been getting fertilized and watered regularly. The spot feels mushy and looks like the fruit is rotting from the bottom. Can you tell us what it is and how to deal with it?

A. The problem you describe is very likely blossom end rot, a physiological problem with tomatoes and zucchini. The first symptom is the appearance of what looks like a water-soaked area at the bottom of the fruit. This area continues to deteriorate, turning black/brown and shrivelling, and leaving a leathery sunken area.

The problem is caused by a lack of calcium—not necessarily that the soil is deficient in calcium, but simply that calcium has not been able to be taken up by the plant.

It could be caused by several factors, including lack of steady moisture during periods of drought. It is critical to keep tomatoes moist at all times, especially when the fruits are setting and developing. The plant needs calcium to develop fruit properly, and that calcium is dissolved in soil water. If water is lacking, then so is the calcium. Thus, you can have a calcium deficiency and yet have a good source of calcium in the soil.

Rapidly growing plants are more prone to the problem, because fast growth requires an abundant supply of water and calcium. Also, excess nitrogen can contribute to the problem by excessively speeding up growth.

Transplanting tomatoes into cold soil may contribute to calcium deficiency because the organisms that convert calcium into a usable form are not as active in cold soils. Cultivating deeply around tomatoes can damage roots and also cause a lack of water and calcium uptake.

Tips to avoid blossom end rot:

- keep soil moist but not sopping wet; excess water is just as bad as not enough
- mulch to help maintain even soil moisture
- shallow, frequent cultivation is best

Basket of peppers and tomatoes.

Q. After reading a column where you talked about heirloom tomatoes, I decided to find out more about these tomatoes. I was pleased to find an heirloom variety at a local greenhouse this past summer. It was 'Brandywine,' and I loved the taste and size. I would like to grow more varieties, but I am having some problem getting information on the varieties of heirloom tomatoes themselves. Do you have any references to recommend?

A. Sometimes I feel that plant breeders were too hasty in looking for the perfectly shaped tomato and lost the flavour along the way. 'Brandywine' is a very good example.

The tomatoes are not the most perfectly formed and may have lots of crinkles and wrinkles, but the taste is amazing.

One of the best references I can recommend is a book entitled *100 Heirloom Tomatoes for the American Garden*, by Carolyn J. Male. The author does a great job of reminding readers that grocery store tomatoes are not really tomatoes at all when compared to some heirloom varieties. Carolyn is also not afraid to criticize some varieties, and I like her balance between the pros and cons. She is well qualified to write on the topic since she has grown more than 1000 varieties of heirloom tomatoes over the past 14 years.

Q. I planted a small tomato plant in May called 'Ultra Sweet.' I had not heard of this variety before this year. I just picked the first tomato from it—the tomato is fully ripe (August 2), weighs 425 g and is 33 cm in circumference. No problems with the plant whatsoever—it is like a great spreading tree, and there are still 32 tomatoes in various stages of ripening on it, and all perfect-looking fruit. Is this unusual? It certainly is to me.

A. I'm growing 'Ultra Sweet' tomatoes as well and getting some tomatoes of the size and weight that you describe. In fact, I just had one for lunch the other day and it was one of the tastiest tomatoes I have had—very "meaty" and firm. My plants are nearly 1.5 m tall and are also covered with many tomatoes, so that would appear to be the norm for these plants. The 'Ultra Sweet' tomato, for anyone who may be interested in trying them, is a beefsteak type and matures in 55–62 days. The tomatoes on average are 280 g in size. The nice thing about this plant is that they are verticillium and fusarium resistant.

This year is one of my best years for tomatoes. In addition to the 'Ultra Sweet,' I am growing 'Ultra Girl' and also 'Sweet 100' for some cherry tomatoes. Production looks to be very good on all plants, and my plants are all taller than they have ever been. I think the hot summer has certainly helped the tomatoes this year.

Q. Is there a good reason to pinch back tomato plants? I have heard that it causes the plant to yield fewer tomatoes but better ones. If yes, would you please tell me how?

A. There are two schools of thought on pinching tomatoes. One school says that pinching the active growth tips will encourage the plant to produce bigger tomatoes. The other school says that is not true and in fact inhibits tomato production. I have tried both methods and tend to agree with the "do not pinch" school of thought. You can still pinch out the sucker growth that comes in the crotch between the stem and branch, but leave the actively growing tips on the top of the plant alone.

Q. I live in a new subdivision and I am growing a beefsteak tomato plant in a container that sits on my south-facing deck. I have added some slow-release fertilizer to the soil, and the plant is growing very well. I keep the plant well watered, although I did have some problems keeping the soil moist when it was 30° C. The plant had many blooms and now has many tomatoes, but they are not very big. I have harvested some and they taste great, but they are only 5–8 cm in diameter. I know beefsteaks are supposed to be much bigger. Why are they so small?

A. Lack of water can cut down on fruit size, and during the hot days of summer, keeping the soil moist is very important. The heat itself can cause stress in the plant, resulting in smaller fruit. Too many fruits may also result in all the fruits being small. Try picking off some of the small ones so the plant can send more of its energy to the remaining fruits.

Q. I clipped one of your columns regarding growing tomatoes indoors. I've followed instructions carefully. My tomatoes are just starting to bloom, but the leaves on some are starting to turn brown and curling under. Do you know what could be the cause?

A. I'm so glad to hear you have the tomatoes to the point of blooming. The browning might be from a few different sources.

Too much fertilizer causes root damage. If you are fertilizing a lot, cut back for a time. I would fertilize at ¼ of the recommended rate every third or fourth time you water.

You may be over- or underwatering. Tomatoes like to be in moist soil but not wet. The soil should be just moist to the touch.

Q. I recently picked off all my tomatoes before they froze and am sitting here staring at hundreds of green tomatoes. I would like to hurry the ripening process along so they do not all mature at the same time.

A. I have found that one of the best methods for hastening the ripening is to place the tomatoes in a brown paper bag along with an apple. The apple produces ethylene gas that aids in the ripening process. By using this method, you can selectively ripen a few tomatoes at a time over an extended period of time rather than having to wait until they all ripen at the same time.

Q. We have a small acreage out of town that we use as our second home. Currently we live in a downtown condo that has no room on the small balcony for any pots. We would love to be able to grow our own tomatoes—we love the taste of home-grown—but don't want to have to dig up a garden patch on our acreage. Do you have any low-maintenance ideas for growing tomatoes in pots? We only go out to the acreage twice a month, so watering and fertilizing might be a concern.

A. Tomatoes are pretty foolproof to grow if they have a reliable source of water during the hot days of summer during the time they are forming the fruit. The water is needed not only for the health of the plant but also to transport calcium up into the plant. Calcium is needed during fruit formation to prevent blossom end rot. A drip irrigation system will solve the problem and allow you to grow tomatoes in a container.

There are a couple of ways to set up the drip irrigation system. One is to connect it to a tap if you have such a source of water, or you can connect it to a rain barrel where you capture rainwater. Drip irrigation systems are rated by the number of gallons of water per hour (GPH) they deliver at a certain water pressure. With a rain barrel, the pressure is determined by gravity so the pressure will depend on how high the barrel is above the irrigation system. To increase the pressure, you need to raise the height of the barrel higher than the drip system. With some gravity type drip systems, as long as you can create and maintain a siphon (the barrel has to be higher than the highest point where the water is being delivered), the system will work. There are battery-powered inline timers available that can turn your water on and off. In this way, you can have a drip system that does not require an externally pressurized source of water.

The other way to increase the pressure is to use a small and relatively inexpensive electric pump. You could connect the pump to the faucet at the bottom of the rain barrel. You can find these pumps in garden centres or suppliers of pond equipment. The next step would be to install an inline timer/controller. Some controllers will not only turn on the flow of water but will also turn the pump on to deliver the water. These and the pump would, of course, need a source of DC power.

A simple drip emitter would be needed in each container, and at a set time the water would flow to the pot. By adding a mulch to the top of the soil in the container, you could help conserve the moisture. On very hot summer days you may want to increase the number of waterings. Normally, a single application of water should be enough, but containers can dry out very quickly on hot, dry days.

Fertilizing the plants is a simple task as well. Slow-release, pelleted fertilizers are a boon to container gardeners. Many of these fertilizers can last two to three months depending on the amount of rain. The alternative, and it is still a reliable one, is to fertilize whenever you are out on your acreage. A good quality fertilizer such as Miracle-Gro applied every two weeks should provide ample nutrients to the tomatoes.

Q. The bottom leaves on my tomatoes are turning yellow. I have been fertilizing with 15-30-15, but perhaps it is not the right fertilizer. What is a good one to use for tomatoes?

A. If the problem is a nutrient deficiency, then the symptoms you describe would be a lack of nitrogen, so use a fertilizer with a higher first number: 15-30-15 is not a bad fertilizer to use on tomatoes, but a formula such as 18-18-21 would be even better.

The yellowing may not be a fertilizer problem but rather fusarium wilt. This fungus has similar symptoms—including older leaves turning yellow—but also the development of brown spots on the leaves and leaf drop. The plant growth is stunted and little or no fruit develops. If it is wilt, you will need to destroy the infected plants. Do not plant tomatoes in the area for a minimum of four years, and plant resistant varieties of tomatoes.

Q. There is a lot of conflicting information out there on the topic of fertilizing tomatoes—from "use all-purpose fertilizer monthly" and "use tomato fertilizer in the early spring," to "do not fertilize when the plant flowers." I purchased two large tomato plants and gave one to a friend. I was most diligent with watering and fertilizing, but after about a month, the leaves started to curl upward. At first I thought it might be the wind, so I asked my friend and she had the same problem. Although they were very sturdy and looked healthy at first, the plants must have been diseased right from the get-go. I assume there is nothing that will revive them.

A. If the leaves are just curling and not yellowing and dropping, it might not be a big problem. Many tomatoes, for reasons unknown, will have leaf curl and still produce good fruit. Wind can actually be one of the causes of the curl so your thinking is right on the mark. Keep a close watch on the plants. If the leaves begin to yellow, especially the older ones, it may be a fungal wilt and that cannot be treated. If the leaves stay curled but do not yellow, the plants might just make it.

Q. Could you please tell me why my cherry tomatoes are splitting before they are completely ripened on the vine?

A. Your tomatoes are likely splitting because of uneven moisture. Splitting usually occurs when the plant dries out and then is really soaked. Tomatoes really like to have even moisture, especially when the fruit is developing. However, sometimes overwatering is also enough to cause the tomatoes to split. The moral here is "even moisture." Don't let them dry out, and don't keep the soil sopping wet either.

Questions and Answers: Onions

Q. I used to use Diazinon and Malathion on onion maggots before I planted. What am I supposed to do to prevent the maggots now that those chemicals are off the market?

A. This problem is faced by countless gardeners. Using Doktor Doom House and Garden Spray may be the solution. This spray contains permethrin, which is a water-based insecticide that was formulated as a copy of the naturally occurring pyrethrins. I have had success applying the spray to the soil in the planting area and then planting or seeding immediately after. You should also reapply at the base of the newly planted plants. If seeding, reapply once the plants emerge from the ground.

The residual effects of the Doktor Doom House and Garden Spray should last for a month in the soil and be effective against the maggots. The eggs of the insect are laid on the soil surface. After hatching, the maggots burrow down into the soil. It is during this hatching and burrowing that the Doktor Doom would be effective.

Q. I have tried growing and storing onions the past few years with little success. Once again this year I went to my cold room in the basement to get some onions and found some of them starting to go soft and starting to rot. What the heck am I doing wrong?

A. It sounds like the onions may not have totally matured before you stored them. In fall when the onion tops begin to turn yellow, push the tops over. Doing so will force the onions into their final maturation state. After about three weeks, they should be ready for harvest. Once you have dug them up, lay them on newspaper in a dry spot for about 10–14 days. My dad used to put his onions on newspaper up in the attic of his garage. It was a very dry and warm spot and perfect for curing off the onions.

Once cured, the onions should be stored in a cool, dry location. Check your cold room for humidity—it may be too humid. The ideal temperature for storage should be around 2–7° C. The onion bulbs should also have good air circulation around them. Some people store them in a mesh bag to allow good air movement.

Q. I noticed that in a recent column of yours that someone asked whether there was a replacement for Later's Onion Maggot control (you said there wasn't). I have had 100 percent success by planting marigolds around my whole garden and near the onions. The marigolds keep away the flies that lay the eggs that maggots come from. The marigolds have to be in bloom when you plant them. One year I bought plants that weren't in bloom, and the flies layed the eggs and were gone before the marigolds bloomed.

A. Thank you also for your excellent suggestion on dealing with the onion maggots. By using the marigolds to repel the flies, you are using a form of companion gardening. This method of gardening is an excellent way of gardening without chemicals. Companion gardening has been in use for centuries.

Questions and Answers: Cucumbers

Q. I think I will have a bumper crop of cucumbers. Should I pinch off the curly ends of the cucumber vines? They are really spreading and taking over the garden.

A. You can certainly pinch back the cukes to keep them under control without harming them. In fact, doing so may benefit the developing fruits— the plant puts more energy into fruit production than growth.

Q. We have downsized our garden this year but we still would like to grow some pickling cucumbers. Is it true that they will grow up a trellis? Any tips on how to do this will be most helpful.

A. Most varieties of cucumbers are vines and they love to climb. Some experts believe that cukes will produce two to three times more fruit when grown up a trellis. Plant the cukes 46 cm apart. Choose a trellis that will give good support because the fruit load can tend to get heavy.

Q. How the heck do you tell a male cucumber flower from a female flower? They only get one or two flowers at a time, and for the life of me I can't tell which is which.

A. In general, male flowers appear first, and you can find them on the main stem. Male flowers are also usually found in clusters of three to five and have a shorter stem than females.

Female flowers are on both the main and lateral stems. The most distinctive feature on the female flowers is the presence of an ovary, which appears as a swelling right below the flower itself.

Q. Can you help me to solve the mystery of cucumbers this year? Many beautiful flowers but no cucumbers at all?

A. Ahh yes, the mystery of cucumbers. This is akin to the mystery of life itself. Seriously, there may be a couple of reasons for your lack of cucumber production. One is a lack of bees or other pollinating insects to pollinate the flowers. Another is that temperature or drought stress can actually cause the plants to produce only male flowers. Male flowers will not produce fruit. The conditions we had this summer with periods of intense heat with drought-like conditions could account for your problem.

Solutions? Hand fertilize the flowers if the problem is caused by a lack of pollination. Use a fine paint brush to fertilize the flowers. Gently wipe the brush across the anthers of the stamens of the male flowers, trying to get as much pollen as possible on the brush. Then apply the pollen to the female flower pistil. Consistent watering will help if the problem is caused by the drought. Cucumbers like moist soil, but not damp soil, to produce the best.

Questions and Answers: Harvesting

Q. We planted acorn squash this year, and it is growing very well. How do I know when the squash are ready to eat?

A. Acorn squash is a deep green with a yellow spot that faces the ground. When the yellow spot turns orange, the squash is ready to harvest. You can also test the rind of the squash. If you cannot scratch the surface of the squash with a fingernail, it is ready to pick. In any case, you should harvest the squash before the first frost.

Q. My wife and I are new gardeners, and we have planted potatoes for the first time and are not sure when we can harves them. Can you please help?

A. Potatoes give signs when they are ready to be harvested. Shortly after the vines bloom, the underground stems begin producing potatoes. You can now get out your soup spoon and start looking for new potatoes if you like, or you can wait until the tops die in fall and then harvest all of the full-sized spuds at once.

Q. I have heard that you need to wait until the tops fall over to harvest onions. Is this just an old wives' tale? When is the right time to harvest onions?

A. There is no such thing as an old wife. They are all holding at 29 years of age. (I think I may have scored a point with my own wife with that one.) Seriously though, it is true that the right time to harvest onions is after the tops fall over. What I do is wait until about 50 percent of the tops have fallen over and then go ahead and harvest all of them.

Q. I have been trying to grow sweet corn for a few years. My success rate is variable, but this year seems to be a bumper crop. I never know when to pick the cobs. Can you give a tip on what to look for when harvesting corn?

A. The silks of the corn will begin to turn brown around three to four weeks after they first appear. When you see this happening, peel back the husk until you expose the kernels. Poke a kernel with a fork or knife and examine the liquid. If it runs clear, the corn is not ready. If it is runs milky, it is time to pick.

Q. Last year we made the mistake of waiting until our peas were mature before harvesting them. The peas were not very good. Can you please tell us when is the best time to harvest peas so they will be at their best?

A. Leaving peas on the vine to mature is not a good idea. They become hard and woody. The best time to harvest peas is when the pods are a bright green and are full. Taking one off the vine and tasting it is really the best way to test if the pea is ready for harvest.

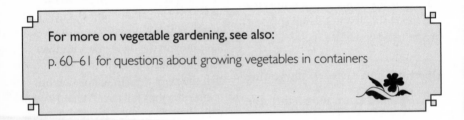

For more on vegetable gardening, see also:

p. 60–61 for questions about growing vegetables in containers

Lawns

Lawns are one of those topics in gardening that are embroiled in a heated debate. The pro side includes those gardeners who love the look of their lawns and are committed to doing whatever it takes to keep those lawns looking their best.

The con in the debate are the gardeners who are eco-friendly and, although they also love the look of their lawn, they are not prepared to use chemicals or waste excess water to have that lawn looking its best. There is a third faction in this debate, and that group includes those who feel so strongly about not having a lawn that they remove their lawns and replace them with either groundcovers or mulches of one form or another. For our purposes, we will look at both traditional and eco-friendly approaches to growing and maintaining lawns.

Lawns can demand a lot of fertilizer, water and time. Despite all the cost and effort, many gardeners are devoted to making the lawn look its best. The search for a balance between eco-friendly alternatives and a healthy lawn seems to be finding some solutions. As always, I offer both sides of the argument and, based on the facts presented, I let you, the reader, decide. While I may offer opinions, the ultimate decision is yours to make. This decision is no longer as black and white as it used to be. Today, many gardeners use eco-friendly alternatives such as natural fertilizers but still use pesticides.

Others use natural pesticides but are comfortable with synthetic fertilizers.

There are people who speak on the virtues of having a lawn. Don Williamson, in his book *Lawns for Canada*, addresses some of the positives, which include the following:

- Lawns draw in carbon dioxide and release oxygen thus benefiting the environment.

- Lawns filter water improving water quality.

- Lawns reduce wind and water erosion.

- Lawns can help reduce dust by trapping particles in the air.

On the other side of the fence, the list of negatives include the following:

- Lawns need far too much water to look their best.

- Nonorganic lawns need far too many chemical fertilizers and pesticides.

- Lawns have a large carbon footprint when considering traditional lawn-care methods. Power mowers, power weeders and transporting fertilizers and chemicals all contribute to this footprint.

I won't pontificate on which side is right. Your own answer may be found in the questions and answers that follow.

Questions and Answers: Eco-friendly Lawns

Q. I am interested in using an environmentally friendly way to control weeds on my lawn. With the upcoming ban (January 2010) on weed and feed products, is there an alternative available that is safe for the environment?

A. The search continues for environmentally friendly alternatives to synthetic fertilizers and herbicides. Corn gluten is a relatively recent introduction on the eco-friendly gardening scene and shows some real promise for homeowner applications for both control of lawn weeds and fertilizer use as well.

Corn gluten is an organic alternative to weed and feed fertilizers for lawns. It has been proven to reduce germination of broadleaf weeds by as much as 90 percent, and it also slowly releases nutrients, working as a fertilizer. According to Mark McNicoll, Parks Leader, Parks South Operation for the City of Edmonton, corn gluten, "is the dried protein component separated during corn starch manufacturing for the food industry. The product contains up to 10 percent nitrogen by weight, which is released following microorganism breakdown, and also has pre-emergent weed control properties. It could be categorized as a 'weed and feed' product but, unlike synthetic weed and feeds, the weed control is pre-emergent as opposed to post-emergent." Corn gluten works by inhibiting sprouting seeds from developing normal roots. Although this does not kill the weeds directly, it does make them weak and prone to dehydration. It does not affect established plants.

According to the Northwest Coalition for Alternatives to Pesticides (NCAP), corn gluten's use as an herbicide was discovered by Iowa State horticulturist Nick Christians. Christians tested the effect of the product on 22 different weeds. The product reduced root development and survival on all 22 species tested. The NCAP also noted that the Environmental Protection Agency in the U.S. has classified corn gluten as a "minimum risk pesticide" that is exempt from having to be registered.

Canada's Pest Management Regulatory Agency (PMRA) has identified a potential health problem associated with corn gluten meal. Corn and corn by-products are known to cause allergies for some people. A few people have serious reactions, including respiratory problems and hypersensitivity. If you know that you or your family members are allergic to corn, it is recommended that you avoid exposure to corn gluten meal. Turfmaize is Canada's only PMRA-approved turf fertilizer with a natural weed preventer.

The City of Edmonton conducted trials using corn gluten on some of its fields, but according to McNicoll, the product was too expensive and not potent enough for large-scale operations. However, McNicoll says, "it is a product that could be well suited as a substitute for synthetic fertilizers used by private homeowners for their lawns and beds."

Q. I am looking to go completely organic on my lawn at my cottage. My plan is to use a compost topdressing instead of any fertilizers. I have two small children who love going out to the cottage, but whenever I fertilize, they have to stay indoors, and that just does not seem right. Do you think that this compost will help the grass look good without fertilizers? Also, how much compost do you think would be enough?

A. There is no question that your lawn will love the compost application. The compost can help the grass plants be more drought tolerant as well as more insect and disease resistant. Your lawn should be able to do quite nicely with only the compost and no fertilizer. You may have to apply the compost two or three times during the growing season to have your lawn looking its best.

The experts recommend applying a thin layer of compost of about 0.65 cm. The thin layer will break down and release its nutrients into the lawn more rapidly as a result. Use a fine-textured compost that will be easy to work into the lawn. Compost containing large clumps tends to break down more slowly and makes the lawn look unkempt for longer. Initially use a shovel to toss the compost out onto the lawn. Then use a rake to even out the application. Once you have it raked out, water it for 15–20 minutes with a water sprinkler to help settle the compost down into the lawn. It is also a good idea not to mow the lawn for seven days to allow the compost to break down.

Compost not only contains the essential nutrients such as nitrogen, phosphorus and potassium but also trace elements that are not usually found in artificial fertilizers.

Some of the other advantages to using compost instead of fertilizer are:

- not having to run the sprinkler for hours to prevent the fertilizer from burning the lawn
- compost works quickly
- compost is completely environmentally friendly
- great additive for the lawn itself, with long-lasting effects
- makes the lawn look great
- safe for children and pets

If you are looking for a source of compost, call your local garden centre. Most carry large stockpiles of compost.

A few years ago, a list of guidelines from Environment Canada entitled "12 Easy Steps to Get Your Lawn Off Drugs" was published. Can these guidelines actually work in creating a lawn that is eco-friendly and yet looks good? Environment Canada starts off with two dramatic statements, "Be a good neighbour! Don't poison the soil, the water or the people in your neighbourhood with chemicals." And "Weed & Feed and other chemical fertilizers and pesticides are not necessary…"

Let's examine some of Environment Canada's list of 12 steps:

1. "Tolerate some weeds." Environment Canada says that you should tolerate "good weeds" like clover because it is beneficial: clover fixes nitrogen, thereby making it available to the lawn. If you can tolerate such weeds in your lawn, go for it. If, on the other hand, you are like me and hate the look of the weeds in a manicured lawn, then you will need to use a herbicide to get rid of the clover. Once your lawn is strong and healthy, it will not allow weeds to establish themselves.

2. "Hand digging weeds." I'm a big believer of hand digging weeds. I use it myself. More than 80 percent of lawn weeds are annuals and can easily be plucked out of the ground

by using a sharp old knife or a dandelion puller. Annual weeds need to be removed before they flower and go to seed. Some weeds with tough root systems, such as clover and chickweed, may require a herbicide, but the majority can be dug out. Dandelions need to have the whole root removed. You may have to dig them out more than once, but be persistent. I find the hand digging to be "therapeutic."

3. "Remove thatch and aerate." Thatch is the layer of clippings and debris on the top of the soil. It should not be thicker than 1.2 cm. Hire a lawn company or rent a power-raking machine to remove the thatch, and then aerate with a core aerator.

4. "Fertilize naturally." Good quality natural fertilizers used to be limited in availability. Several good quality organic lawn fertilizers are now readily available. The first is a lawn care product line by Myke. The lawn foods are completely organic and are slow-release formulations. There is a three-part strategy to the Myke system. In spring, you fertilize with a 10-3-3 application; in mid-summer, you use the 9-4-2 blend; and finally in fall, you use the 3-3-8 formula.

Second on our list is a product made by Groundskeeper Pride that is a certified organic lawn food (10-3-3) and is advertised as safe for children and pets as well. This product is also slow release and

is doesn't burn. Finally there is an organic product called Alfalfa Green (3-0-2). The manufacturer of this product bases its efficiency on the fact that alfalfa contains a hormone (triacontanol) that is a plant growth and root stimulator that can increase yields 30–60 percent. Alfalfa Green also naturally enhances the friendly bacteria and microorganisms in the soil. The interesting thing about this product is its claim to having anti-compaction properties, which would be helpful on lawns that are planted on clay soils.

I think that all of these products can get the job done and give you that great-looking lawn without the use of synthetic fertilizers. Many of these organic fertilizers will add to the organic content of the soil. This addition encourages the increase in beneficial microbial activity of the soil. Synthetic fertilizers do not offer this benefit.

5. "Leave lawn clippings." Lawn clippings will begin to break down almost immediately and will provide the lawn with a 4-1-3 NPK (nitrogen, phosphorous, potassium) feeding every time you mow your lawn. You don't even need a mulching mower. Any regular mower where you can close the door to the grasscatcher will work. Set your mowing height a little higher than normal (7.5 cm instead of 6 cm, for example) and close the door to the grasscatcher. If you would

A healthy lawn.

rather not mulch your lawn, consider using the grass clippings as a mulch around tomatoes, in between rows of vegetables or even around annuals and perennials. The clippings help to conserve moisture and keep weeds at bay.

6. "Mow at proper height." Environment Canada recommends cutting the lawn to a height of 6–7.5 cm to help with moisture retention and crowd out weeds. I like the look of a groomed lawn and cut mine at a height of 7.5 cm. Yes, I cut my lawn every 3–5 days because I don't want to cut too much off the top of the grass. If you cut more than one-third of the height of the grass at one time,

it may go into shock. Another key is keeping your lawnmower blades sharp.

7. "Water deeply and less frequently." I've been preaching this one for years. Your lawn will have a better root system if you soak it deeply and don't water frequently. Frequent watering encourages fungi, diseases and shallow roots.

8. "Control pests naturally." I am a big fan of this one, but I also am realistic about this statement. If my lawn has a major insect problem, I will try all organic means available, but then will resort to a pesticide. If I have to use a pesticide, I like Doktor Doom products because they are made either

with pyrethrins, which are a naturally occurring pesticide, or permethrin, which is the synthetic version.

So how tough is it to grow that lawn organically? Looking through the list, it occurs to me that many of us have been doing this organic thing all along without ever knowing it. If we start using organic fertilizers, we will have accomplished what many thought was impossible only a few years ago, and that is a magnificent lawn the organic way.

Q. I would appreciate your advice on how to get a fuller, healthier lawn. My lawn is five years old, is a little patchy and has an inconsistent colour. I suspect lack of topsoil.

A. Topdressing and overseeding will definitely help. Topdressing is simply adding soil to the top of the lawn. It should be done in small increments, because adding too much soil in one application can kill the grass. I would not add more than 2.5 cm of topdressing at a time. The topdressing can be just topsoil or it could be compost or a combination of the two. I strongly recommend using pure compost or the combination rather than straight soil. The compost will help improve the organic content of the topsoil, which will help a great deal with adding the ability to retain more water.

Simply rake the topdressing into the grass, but don't smother the grass.

Use your rake to knock off any soil that is attached to the grass blades, or just water the lawn. Topdressing is normally done in summer or early fall when the grass is tall and actively growing, but could also be done in late spring. Adding this topdressing will, over time, build up the level of the existing top soil and should help to make the lawn healthier. To increase the benefit of topdressing, consider aerating the lawn before applying the topdressing. Aerating will help to work the topdressing down more deeply as you rake it in.

By adding 2.5 cm of topdressing each year, you can get a nice thick layer of topsoil in a few years. The bonus in using this method is that the lawn will benefit immediately from the nutrients in the soil/compost, thus reducing the need for fertilizer applications. It is a very natural and eco-friendly way to fertilize the lawn.

Seed the lawn after topdressing it, thus making for a thicker, richer-looking lawn. This technique is called overseeding. Apply a good quality grass seed mix right over the topdressing. Very gently mix the seed with the soil so the seed has good contact with the soil, and keep it well watered. Topdressing and overseeding is an excellent way to rejuvenate an old lawn or to keep any lawn in top condition.

Q. We inherited a lakefront cottage with a massive lawn that runs right down to the waterline. I know my dad used to spread manure and compost on it for many years. He never used commercial fertilizers. The problem is that it is full of dandelions that really spoil the appearance of the lawn. Is there anything I can use on these dandelions that will not be harmful to the lake but will do in the weeds? I have a feeling I already know the answer to this one but thought I should ask anyway.

A. There are no herbicides on the market that will act on the dandelions but are not harmful to the lake. I do have several suggestions. First, how about organizing a dandelion bee? Several friends with dandelion pullers could make short order of the weeds, and you could have fun doing it. It's great for the environment too. Second, and it was my brother who made me a believer in this method, simply cut the grass short. By cutting it shorter, you actually don't even notice the weeds in the grass. The bonus is that the weeds are weakened, and some die out. The trick to this method is to cut the grass regularly, especially when the weeds are actively growing. If they are blooming, cut them even more often to keep them from going to seed.

Lastly, a weed burner torch is actually kind of fun and gives great satisfaction. Any grass that is singed in the

process may regrow, but if it does not, it can be easily reseeded.

Q. I have an unusual situation with my lawn. About three years ago I built my lawn using topsoil from an old, dried-out slough and then seeded it. The following year, I discovered the soil had a huge nutrient deficiency. I used the same soil to make my garden, but I was able to rectify the problem by adding compost, sand and old, rotted manure. My problem now is what to do with my lawn—most growth has changed from grass to our three favourite invaders (thistles, dandelions and clover). I have a lot of grass, so the thought of removing the sod and topsoil is not a welcome one. The other problem is that the soil has been heavily compacted by a bobcat. Can I overcome my issues by renting an aerator, punching a lot of holes in my existing lawn, removing the plugs, topdressing with 2.5 cm or so of good quality topsoil and reseeding?

A. The problems you describe are major issues when it comes to the health of your lawn. The nutrient deficiency is in itself a huge problem, but it is compounded by the compaction caused by the bobcat. The fact that the weeds have moved in is not a surprise—they have no competition from the grass. Your suggestion of aerating, then topdressing and reseeding will not address the immediate problem of the deficiency. Over a number of years this topdressing scheme may eventually prove successful, but it may not. Because the problem is deep into the foundation of the lawn, namely the soil, and also because of the compaction, I think your best bet is to start from scratch.

Q. I would like to know which is better for the lawn, core aerating or de-thatching? Which one should I do for the most benefit or do I really need to do both? This lawn is my first lawn (it is an older home), so I want to do things right.

A. Perhaps we need to start by defining what thatch is. Thatch is the light brown layer above the soil surface and below the grass blade area. Thatch accumulates naturally as the grass leaves die and are replaced by new ones. Grass clippings will accumulate after each mowing even if a mulching mower is used. So a thin layer of thatch is not only natural but is needed. It is only when the thatch becomes too thick that a problem can develop. Water, air and fertilizers (nutrients) cannot penetrate quickly. During hot, dry spells, the thatch dries out, and any grass roots within suffer accordingly. During wet weather, the thatch holds water, creating an environment in which disease organisms are able to thrive.

What is considered too thick for thatch? If the thatch is more than 2–3 cm thick, then the lawn should be de-thatched. You can examine the layer yourself to determine the thickness of the thatch. Use a sharp knife and do a small cut in the lawn to view a cross-section of the grass and thatch. De-thatching is best done with a motorized de-thatcher, because raking thick thatch by hand is a demanding job.

Coring aeration helps with a lawn that has become compacted. Over time and use, the lawn will compact, resulting in poor growth. Lawns that are frequently walked on or ones that have been planted on soil with a clay base are prone to compaction. Water has trouble penetrating and may even puddle on the surface.

Coring aeration removes plugs, or cores, from the lawn. Leave these cores on the lawn—do not rake up and remove them. They will disappear over time with rain and watering. Coring aeration allows better movement of water, air and fertilizers (nutrients) to the grass roots. The process is best done with a motorized aerator. Aerate only every two years, unless the lawn is severely compacted. It would not harm your lawn to have it aerated, since you do not know what condition the previous owner left it in.

Q. I recall your talking before about removing dandelions by digging them out rather than treating them with chemicals. Is it really practical to do and does it work?

A. It is the only method I use. I have a good quality weed puller, which is nothing more than a thin rod with a forked end and a nice handle at the other end. The idea is to insert the puller in next to the dandelion and push it down then pull down on the handle and hopefully the root will pop out intact. It does happen with smaller dandelions, but with the larger ones the root usually breaks, which means that the weed will grow back from the broken piece left in the ground.

However, the next time the dandelion grows back, it does so as a smaller plant and is much easier to pull with the weed puller. It does work. I find it relaxing to sit on the lawn on a sunny day pulling dandelions.

Q. I am one of those gardeners who still enjoys having a lawn, but I am hoping you can give me some tips on how I can be more earth friendly when it comes to watering.

A. In summer, watering grass and other outdoor uses can account for up to 50 percent of home water consumption. Studies show that this amount of water use is wasteful, and that the same results can be accomplished with far less water. Here are a few tips for conserving water:

- Many experts feel that 2–3 cm of water per week is enough to sustain a lawn. Leave a measuring container in the yard to measure rainfall and to also gauge how much water is being delivered from a sprinkler. If the 2–3 cm has been provided through a rainfall, skip the watering schedule that week.

- Use a sprinkler that has a low angle or is a pulsating type. Don't use sprinklers that shoot the water high into the air or ones that have a fine spray or mist. With these types of sprinklers, the water can easily evaporate before it even hits the lawn.

- Set the sprinkler to water the lawn, not the sidewalks and driveways. If you have to move the sprinkler from time to time to cover the whole lawn, then make the effort to do so.

- Check your hoses, sprinklers and the connections to ensure that water is not leaking out. For example, a dripping outdoor tap can waste as much as 1 L of water per hour.

- Watering the lawn deeply and less frequently will encourage deep roots in the lawn. A lawn with a deeper root system can withstand periods of drought or less water much more readily than a shallow root system.

- Water the lawn and other plants early in the morning, preferably before 9:00 AM, to help reduce evaporation and scorching of the leaves in the sun. Always water when the winds are calm to reduce water loss as well. If you need to go to work and can't water early in the morning, invest in an inexpensive watering timer. These timers connect at the tap end, and you simply set the sprinkler in place the night before, and the timer will turn the water on and off at a preset time.

- Don't cut the lawn too short. Lawns that are at least 6 cm tall can shade the roots of the grass more easily and retain water better.

- Dig out weeds in the lawn or in beds with a hand weeder. Weeds steal moisture from desirable plants.

Q. I am one of those guys who has been starting to feel guilty about the carbon footprint of my lawn and its care and upkeep. I am concerned with the amount of gas my power mower uses and the pollutants it sends into the air. I think I will get rid of the thing and get a push mower instead. Do you have any experience with push mowers? Will a push mower do the job just as good as a power mower?

A. There are many gardeners who mow their lawn while surrounded by a cloud of smoke pouring out of an old lawnmower. Do you also have a garage full of two-stroke monsters like trimmers, leaf blowers and roto-tillers? The small engines on these garden machines are far less regulated than their larger automobile cousins. The result is that they pump much more pollution into the air.

According to the U.S. Environmental Protection Agency (EPA), a new walk-behind mower spews out as much pollution in one hour as 11 new cars. Riding mowers, according to the EPA, pollute as much as 34 new cars! One staggering fact is that there are 52 million lawnmowers in the U.S. that use 800 million gallons of gasoline each year. In Canada, 500,000 lawnmowers are sold every year. Of those, the vast majority are gas-powered or electric. Only 26,500 are push mower—the type where the blades rotate when you provide the impetus by pushing. However, push mowers are beginning to make a comeback. Sales in the U.S. are up 150 percent. Push mowers offer a healthier environmental choice as well as a healthy lifestyle choice. They cut the grass blades cleaner than rotary power mowers, the blades of which are often dull. Push mowers actually clip the grass blade like a pair of scissors would.

If you have a huge lawn and the thought of using a push mower leaves you breathless, remember that even electric mowers are a better environmental option than two-stroke engines.

Alternatives to other power gardening tools include raking the leaves in fall instead of blowing them. Besides, I never did understand the rationale behind leaf blowers. If you blow them away, they just blow back in the next wind. Trimming the lawn by hand eliminates the need for string trimmers. As a kid, it was always my job to crawl on my knees along the fence and borders to trim the lawn after my dad had cut it. We used a pair of hedge trimmers, and it worked very well because it cut a long swath of grass in one motion. Turning the soil in fall and allowing the lumps to break down naturally over winter is a green alternative to rototillers.

If you hire a lawn clean-up service every spring, consider the pollutants coming out of their power rakes, mowers, tillers and string trimmers, and in the gas used and pollution from their trucks to get to your home. Hand raking with a thatch rake instead of power raking is a good way to get a workout. You can buy spikes like elongated golf shoe spikes that attach to the bottom of your shoes to help in aerating your lawn.

Q. I am in the process of killing off the grass in my front garden and want to use stone, gravel and rocks to make a lawn-free garden. I have fir trees and some shrubs that I wish to keep. Can I use rocks and gravel around these trees, and can I plant new shrubs and perennials into the new base? I will put down a weed barrier over the soil before covering it with small stones and gravel.

A. You can use rocks and gravel as a mulch around the base of existing trees and shrubs as long as you keep the gravel from touching the trunk/branches of the plants. If the gravel does touch the plant on a hot day in summer, it can easily damage the plant by burning it. I would keep the gravel 15 cm away from the trunk/branches. Another consideration is the depth of the gravel mulch. Applying too much mulch can suffocate the roots of existing plants. My mulches are no more than 5 cm deep, and that is a safe depth for most plants.

Yes, you should use a good quality landscape fabric under the gravel. Landscape fabric comes in different qualities. Some last only 3–5 years, while the better quality fabric can last up to 20 years. I strongly suggest investing in the best quality fabric you can afford—laying down the fabric and gravel is not a job you would like to do every 3–5 years.

Do not use black plastic as it can cause moisture problems.

As for your question about planting new shrubs/trees, that is not a problem. Simply scrape back the gravel and expose the fabric. Cut an X-shaped opening in the fabric and enlarge it into a circle of the right planting diameter for the plant, and then plant as normal. I constantly add new plants to mulched areas.

Q. I have a question about my standard poodle. I'm getting pretty good at reseeding the spots left behind by her peeing, but what can I do to stop her from burning my lawn? My backyard looks like a land mine.

A. One thing you can do is to water the area that she urinates on immediately after she goes. That will help to dilute the urine and may help to prevent it from burning the lawn. There are a few things you can try in amending your dog's diet or behaviour to help with this problem. A word of caution: consult your veterinarian before trying any amendments to diet.

There is an excellent website by Dr. Steve Thompson, DVM, of Purdue University Veterinary Teaching Hospital. This website deals with all concerns relating to the dog burn problem, and I highly recommend checking it out. It contains far more detailed information than space here would permit. The address is www.peteducation.com. Once you are at this website, type "lawn burn" in the search box.

Q. My husband and I are having a dispute over mulching the lawn. We currently have a healthy crop of dandelions and a poor quality lawn. He says we shouldn't mulch when we mow until all the dandelions are gone, because it will just distribute the seeds. I say we should because it will increase the health of the lawn and help it repel the dandelions. Can you please settle this dispute for us?

A. I will say that you are both right. If the dandelions are in seed, you will distribute the seed over the lawn by mulching. However, if they are not in seed (meaning the flower heads have not yet formed the white seeds that fly about), you will not do any harm to the existing lawn by mulching. You are quite right in saying that the mulching will help to increase the vigour of the lawn and will help to prevent weeds from finding their way into the lawn in the future.

Q. What do you do for your lawn in spring? Do you hire someone to power rake?

A. Spring is such a busy time for me with my appearances and talks. I always hire a landscape firm to do spring maintenance on my lawn. I thought I might share a story that happened to me this year. I booked the landscape company back in the middle of April. I was told they would be there in a week. It poured buckets the day they were due to arrive. Two weeks passed, and still no spring clean-up. I decided it was time to take matters into my own hands. I'm sure some of you have had this happen in the past or had it happen this year. Here is what I did, and you can do this as well.

Cut the lawn very short (2–2.5 cm) to remove much of the dead grass. After this short cutting, rake the lawn by hand to remove even more of the dead grass. I like to use a metal, spring tine rake. The reason I used this rake is that I did not want to damage the actively growing grass but only remove the dead grass, and it does a great job. I only core aerate my lawn every two years, and since I had it done last year, I was now ready to fertilize. I had a great time reliving my old days as a landscape contractor, and the $100 I saved will go toward buying more plants!

Q. Parts of our lawn are being over-taken by chickweed. Do you have any suggestions (preferably organic) for getting rid of it?

A. The only organic control that I know of for chickweed is getting down on your hands and knees and pulling it out by hand. Will this work? The answer is yes, in time. However, you will need to be persistent in pulling it out whenever you see it.

The good news is that chickweed is shallow rooted and very easy to pull up. Once you pull it out, reseed the area with grass seed and keep it well watered. If you see any chickweed sprouting along with the grass seed, be sure to pull it right away.

Keeping your lawn healthy is the key to avoiding future weed problems. That means using a fertilizer—yes, organic lawn fertilizers are available— and watering regularly.

Questions and Answers: Traditional Lawns

Q. I would appreciate your opinion on the frequency of power raking of lawns. We had ours done last year, and it seemed to take it a while to recover. There were huge brown patches in the lawn that seemed damaged.

A. I was asked this question frequently when I was a landscape contractor. Many people believed that power raking was somewhat of a gimmick and a bit of a moneymaker for contractors and lawn maintenance companies. It is not. I power rake my lawn every spring without fail. In the area we live in, there is a lot of dead grass to contend with every spring. Power raking is the best way to get that dead grass out.

The ideal power rake should leave the lawn looking clean but with-out the signs of the knives cutting too deeply, which can be seen as dark brown patches or even bare soil. If you are doing the power raking yourself and it is taking your lawn some time to recover, you may have the knives on the machine set a little too low. If someone is doing it for you, ask them to raise the power rake a little higher. Your lawn may have lumps and bumps that the power rake is cutting into too deeply, or it may be that the knives on the machine are just set too low. While it is normal to have some brown patches, it is not normal to have most of the lawn brown.

While I am at it, if a company or contractor is doing the work for

you, ask the staff if they disinfect the knives on the power rake or the tines on their aerators between jobs. If they don't, they could be spreading fairy ring.

Q. Can you tell me what time of the day is best for watering my lawn?

A. There has been debate for many years as to when is the best time to water lawns. Some experts have said that watering in the evening is the best way to go since the water will not evaporate as quickly as it does when watering during the heat of the day. That means that you don't have to water as much or as often. However, most turf experts agree that watering is best done during the early

A healthy lawn bordered by flower beds and a shrub fence.

JUST ASK JERRY

morning hours. It is still relatively cool at this time of the day and the sun is not at its strongest. The water will have a chance to penetrate the soil rather than be lost to evaporation if the watering is done later when it is hotter. Watering early also allows the grass to have a ready supply of moisture in the individual plants to get through the hotter parts of the day.

There are other advantages to watering during the early morning rather than at night. Lawns watered during the evening lay dormant overnight and the water pools on the leaves. That encourages fungal growth and other turf diseases. The other advantage to watering in the morning is that the grass can absorb the moisture and use it when it is actively growing during daylight hours.

Q. Can you please tell me what fertilizer you use on your lawn and what schedule you follow in its application?

A. I like to use Scott's Turf Builder because it is a slow-release formulation and is designed not to burn the lawn. I apply the fertilizer in spring (mid-May) and twice in summer (early July and early August).

Q. I would appreciate suggestions for fall applications of fertilizer for my lawn and garden.

A. I'm on record as saying that I am not a big fan of fall fertilizers for the lawn. There are a few reasons for

my feeling this way. First, timing the application of fall fertilizer is critical. It has to be done after the lawn has stopped actively growing in fall. If you apply it any sooner, you run the risk of stimulating the lawn into being actively growing when winter hits. You can damage your lawn if this happens. The second reason is linked directly to our weather conditions. If applied correctly, fall fertilizer is intended to sit on the lawn until spring at which time the moisture from spring thaw activates the fertilizer. The problem is that if the ground has not thawed when the snow is melting, a majority of the fertilizer runs off the lawn along with spring thaw water.

Our lawns in this area of the country do not begin serious growth until well into spring. I find it best to fertilize then rather than using a fall fertilizer and hoping it makes it intact to the right time of spring when it will be effective. I think using a fall fertilizer is a waste of time and money.

Q. We sodded a new lawn last spring. Is it is too late to apply a fertilizer in late August?

A. Do not fertilize a lawn after mid-August because it will encourage the lawn to actively grow into fall as the freeze-up approaches. A lawn that is actively growing can be damaged during freeze-up. My rule of thumb is that no fertilizer should

98

be applied after August 15, to help the lawn slow down growth naturally as fall approaches.

Q. Can you tell me how to get rid of clover in the lawn?

A. Your clover problem can be controlled by looking for a lawn herbicide that contains either mecoprop or dicamba. Either will effectively eliminate the clover.

Q. We just moved into an older home and have a terrible problem with dandelions. Although we prefer to use natural methods such as digging up weeds, this problem is far beyond our ability to dig each dandelion up. The yard would look like a war zone with all the holes. What is the most effective way to treat such a large area with so many dandelions?

A. The fastest and most efficient way to deal with your problem is by using a 2-4D impregnated wax bar. This bar is readily available in most garden centres. Just ask for a dandelion bar. With this system you attach ropes (most come with the ropes) and drag the bar behind you as you walk across the property. Apply in a cross pattern. For example, walk east to west first and then north to south. Walk at a normal pace and not too slowly.

The one warning with this application is NOT to use the bar if it is a hot day. Do not use it if the temperature is above 25° C because the wax becomes very soft and comes off the bar at a much quicker rate. The 2-4D being applied at a higher rate may damage an existing lawn.

Q. Can you tell me if there is anything I can put on my lawn to kill dandelions but won't harm pets or children?

A. Unfortunately, no. I suggest pulling the weeds by hand or using one of the new types of weed pullers. These new generation weed pullers allow you to pull the weed while standing. It saves a lot of backache. They do work.

Questions and Answers: Lawn Problems

Q. This spring we moved into a house where the previous owner had a dog. As a result, the lawn has circular patches all over the place. What are my options?

A. I get asked this question a lot, especially in spring. I know we have addressed this issue in the past, but it bears answering again. Allow me to describe the causes and cures.

It is the high nitrogen, ammonia and acidity levels in dog urine that cause the problems with the lawn. Basically the dog is over-fertilizing a spot to the point where the grass is burned and dies. If you look closely, you will see that the surviving grass on the edges of the spot are actually greener than the other parts of the lawn. That is because the grass at the very edge has not received enough "fertilizer" to burn but has received a higher dose of nitrogen than surrounding areas and thus looks greener.

Some preventive products available through your veterinarian claim to work on reducing the concentrations of acidity and salts to prevent extensive lawn damage. Discuss these products with your vet. There is nothing that can be applied to the lawn as a preventive measure other than training the dog to go somewhere else.

As for treating the areas now, the best way to start is to flood the spot with water in an attempt to flush out the salts, etc. Once the area has been well watered, dig out the soil to a depth of approximately 5 cm. Add topsoil to bring the level back even with the surrounding grass and seed the area. I like to sprinkle a fine layer of compost (3 mm) on top of the grass seed. Keep the spot well watered; in short order you will barely notice it.

Q. We have an established lawn, which is otherwise healthy, green and lush, but sadly inundated with fairy ring. We have been in this house for a year, and we do know the previous owner was using the "poke and soak" method. We continued with this approach, and we also used dish detergent and a "home remedy" from a farmers' market. We are at our wits' end.

Up until now we've been able to mask the problem to a certain extent, but now that we've used dish soap, the rings have yellowed, and the whole area looks just horrible. I removed the dead thatch from the rings and continue to aerate and water faithfully, but I'm starting to wonder if I should just consider it a lost cause, dig out the whole mess and redo the lawn. I do understand that is not without risk as you must get all the underlying "roots" of the fungus. Please share with us any advice on how to manage this problem. I am not enjoying my yard very much this year to say the least.

A. There is still no registered chemical control for fairy ring that I am aware of. The problem with fairy rings is the fungus that is the root of the problem is very efficient at blocking water from penetrating into the affected area. Because water cannot penetrate into the fungus, neither can the fungicides. Getting water into where the fungus lives is the key to controlling the problem.

I have had success using a root feeder to control the rings. Root feeders are readily available in most garden centres. Stick the root feeder into the middle of the fairy ring and a few feet down, and let the water run at a slow trickle for several hours. Then, move the feeder a foot or so into a new location on the ring and repeat the process. Keep repeating this through the entire ring. Also, every time you water other plants in the yard, water the ring. You want to literally drown the affected area. After three to four weeks, you will begin to see changes in the ring, and eventually it will disappear. The key to this whole problem is patience and perseverance. If you sprinkle the area lightly every second day or so, you will not see any results. You have to be at this thing every day and sometimes two to three times a day if you can.

Q. Our lawn is not level all over. There are little bumps here and there. Someone said that the lumps are ants, but we do not see ants in all of them. Are these anthills?

A. The lumps in the lawn may be sod webworms. Dig up a few of the lumps and look for the earthworm-like dew worms. You should find them in larger numbers than normal if it is a problem. Because of the government taking many chemicals off the market for ecological reasons, some of the controls are no longer available. Carbaryl is one chemical that is registered for use on dew worms. A brand name pesticide that has carbaryl in it is Sevin. The problem with using carbaryl is that it will only reduce the number of worms and most likely will not eliminate the problem. One of the reasons for this is that the worms are likely in other areas around your property as well. They will simply move back in after the chemical treatment is no longer effective.

Culturally, you can try the following:

• core aerate your lawn regularly
• maintain even and deep soil moisture (2.5 cm every 7–10 days)
• do not water in the evenings

Q. I have noticed that when I walk across our lawn, little white moths come flying out of it. What are they? What can I use on the lawn to get rid of them?

A. The problem is sod webworm. The small, whitish or greyish moths that are seen flying over the grass are the adults. They hide in the grass during the day and fly in a zigzag pattern when disturbed. They can be easily recognized by their habit of folding their wings closely around their bodies when at rest. They lay eggs throughout the lawn.

The young larvae (webworms) mine the leaf surface as they work their way to the soil to build tunnels. Webworms stop feeding in fall and overwinter in the soil or thatch. They pupate in spring and emerge as moths. The damage they cause is evident as irregular brown patches in the turf. These patches grow larger and can cover entire lawns. Damage is most severe in mid- to late summer. All grasses are attacked, especially bluegrasses and newly seeded lawns.

Seeing the moths fly up does not indicate that damage is being done. Many times, the infestation is not bad enough to warrant chemical control. You can check the numbers of webworms by mixing a solution of 2 tablespoons dishwashing liquid in 8 L of water. Apply this solution over a square metre of turf. Within a few minutes, the flesh-coloured, spotted larvae will surface. If you have more than 10–15 per square metre of turf, you need to treat the lawn. If you don't have that many webworms, do what I do and just fertilize the lawn and water well. A healthy lawn can survive the impact of a few sod webworms with no problems.

If you do have a problem, you will need to treat the lawn with carbaryl. I asked my good friend Gail Rankin of Rankin Horticultural Services about this problem because she is an expert in pesticides and their application. Gail confirmed that carbaryl is the chemical of choice for treating the webworm problem. Follow the manufacturer's directions very carefully for applying the carbaryl.

Q. We have brown spots in our lawn where the grass is mostly dead. Our neighbours have the same problem. It usually starts about the first part of July and lasts until late fall. We have tried a herbicide, pesticide and more fertilizer, but they didn't seem to help. The spots are anywhere from 8 to 10 sq ft and smaller in half a dozen spots.

A. The problem could be from several causes. The two most likely are sod webworm or brown patch. First test for webworms. If the test fails and it is brown patch, then it is a fungal issue (*Rhizoctonia solani*) that is caused by environmental and cultural factors. It starts as a "smoke-ring" of grey-black mycelium from 1.5 to 4 cm wide that develops around the active patch. The grass will turn black and then light brown as it dies and dries up. Patches can be from 2 cm to 1 m and spread rapidly. Hot and humid weather add to the problem with higher night-time temperatures around 18° C. Unbalanced nitrogen fertilizer applications can also be a contributing factor. Frequent mowing can also be the culprit as the fungus can gain easy entry through the wounds after cutting. Avoid unbalanced fertilizers if your lawn has a history of this problem. Reduce the frequency of mowing, and do not water late in the day or evening.

Q. I have a house that we use as a summer home in northern Alberta, and the lawn backs onto bush. The lawn along the edge of the bush is dying, and moss is creeping into the lawn. Any solutions?

A. Moss occurs in lawns when conditions are not suitable for growing a dense, healthy turf. Infestations of moss are associated with low fertility, poor drainage, too much shade, soil compaction, wet conditions, poor air circulation, or a combination of these factors. Contrary to popular opinion, low soil pH is seldom responsible for moss invasion.

You will need to follow the following suggestions to keep moss out of the lawn permanently:

- Maintain good soil fertility. Lawns should be fertilized at least once per year and preferably three times: once in early spring, once in early summer and once in late summer before August 15.

- Improve drainage. Soils that are constantly wet because of poor drainage should be contoured so that water will drain away from the wet areas of the lawn.

- Improve air circulation. Low-branched trees may cause poor air circulation and dense shade. Lawns surrounded by buildings and tall vegetation with limbs close to the ground will require considerable effort to provide adequate air circulation necessary for the growth of a good lawn.

- Provide for more light. In some cases, a choice between trees and a good lawn must be made. If the lawn is completely shaded, removing some of the least desirable trees may be the only answer in order to grow a good turf. Other times, removing low branches and thinning the crowns of trees will allow enough light to reach the ground surface so that a good turf can be produced. If you are not willing to remove enough vegetation so that direct sunlight reaches the ground during part of the day, consider substituting a ground cover for grass. In addition, plant grasses that are shade tolerant.

- Loosen compacted soil. Aeration will help a lawn where it is undesirable to disturb the soil surface.

Q. I have a problem with my lawn. It is about 30 years old. I have given it two applications of liquid Golf Green 20-3-4, one at the end of May and one at the end of June. It perks it up for about two weeks, and then it seems to have no further effect.

A. The problem is likely the fertilizer itself. Liquid fertilizers are great for adding immediate punch to a lawn because they are readily absorbed into the plants, but they fizzle out relatively quickly. You may need to look at a slow-release fertilizer such as Scott's Turf Builder, which will provide nutrients to the lawn over a much longer period.

Q. My question relates to my four-year-old lawn. The front faces east and the backyard west, protected by many trees. Both lawns are in good to great condition, but the backyard lawn is plushier (I believe because of the tree protection). Both have developed grass that sprouts what appears to be seeds at the top but only when I allow it to reach heights over the general cut length or extended cutting periods. I do cut my lawn mid-long length, and I like to believe it looks better than most. Are the seeds an issue, and, if so, what can I do to solve the problem? I have been given mixed comments from friends.

A. This question was asked a few years ago, and I consulted the greens-keepers at two local golf courses for the answer. I knew that stress can cause bluegrass to go to seed. Some of the stresses are caused by drought, too much potassium and trying to cut it all down in one pass after leaving it to grow longer. Both greenskeepers agreed with my list of causes but also reminded me that mid-spring is a normal time in the grass' cycle for the lawn to go to seed even without any stress.

One greenskeeper said the grass at his home went to seed in May, and he did not have it very long at all. He told people that it is a normal process and is not harmful to the lawn. I asked the greenskeepers for some home-care advice, and they agreed that homeowners should not water too often. Lawns can recover from dry conditions quite nicely. If you use a mulching mower when cutting your lawn, the grass seed will go back

into the lawn. (Don't mulch if you have quackgrass in your lawn and it has gone to seed.) I used a mulching mower on my own lawn, which had gone to seed, and the only issue was that the mower was set fairly high and blew the seeds into the flower beds. I had some extra work pulling out all the grass seedlings.

Q. I hope you can help with a problem in my front yard. I have been trying to save the lawn that is growing—or trying to grow—under a very large, old spruce tree. I water the lawn very well every week and have topdressed and overseeded it. It looks okay for a time but by mid-summer it starts to look bad again. Can I do anything to help the grass grow there?

A. Your question definitely ranks in the top 10 of the most asked questions. Trying to grow grass under a spruce tree is a problem for a few reasons. The spruce, with its extensive root system, is very good at sucking up every last bit of moisture in the area under and around the tree. The grass that is trying to grow under the tree has a root system that is very shallow and not nearly as efficient as the spruce in competing for the moisture.

Topdressing and overseeding will only last for so long unless you water almost constantly. As the heat of summer descends, the grass will begin to suffer because of the moisture loss to the tree. Unfortunately, there is no easy solution or magic bullet that can make grass grow under such a tree. Most people think that the reason for the lack of growth in the lawn is the acidic conditions under the tree. While it is true that the soil under an evergreen is more acidic, that is not the main problem. The lack of moisture is the number one problem.

My best advice is to stop wasting time and money in trying to grow a lawn in a spot where it will simply not grow well. Laying down a decorative mulch is the best way to handle this area.

Q. My lawn is 40+ years old. It has become infested with seven separate fairy rings. We have decided to completely replace it and would like to know what season is the best to do the work. Some people suggest fall and others spring. Also, how does one go about choosing a company to do this work?

A. Replacing a lawn does not have to be a traumatic experience. All you need is the right sod to do the job. I'm sorry, I couldn't resist the pun. Seriously, though, sod can be laid in spring or in fall with equal success. I prefer spring because the grass roots have no time restrictions on sending out new roots. Laying sod in fall depends a bit on when the cold weather or snow arrives. If the grass

has at least some chance to send out new roots, there is no problem. If it doesn't have enough time, some dead spots may develop but that is usually rare.

As for choosing a company, there are many reputable firms out there. Start by phoning a few to get some estimates. Asking for references is an important part of the process. Along with the references, ask if you can see jobs that were done to give you an idea of the quality of their work. Also, being able to speak to previous clients can offer insight into the work ethic of the company.

Q. The thatch in my lawn is 7.5 cm thick in some places. We moved into the house three years ago, and I have been picking up my grass clippings, aerating the lawn and using a power rake on it. Is there any way to speed up the process of getting rid of the thatch?

A. Thatch is a layer of undecomposed stems and roots that accumulates near the soil surface. Grass clippings do not contribute to thatch accumulation. The rate at which thatch accumulates is determined by the type and vigour of the grass in the lawn. A bluegrass, for example, forms thatch more rapidly than other grasses.

Thatch is a normal part of any lawn, and only becomes harmful when the thatch layer is thicker than 1 cm.

When thatch becomes excessive, the lawn may root into the thatch rather than the soil. Thatch does not hold moisture, so lawns rooted into thatch will not tolerate dry weather or cold temperatures.

If you have underground sprinklers, the easiest management technique is a 20-minute watering at mid-day, every day, to help control thatch by keeping it wet.

If you don't have underground sprinklers, the three other options are power rakes, core aeration and topdressing. Obviously, you have used the first two methods with no success. The third option, topdressing, means applying a thin layer of soil over the lawn to help decompose the thatch layer. This topdressing may also be combined with coring. The soil introduces micro-organisms that help decay the thatch.

Q. Last year I moved onto a property that has an automatic irrigation system. We cut plugs out of several areas of the lawn and the thatch is very thick, 5–7.5 cm thick in some areas. I'm pretty sure the previous owners watered the lawns frequently and shallowly. Because there is so much thatch I hesitate to get someone in to do a mechanical de-thatching— too much material would get pulled up and the lawns would look terrible afterward. Would topdressing with compost be more beneficial to encourage microorganisms?

A. Wow! That is a lot of thatch. Normally thatch should not be any thicker than 1 cm. I believe the best and fastest solution to the problem is to have the lawn mechanically de-thatched, even though you are hesitant to do so. Waiting for a biological de-thatching agent to work could take too long and the existing grass may start to die. Topdressing would really not accomplish anything. In fact, it would probably compound the problem by further smothering the roots of the grass.

When I talk about mechanical de-thatching, I am not talking about the spring tine approach to your thatch problem. A roto-rake will do far more damage than good in this situation. I recommend hiring a professional to de-thatch your lawn. The pro will come with a specialized de-thatching mower with rotary knives that will slice through the thatch. This de-thatching should be followed by a good, thorough power raking.

Tell your lawn-care professional that you need some special attention given to your lawn. If he knows your situation, he will adjust the de-thatching mower to a higher height to keep the mower from tearing the thatch rather than cutting it.

He may need to make a few passes over the lawn, dropping the height each time, until all the thatch is gone.

While the lawn may not may look great this season, it will start to come back rapidly once you have it on a regular fertilizing and watering schedule. If you have some bare patches you can easily fill these in with some compost and lawn seed.

Q. One lawn maintenance company said it is best to aerate a lawn in fall and didn't want to do it in spring. Another said it's best to do it in spring. Both companies said it had to do with getting water into the soil at the right time. Is there a right time?

A. There is no difference whether you aerate the lawn in spring or fall. Aerating the lawn is beneficial for the following reasons:

- improved air circulation
- better fertilizer uptake and use
- reduced runoff
- stronger grass roots
- eases soil compaction
- helps thatch break down

All of these benefits can be achieved by aerating in spring or fall. If you choose to aerate in fall, another benefit will be that you will see an improved spring green-up and growth.

Q. Is there a cure for mushrooms in a lawn? Not fairy ring mushrooms, but a cluster of tall white mushrooms in one spot, some black ones in another, and some beige mushrooms in yet another. After I dig them up, they go away, then a week or two later pop up in another place, usually in August and September. Is there something I can spray on them?

A. Nothing you can spray on your lawn will kill these mushrooms. In reality, the primary fungal organism is a rather extensive system of mycelium located in your soil system. This type of fungus is simply decomposing organic matter located in the soil—which is a good thing. If the short-lived and temporary mushrooms bother you, just kick them over and remove them. If you knock them down before they sporulate (release their spores), they will not return as easily next year. I always kick mine over as I mow the lawn, and it works very well in keeping them at bay.

Decomposing mushrooms are not an indication that anything is wrong or out of balance. They cannot harm your turf. Rain triggers the reproductive cycle for many fungal organisms because their spores require water for successful germination.

Q. What causes the white powdery mildew on certain spots on a lawn? It seems to occur in the same place each year and doesn't spread.

A. Powdery mildew on a lawn is usually the result of poor air circulation. You probably have some large shrubs that are encroaching on the lawn. Try pruning back the shrubs to open up the lawn space for better air movement. Overwatering and over-fertilizing can also contribute to the problem.

Q. I have a strange question. I am fairly new to gardening so I have never seen this situation before. During the winter, I walked over the snow on my lawn while I was installing my Christmas lights. I noticed in the spring that each footstep in the lawn had a white growth on the top of the grass. What is this growth, and why is it growing in the footprints only?

A. What you describe is a type of snow mould. This fungus or combination of fungi grows in wet areas, and the bottoms of your footprints are the wettest areas. As soon as you see this mould, you should simply take a garden or lawn rake and disturb the grass where the mould is growing. The matted fungi will break up, and air will get in to dry out the grass.

Q. I have snow mould in my lawn. I tried to rough up the grass where the snow and ice let me. Near the snow mould are some bright yellow/white spots of grass. This pattern occurs throughout part of my lawn.

I don't think it is snow mould. It looks like dry grass. I have it in my front and back yard. The funny thing is that neither neighbour has this problem.

A. I have the same problem, and this is the first time the problem has been as extensive. What you describe are patches of grass that have been damaged as a result of the snow mould. In most winters, grey snow mould, which is likely the culprit, does not damage the lawn, but this winter it has. The damage is more likely to happen in winters where snow falls early on unfrozen ground, stays for long periods and is compacted. That describes perfectly what we have experienced this past winter. It also happens more often in areas that are shaded and where the snow melts slowly. Raking to get the grass to stand up and allow air in usually keeps the mould at bay, but the snow has been down for so long this year that the damage was already done before we could rake.

Give these dead patches a little more attention with fertilizer and water this spring. If you don't get new growth showing fairly soon, you will have to reseed the areas.

Q. As the snow has been melting, we are noticing that the lawns throughout the neighbourhood have tunnel-like pathways through them. Any information I can find indicates that the tunnels may be caused by voles. Do you have any suggestions for eliminating the problem, lawn care after the fact and future steps to take for years to come? We back onto a green belt, and I don't know if that makes things worse, and we do have children and want to be able to play safely in what's left of our backyard.

A. Controlling the problem takes a bit of work, but it can be done. Piling snow up along the edges of your property and then watering the piles down to turn them into ice is a solution. The ice acts as a barricade and prevents the rodents from getting into your yard. You can also use a wire mesh (1.5 cm) barrier. The wire would have to be 45–60 cm high to prevent the beasties from crawling over it easily. This more costly solution (because you would need to use the mesh all along your property line) may be the best solution if the snow cover is not very deep.

The damage rodents do to the lawn is more cosmetic than anything. The lawn will be unsightly for a time in spring after melt but should not be permanently damaged. Only the blades of grass have been consumed, and they will grow back in short order. As for your observation, yes, the green belt is the likely source for the invaders, and their numbers are higher there.

Q. I have a huge problem with ants in my lawn. There are anthills

everywhere. I have tried just about everything to control them—nothing seems to be working. Can you help?

A. As many of my readers know, I like to recommend products that I try myself and know they work. Doktor Doom is one of those products. Just last week I was out treating an ant problem that I had. The telltale piles of dirt began appearing next to my sidewalk, and after I watched for a few minutes, hundreds of ants could be seen. I reached for my Doktor Doom Residual Insecticide. One application and my problem was gone within one day. I have checked the area several times and not one ant could be found.

I like this product for several reasons. First, the product works very well. Second, I like the applicator. The spray comes with a small tube that can be affixed to the nozzle. With this tube I can inject the spray right into the mounds or where I observe ants emerging. Finally, the residual action of this product means it stays effective for a longer period of time. I also spray around the hill so that any stragglers walking through the area will come in contact with the insecticide.

Q. Quack grass is invading my lawn! Are there any more or less painless solutions to their removal? Along with the quack grass, there are a multitude of dandelions, which I have begun to dig out.

A. There is no treatment for quack grass that will not kill the grass around it as well. Nonselective glyphosate products such as Round-Up will kill the weed but will also kill the lawn around it. There is a method to deal with this problem, but it takes time—be prepared because you might look silly doing it. Get a small artist's brush and "paint" the Round-Up on each blade of the quack. The Round-Up will kill the weed right to the root and will not leach across the soil into the lawn. It works. I've done it—but the mail carrier and every neighbour who happened by stared at me as I painted my lawn. Making sure your lawn is well fertilized and watered helps keep the good grass strong, which also helps keep out the quack grass.

Q. Is it really necessary to roll sod when installing it? I seem to remember a pamphlet from the University of Alberta on lawn building that said it was of no benefit.

A. Like so many other topics in gardening, there may be more than one definitive answer to the question. I have always rolled my sod and will continue to do so. I feel that I get better root-to-soil contact with rolling. Often sod gets kinked and bent as it is cut and stacked. When you lay it, there may be sections that do not touch the soil because the sod section had been bent. Rolling helps press these sections down into the soil.

There is no need to roll with the full weight of the roller. In other words, if you are using a water-filled roller, drain away two-thirds of the water before rolling. You are looking for light pressure only.

Q. Last spring I laid sod at my new house. It grew very well, but I soon noticed some problems. The sod was laid on a rainy day, and wherever someone steps on it, depressions occur in the sod as they sink in the wet soil. There are also gaps where two edges of sod come together, and the edges are turning brown. I spent a lot of time and money on the sod, and now it looks horrible. What can I do other than ripping it out and starting over?

A. Take a deep breath. There are some things you can do to correct the problems. If the gaps between sod edges are larger than 1 cm, sometimes the edges of the sod can die if the sod is not watered very well each and every day. This dieback combined with the original space can create the situation you describe.

This problem can be easily solved. Get a good-quality topsoil and spread it into all of the gaps. Rent a small lawn roller and fill it half full of water. Roll the entire lawn when it is slightly damp but not sopping wet. Next, seed the areas with a grass seed that matches the type of sod you have. Keep the seeded areas moist, but not too wet, until the grass sprouts, then keep up the watering until the grass is established.

Rolling will help tamp the topsoil in place and smooth out some depressions. If the depressions are too deep, topdress those spots by adding topsoil 5 cm at a time into the depressions. Allow the grass to grow up and through the soil and then add a little more soil. Keep adding a little more soil until the depression is even with the rest of the lawn.

It sounds as if the base of the lawn was not prepared properly. It should be rolled or tamped so that the soil is firmed up and not loose. Many homeowners simply install new soil and lay sod on top of that soil without the compaction that is important in preventing the types of hills and valleys you speak of. If the soil is properly rolled and tamped, you can install sod even on the rainiest day without sinking in too deeply.

Q. I have a question about my front lawn. A few years ago, a tree service removed a dead birch tree. I also had the stump removed. I put in what I thought was good topsoil where the stump was and seeded it. The grass has never grown particularly well there. It grows all right, but it never gets to be a rich dark green. It looks rather a sickly yellow green. I was wondering if the stump removal people put some chemical in the soil that the grass does not like. Or could I possibly have used some type of soil that had the wrong pH?

A. If you had the stump ground out, the tree service would have had no need to use any chemicals. I would be more suspicious of the soil you added into the area. It might be worthwhile to buy an inexpensive pH testing kit at a garden centre and do a quick test of the pH level. Other questions to consider are whether you are fertilizing the area and does the spot get enough light, or is it perhaps screened by other trees?

The other causes of the yellowing might be from overwatering or chlorosis caused by an iron deficiency. Iron chlorosis is caused when the pH of the soil is too high. The ferrous ions are available to the grass when the pH is in the 5–6.5 range. High pH or soils with excessive phosphorus can bind up the iron and make it unavailable to the grass—another reason to have the pH checked.

Q. Our lawn has fairy ring and other problems, and we have decided to replace it. We were planning on putting Round-Up on the entire lawn, then rototilling and putting in new sod in spring. The question is, will Round-Up kill the fairy ring fungus that lies beneath the sod, or should we attempt to dig out the fairy ring first? Our lawn gets a lot of sun; is there any particular type of sod that is more sun/drought tolerant than others?

A. Round-Up will not kill the fungus that causes the fairy ring. You will need to dig down 20–90 cm depending on how large and well developed the fairy ring is. Remove the affected soil and dispose of it in securely tied garbage bags.

As for sod that is tolerant of the sun, talk to the staff at the sod farm where you are planning on buying the sod from. They can tell you the grass blends they have available. Most grasses used for sod are quite tolerant of the sun and actually thrive in more sun.

Q. I've just moved into a house after years of living in an apartment. I'm at a loss at what to do with my lawn. It is very uneven (mounds and holes everywhere), and it is also very patchy. The grass in the lower sections—the holes—is lush, and the grass on the mounds is sparse. The holes are about the size of your foot (around and deep). The mounds vary; some are large (about 60 cm around at the base and about 15 cm high), and the rest are smaller. Needless to say, it's difficult to mow the lawn without catching the lawnmower blade on the mounds and missing the grass in the holes.

Maybe I'm looking for too much, too soon, but I would really like to have a nice, lush yard next spring. Also, do I use sand or topsoil to level out the yard?

A. The valleys you described are too deep to topdress in one fell swoop. If you added 15 cm of soil immediately, you would kill the grass growing underneath. Sand is not an option; topsoil is the best way to go. Proper topdressing involves adding 2.5–5 cm of soil on top of existing grass. With the amount of topdressing you would have to do, this process could take several years.

I would advise hiring a professional to level the property properly and then reseed or resod. If cost is a consideration, you can level the property yourself, but it will not come without a great deal of effort. You will need to level the mounds by removing them completely. Cut them down so they are even with the surrounding lawn, then seed or sod these bare areas.

Q. I have a healthy 10-year-old lawn that gets pampered with fertilizer/ sprinkler and regular cuts with a sharp mower. Over the past few years, I've noticed a fine, lighter green grass of a circular stem nature showing up in several locations throughout the lawn. It is also present in the neighbour's and is apparently propagating through our yards. Could you suggest what this growth is and how to rid our lawns of it?

A. It sounds like the problem is *Poa annua*, an annual bluegrass that can invade lawns. It has the "boat-shaped" leaf tips, which curve up not unlike the bow of a boat. It is lighter green and more shallow rooted than Kentucky bluegrass. There is no selective herbicide available to treat *Poa annua* specifically. But Round-Up will kill it. Try painting the Round-Up on the *Poa annua,* or simply treat the whole area and then resod or reseed.

You can prevent the *Poa* from invading by doing the following:

- Do not cut the lawn too short. Lawns taller than 6 cm never have much *Poa annua* in them.

- Do not overwater, especially in shady areas as this encourages the *Poa* growth. Water infrequently but deeply.

- Aerify the lawn frequently, as compacted soil conditions also encourage *Poa* growth.

Q. The grade around our two-year-old house is really messed up (a lake is in the middle of the yard). We had a landscape company come out to give us an estimate. The existing grass is very bad—all dandelions and who knows what else. Would it help the weed situation to remove the sod, lay new topsoil, then resod, or will the weeds just continue to grow? We have a lot of kids, and I try to be earth-friendly.

A. If the weed situation is as bad as you describe, then, yes, it may be best to resod. The completely eco-friendly method is to lay down landscape-grade black plastic over the lawn, secure it in place and let the grass and weeds die from a lack of sun and the heat that is generated under the plastic. This method will definitely kill all the weeds so they will not be a problem in the new sod.

To solve your problems with the grade in your yard, you may have to add more soil; resodding is a logical progression. Once you have killed the weeds, I suggest rototilling in the dead weeds and grass, and then adding fresh topsoil on top. Many people ask how much soil they should add when installing sod. Ideally, 20 cm of topsoil is best. That gives you a base that will support a healthy lawn for many years. If cost is a concern, the minimum amount of good quality topsoil depth should be 10–15 cm.

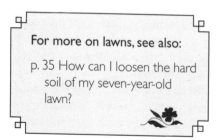

For more on lawns, see also:

p. 35 How can I loosen the hard soil of my seven-year-old lawn?

Perennials

One of the most versatile groups of plants has to be perennials. For the most part, these plants require little in the way of maintenance, and many bloom for long periods of time while others have interesting foliage colour, texture or form.

There is a perennial for almost every area in the garden, from full sun to deep shade and from dry to wet. A perennial bed will offer years of enjoyment with only the basics to keep the plants happy.

If you are planning a perennial bed or thinking of redoing one, the most important consideration for such a bed is the soil. Taking the time to properly prepare the soil for your perennials is crucial if your ultimate goal is great-looking plants without a lot of extra work. Taking the time and spending the money necessary to do this part of the job right will pay dividends for years to come. Begin by

digging down 30–40 cm. This chore can certainly be a lot of work especially if you are hand digging the area, but try doing it in sections so that you are not overwhelmed, especially if the bed is a large one.

If you run into clay at the 20 cm depth, dig down until you hit 30 cm and get rid of that clay! Your plants will thank you for it with their performance. Next, add one bag of compost and one bag of well-rotted manure per 20 sq ft of garden bed. Work this mixture in well with existing soil. Doing so will allow for good drainage. More perennials die each year from poorly drained soil than from any other reason. It is critical to their growth, whether the area is in sun or shade. If the area is hardpan clay and impossible to dig, consider a raised bed where you will place good quality soil mixed with compost and manure on top of existing soil to a depth of 30 cm. Sometimes raised beds will suffer more in winter than beds in the ground. Usually the plants on the outside edge suffer most. Mulching can help the plants that are most prone to winter damage.

My purpose in this book is not to present the best perennials or even a comprehensive listing of perennials but rather to offer a compendium of problems in growing these plants and some possible answers to those problems.

Questions and Answers

Q. I was outside yesterday surveying the damage done by the cold weather we had at the end of April. It appears that several of my perennials have taken a hit of frost. They have fallen over and are looking much the worse for wear. Will they come back? Is there anything I can do to help them along?

A. We had several evenings where the temperature was well below zero, and many perennials that had made an appearance because of the warm weather earlier in the month were zapped by the frost. In most cases,

they should make a comeback. Do not cut or prune them back until you are sure that the affected area is dead. Perennials are a hardy lot, and while they may be set back a bit with this frost, they will come back.

Q. I bought some boxed perennials at a big box store in early spring and just looked at them (in late April), and they are sprouting. What can I do with them until it is time to plant?

A. You will need to pot the plants up for them to survive. Boxed plants are usually packaged with a minimum of soil and most often they sit in just some bark chips or peat moss. If they are sprouting now, they will die before it is time to plant. If you have some leftover pots kicking around the garage, pot the plants in them. If not, make a trip to the garden centre and pick up some inexpensive plastic pots and some potting soil.

Choose a pot that is large enough for the root system. Fill the pot with potting soil that you have moistened. Dig a small hole in the soil for the roots. Insert the plant into the hole and fill in with soil, making sure that the plant is at the same level in the soil as it was in the box. Place the pot(s) in a sunny window and keep the soil moist but not wet. If the plant starts to get spindly, cut back some of the new growth to encourage the plant to bush out. Cut the plant back approximately 5 cm.

When ready to plant outdoors, you will need to "harden off" the plant by introducing it slowly to the outdoors. Putting a plant that has been indoors into full sun and leaving it there will result in the plant going into shock and/or actually burning and bleaching from the intensity of the sun. Put the plant into a shady spot to start with, and move it back indoors at night. Move the plant into the sun gradually, adding a few hours each day to the time it is exposed. When the plant is hardened off, it will be ready for planting.

Q. I am planning a new landscape and I am looking for a good-looking, flowering perennial that will be very low maintenance. Am I asking for the impossible? The size does not matter, and the exposure is south facing.

A. Daylilies are the answer. Brown and green thumbs alike both agree that these versatile plants are the answer to so many landscaping problems. The name "daylily" comes from its Latin name *Hemerocallis,* which means "beauty for a day." Each bloom lasts only a day, but new blooms are produced every day over a long flowering period. An established daylily clump can easily produce 200–400 blooms over its flowering period. Most will flower for three to four weeks.

The flowers are borne high above the long, spiky foliage on tall stems that make them easy to harvest as cut flowers. Even when daylilies are not in bloom, the foliage is striking on its own, creating an almost tropical appearance with the long, gracefully arching leaves.

There are over 46,000 daylilies that have been named, officially registered and marketed. The blooms come in many different forms, including ruffled edges and borders, round and full forms, miniatures and doubles. The bell-type flowers may be deep and trumpet-shaped or more shallow and cup-shaped. Flower colour can range from creamy white to deep mahogany, with nearly every shade of

Daylily 'Bonanza.'

yellow, orange and pink in between. There are also multicoloured varieties, with blends of related shades, and bicolour and eyed flowers that combine different hues. Flower sizes range from a few centimetres to 25 cm. The most common are in the 2.5–15 cm range. The fragrance ranges from little or no fragrance to those that are highly fragrant.

Whether you have a large garden or only room for a few containers, daylilies can fit the bill. These plants come in a wide variety of sizes. The miniature or dwarf forms available grow to a height of only 30 cm, ideal for small beds or containers. Daylilies are also available in medium to large sizes reaching a height of 1 m or more.

These lovely plants can transform a previously unused spot in the garden into a true showpiece. They will grow best in full sun or partial shade and will grow in a more shady spot as well but may not flower as prolifically. Dense shade is the only spot they won't do well in. For these plants to give optimum bloom, at least six hours of sunlight is required. Daylilies will grow in almost any soil. They will be at their best in a rich, well-drained soil but will tolerate even clay soils. When planting in clay, add a soil amendment such as compost to help break down the clay, and add organic matter. If planting in a container, using a timed-release fertilizer is ideal. Add this fertilizer at planting time. If growing in a bed, applying a 5-10-5 or other bloom fertilizer at regular intervals prior to bloom will help produce a good show of flowers.

Because these plants multiply and spread, they are excellent for filling in a spot all on their own. They make an excellent plant for containing erosion on slopes. Plants can be planted as soon as the ground is workable in spring or in fall before freeze-up. Once established, they are very easy to split and divide, and with many varieties hardy to zone 2, their hardiness makes them ideally suited for the prairies. They are also able to withstand drought conditions better than most perennials. With the modern focus on reducing water usage in the garden, daylilies make a great addition to the xeriscape (conservation of water and energy through creative landscaping). An added bonus to the versatility of daylilies is their resistance to most diseases and pests.

Daylilies can be used in a wide variety of applications. The larger varieties are ideal as background plants in any perennial bed. They make beautiful foundation plants around a home. Because of the appearance of the foliage, they make a striking statement when used in and around a water feature. When planted around a pond, the arching leaves add a graceful touch. Use the miniature varieties in border plantings or in rock gardens.

Consider planting daylilies in clumps, or "drifts," of the same varieties to create a more natural look. Also consider using a variety of daylilies that bloom at different times of the growing season to ensure that your perennial garden always has some daylilies in bloom. The use of daylilies in containers increases their versatility even more. Once containerized, they can be moved to any spot to create a focal point or grouped to make an even more dramatic impact.

Some of the newer varieties to try are listed here:

Dwarfs and Miniatures

- 'Buffy's Doll': grows to 30 cm; flowers 7.5 cm across; pink with red eye zone and red ribs on each petal

- 'Stella D'Oro': grows 30–45 cm; one of the first daylilies to bloom in June; masses of golden yellow, ruffled blooms

Mediums

- 'Night Beacon': grows 62.5–75 cm; flowers 10 cm across; maroon-purple with a chartreuse centre and a green throat

- 'Strawberry Candy': grows to 62 cm; flowers 10.6 cm across;

Daylily 'Stella D'Oro.'

strawberry pink blend with rose-red eye zone and a golden green throat; truly stunning planted en masse

Large

- 'Big Bird': grows to 85 cm; flowers sunshine yellow with large ruffles accenting re-curved petals; cream-toned edges, slight green throat
- 'Pink Tangerine': grows to 85 cm; flowers pink and tangerine combination with ruffled petals

Daylilies are beautiful, easy to grow, resistant to diseases and pests, drought tolerant, bloom continuously, are adaptable to most soils, will grow in partial shade, make excellent cut flowers, have nice foliage and many are fragrant. They truly are the perfect perennial. If you can't tell by this long-winded (even more verbose than I usually am) answer, daylilies are a favourite of mine.

Q. We are doing a major makeover in our backyard, and I have many questions.

1. I have quite a few trees, shrubs and perennials yet to plant. Is it too late in October?

2. I have quite a few shrubs and perennials that I have planted in pots. In the past, I always dug them into my kids' sandbox, and they always survived the winter. We no longer have a sandbox, and my garden spot will not be ready this year. Can I keep these plants in an old garage that we have out back? It is insulated but not heated and has one window. If so, do I have to insulate them, or what do you recommend? The plants I have include a tree rose, boxwood, globe caragana, two globe cedars, hostas, stonecrop, silvermound, barberry and some mix and match pots with various miniature evergreens.

3. I am planning on putting mulch down in the new flowerbeds that I have made. I have planted various groundcover plants (stonecrop, vinca, pinks, etc.). Will they still spread? Can I put fabric underneath the mulch, or is that not a good idea?

A. 1. You can plant up to freeze-up.

2. The plants may or may not survive in the garage. It depends on winter, temperatures, etc. Insulating them with fibreglass insulation is a good idea. The tree rose and boxwood will be the most difficult to overwinter.

3. Groundcover plants are so named because they do spread, yes. The vinca will spread fairly quickly. I never use landscape fabric under my mulch. I use shredded cedar bark mulch. I would not recommend using a fabric if you want the groundcovers to spread.

Q. Would you please tell me if it is safe to transplant perennials in fall, or should I wait until spring? I have a couple of delphiniums to transplant as well as some ferns and hostas.

A. Fall is a great time to transplant perennials. Having said that, the only caveat is if the perennial is a fall bloomer. If it is, and it's blooming, wait until spring to move it. Other perennials can be safely moved right up until about three weeks before freeze-up. I would recommend cutting back the tops by one-third to allow the plant to work at establishing itself rather than working at supplying water to the foliage.

When transplanting, make sure you dig a fairly large area around the base of the plant you are moving. Taking as much soil as possible will go a long way to making the transplant a success. Try not to disturb the roots if possible. It is also a good idea to add about 10 cm of mulch around the base of the plant to help to conserve moisture, insulate the newly transplanted perennial and promote root growth. Give the transplants a good drink of water as well.

Q. It does feel like fall is here, and as a new gardener, I'm not quite sure which of my plants must be cut back before the cold sets in. Is there a "rule of thumb" to observe regarding cutting back plants?

A. I assume you are talking about perennials. There is no general rule as to what you can cut back in fall. I leave my perennials as is until spring, and then I do clean-up. The leaves and stems can act as insulators over winter and in some cases tell you where a plant was so you don't accidentally dig it up in spring. If you are intent on cutting things back in fall, make sure you wait until the plant has been killed back by the frost. If you cut back an actively growing plant, you can damage it.

Some experts tell you that by cutting back in fall and cleaning up, you remove the parts that will rot in a wet spring and that may harm emerging plants in spring. They may be right—but my feeling has always been that if I get out there early enough in spring, I will clean things up before they have a chance to rot. Getting out early in spring has never been a problem for me. I'm out there in the snow looking at things and pulling things out that need pulling. I like seeing where the plants were growing, and over winter I actually like seeing the snow and/or ice sitting on the spent plants. It creates winter interest in places where there would only be snow.

Q. I covered all perennials including many roses with a mulch of peat moss and dried leaves. The roses are up against the house on the south side and are showing signs of growth now that it is spring. When should I remove this covering? Last year I took it off too soon, and the new growth froze, but I also do not want to limit the growth of the plants.

Also, I need to amend one of my large perennial flower beds as the soil is quite hard, and it is difficult to work around the flowers during summer. What should I add to the soil to make it more workable?

A. I have struggled in the past with when to remove mulches as well. Recently, while doing some reading, I ran across an article with a great idea that I plan on using myself, and I would like to pass it on to my readers. The article said to monitor native trees, and when they showed signs of budding out, that was the sign to remove the mulch. Truly, this makes a great deal of sense as the trees will only bud out when the ambient and ground temperatures are right. Of course, Mother Nature can still throw a curve weather wise, but I still feel this is a very good indicator as to when to remove the mulch.

As for what to add to your soil, compost is the best organic matter to add to recondition soil. Add compost to a depth of 5 cm and work it in around the plants. Take care when cultivating very close to plants so as not to damage the roots.

Q. I have a question about my perennials. Last year we had little or no snow cover, and I'm wondering what to do if it happens again this year. I'm thinking of using some fibreglass insulation to cover some of the more delicate perennials. What is your opinion?

A. The lack of snowcover and cold may harm many plants. Laying down a layer of insulation will help protect the roots from dramatic swings in temperature, especially for perennials in their first year. Many types of insulating materials are available. Snow, of course, is one of the best, but if snow level is poor, you can also use dried leaves, dried grass or hay/straw. For perennials, lay the insulating material directly on top of the area the plants are in. There is no need to use boxes filled with the insulating material as you would for protecting a rose, for example.

If you are concerned about the leaves and/or straw/hay blowing away, place the material on the bed and cover it with some landscape fabric. I like to use landscape fabric pins to hold it in place. It is much better to use the fabric than plastic because the fabric breathes. Plastic can cause overheating on a warm, sunny day, and the lack of air circulation can cause mould and rot.

The insulation will also help avoid frost heaving, which is a problem especially with plants planted near houses or other buildings. The soil temperature may rise dramatically during the day and then freeze rapidly at night, causing the ground to heave. This process may even partially lift plants out of the ground.

Q. There has been a lot of talk in your column about watering trees and shrubs during a dry winter, but what about perennials? I have 300 perennials; should I be watering them?

A. Yes, you certainly should be watering the perennials. If the ground is not hard frozen, watering the plants once or twice a month will go a long way toward their survival in spring. While that is true for all perennials no matter where they are planted, it is especially true for perennials that are planted close to a house, garage or other outbuilding and particularly those in south-facing spots. Watering now is also very important for any newly planted plants.

Also consider applying mulch if you have not already done so. The mulch will help in two ways. First, it will help to keep the moisture in the soil around the plant. Second, it will help to prevent frost heaving, which is a real problem with no snow cover. I have had plants literally uprooted from the heaving if no mulch is applied.

When I was out watering on the weekend, I watched in amazement as the water soaked into the ground around my newly planted flowering crab. I expected to see the water pool and drain slowly, but it was like pouring water on a sponge—that is how dry the soil was.

Q. When deadheading flowers, do you pull only the petals or the whole head? I assume it should be the whole head to remove the seeds that use up nutrients from the plant to develop.

A. Deadheading is a technique to remove spent flowers. It serves two purposes. First, it serves an aesthetic purpose by keeping the plant looking neat and tidy. Second, it stops seed production. In many plants, once seeds are produced, flowering will decline. While different plants respond to different techniques, the general rule is to remove the spent blossoms, making sure that you remove the seedpod developing directly behind the flower or in the centre of what was the flower. Don't just remove the flower petals.

This technique is most often used with annual flowers, but it can be effective with many perennials. While most perennials have a shorter blooming time than annuals, deadheading can still increase the flowering period for many perennials.

Q. I have a spot in my backyard that does not drain as well as other areas. It tends to stay quite damp, and I am having trouble finding a plant that will grow well in this spot. A friend told me that Queen of the Prairie would grow well in this spot. I have been unable to find any information on the plant and how to grow it.

A. Queen of the Prairie, or *Filipendula rubra*, is hardy to zone 3 and grows in full sun to partial shade. It will tolerate almost bog-like conditions, so that makes it a perfect candidate for your wet area. It is a herbaceous perennial that can grow to 2 m tall and 1 m wide. It has the most beautiful pink flowers in mid-summer. They look like pink cotton candy and are held high above the plant itself. The flowers are 22.5–30 cm in height. This plant is one of my favourites and is one that needs to be used in more gardens.

Queen of the Prairie.

Q. I am moving at the end of November and want to take my perennials with me. I would like to dig them up in mid- to late October and put them in containers to be replanted in spring when the frost is out of the ground at the new house. Is this a good idea? I am open to your suggestions, but I do not want to leave the perennials at the old residence.

A. You can certainly transfer the perennials to containers to take with you in October. However, I recommend planting the plants in the ground at the new house this fall if possible. You can plant the perennials right up to freeze-up in their new locations. If you haven't decided yet where to put them, just put them into a spot temporarily. I say this because overwintering plants in containers is more difficult than planting them in the ground. You can even leave them in the pots. Just put the plant, pot and all, in the ground.

If you cannot plant them immediately or need to overwinter them in the pots above ground, then keep them in the garage if you have one. If not, place them in a sheltered location away from winter winds and wrap them with insulation or cover the pots with dried leaves to a depth of at least 25 cm.

Q. I have recently moved from the coast and am not sure how to winter all the perennials that I started this

Peony 'Coral 'n' Gold.'

summer. Should I cut them back now or wait until spring? What is the best way to protect them, especially the ones that might be outside their hardiness zone? Do you suggest adding any granular fertilizer around the periphery of the plants in fall? I want to move some hostas; is now a good time?

A. You can cut down your perennials now or wait until spring. It really does not matter. Some people think it makes the bed look tidier first thing in spring, and by cutting them down in fall, you don't have to contend with the rotting leaves of the previous year. Make sure you wait until they have blackened and died back before doing any cutting.

Water the plants in well before freeze-up and cover the sensitive ones with a layer of straw or dried leaves to a depth of about 15 cm. A good snowcover will help the tender perennials to survive. A poor snowcover this year may mean that you'll have to shovel snow from other areas onto the tender plants. Snow has wonderful insulating properties.

I would not bother adding the fertilizer until springtime. Spring runoff can mess up your best intentions by removing the fertilizer.

Hostas can be safely moved until freeze-up. I just finished planting a dozen hostas, and as soon as I planted them, the winds ripped off whatever leaves were left, so I carefully inserted the plant identification tags so I will know where the plants are next spring.

Q. We have a relative who wishes to give us a peony. What is the ideal time of the year to transplant it? Should it be placed in a sunny location? What soil conditions does it prefer? When we transplant it, should bone meal or a slow-release fertilizer be added to the soil?

A. September is a good time to transplant peonies and other perennials. Peonies should definitely have a sunny location, as they perform best in full sun. The soil should be rich in organic matter, so when planting, work in lots of compost or well-rotted manure. The area you are planting in should also be well drained. Peonies do not like to have their "feet" wet. I always used to put a handful of bone meal into my perennial planting holes, but now I cut back on the bone meal to half a handful and add some Myke (biological growth supplement).

When planting the peony, don't plant it too deep. The top of the roots should not be more than 5 cm below the soil surface. If planted too deeply, the peonies will not bloom.

Q. I would appreciate it if you could talk a little about fertilizer. We plan on transplanting some of our perennials. We also will get some annual bedding plants and do some container gardening. We also have several fir trees and a mountain ash in the backyard. When do we use bone meal? Should we use a starter fertilizer when planting annual bedding plants. What combination? 10-52-10? Someone said to use 14-14-14 for planters and hanging baskets. Is it enough to use the all-purpose fertilizer 20-20-20 for all of it?

A. I have been getting many, many questions on fertilizers this year. Part of the problem, I believe, is that manufacturers are swamping the market with different NPK (nitrogen, phosphorus, potassium) combinations and confusing the consumer in the process.

I will share my own opinions on this issue, but I also called on my friend Bob Sproule, at Salisbury Greenhouses and Landscaping, for his thoughts as well. Bob says that he believes most gardeners can do quite nicely with three basic fertilizers, and I agree. Using a transplant fertilizer such as 10-52-10 is an excellent idea not only for annuals but also for any plant you are planting or moving, including trees, shrubs, perennials and annuals.

Single stem of bleeding heart flowers.

As Bob puts it, "If I were going to the moon and could only take one fertilizer, it would be 20-20-20. Although it is a little high in nitrogen for most purposes, it is still an excellent, all-round fertilizer for trace elements."

Using a fertilizer with a higher second number, such as 15-30-15, is excellent as well for annuals and other flowering plants and vegetables.

Regular bone meal is one of those great fertilizers, too. The NPK formula, according to Bob, is 2-13-0 and is an excellent choice for boosting roots. It can be worked in when planting or added to the soil surrounding existing plants and worked in. The bonus is that it will not burn. Don't

confuse regular bone meal with Bone Meal Plus, which has other additives.

The bottom line is if you have 10-52-10 for transplanting, 15-30-15 or 20-20-20 and bone meal, you are good to go no matter what type of gardening you plan to do. As to how often to fertilize, Bob recommends that every time you water, "colour the water." Don't be too concerned with following the recommended application rates. If you add a little to each watering, the plants will benefit.

Q. I am looking to plant a perennial border as a foundation planting at the front of my house. While my wife and I enjoy gardening, neither of us has much time to devote to it. Can you give us a quick list of perennials that will perform well with a minimum of attention?

A. Low maintenance is a common theme in today's gardens. Fortunately, plant breeders are supplying plants that are lower in their maintenance demands. Some examples of low-maintenance perennials that are excellent in foundation plantings are:

- Bleeding heart (*Dicentra* spp.)

- Blue Fescue grass (*Festuca glauca*)

- Coral bells (*Heuchera* spp.)

- Daylily (*Hemerocallis* spp.)

- Feather reed grass (*Calamagrostis aculiflora* 'Karl Foerster')

- Hardy geranium (*Geranium sanguineum*)

- *Hosta* spp.

- Russian sage (*Perovskia atriplicifolia*; part shade)

- Siberian iris (*Iris sibirica*)

- Spiderwort (*Tradescantia* 'Sweet Kate'; shade)

- Threadleaf *Coreopsis* (*Coreopsis verticillata*)

These perennials made the top 10 list for several reasons. While some offer blooms, they also offer foliage that adds interest even when the plant is not in bloom.

Q. Our backyard borders onto a pond that has tall swamp plants; I think they are bowrushes. A chain-link fence separates our property from the pond. From the fence, we began our landscaping with about 2 m of rock, which runs across the entire width of our property. We put landscaping fabric under the rock, hoping to kill off the pond growth. Under the landscaping fabric there is some soil that has lots of clay mixed in it. Although the growth from the pond is less, we are still getting a few plants that pop up here and there. I should mention that after putting down the 2 m of rock, we have a pretty nice lawn.

Is there any type of perennial that prefers those conditions? It doesn't matter if it's tall or

Iris sibirica 'Roanoke's Choice.'

a groundcover, but I would prefer something that flowers. At times it is fairly damp back there, and depending on how much rain we have, the pond sometimes rises. Otherwise, it is in full sun. Would it be better to clear rock from the centre of all that rock and simply plant in that area, or are there plants we could plant here and there? I hope this question doesn't leave you "stumped."

A. HA HA! "Stumped" indeed! This question is difficult, but I think I have the answer. First, the plants you refer to are called bullrushes, or common cattails, and can be incredibly invasive. You are doing well if you only have a few popping up here and there. I hope you chose heavy-duty landscape grade fabric to put down under the rock. The nylon fabric will work much better than the cloth types when dealing with plants as tough as the bullrushes.

There is actually no reason you cannot have a very attractive perennial garden in the area you have described. The following list of plants will grow well in wet conditions. They also vary in height, so you can plant the taller ones at the back and work your way down to the shortest ones in the front as you would with any perennial border.

Here is the list and some brief descriptions:

- Marsh marigold (*Caltha palustris* 'Flore Plena'): low-growing perennials with brilliant yellow flowers; loves wet conditions; plant disappears after blooming only to reappear in spring

- *Allium* 'Gladiator': 90 cm–1.2 m tall with globe-shaped purple flowers; tolerates wet conditions

- Bee balm (*Monarda didyma*): 60 cm–1.2 m tall with red or pink flowers; found growing naturally along stream banks

- Hardy geranium (*Geranium sanguineum*): low-growing perennial with a variety of flower colours

- Wild ginger (*Asarum europaeum*): dark green, leathery glossy leaves; foliage is the feature; flowers are dull brown

- Daylily (*Hemerocallis* spp.): 46 cm–1.2 m tall; long, spiky leaves look great next to water; blooms come in a wide variety of colours

- Bog rosemary (*Andromeda polifolia*): low, spreading perennial; finely textured, bluish green foliage; leaves look like rosemary; masses of pink, globe or urn-shaped flowers in spring

- Cardinal flower (*Lobelia cardinalis*): 30 cm–1.2 m tall; grows easily in wet soil; electric-red flowers in summer

- Joe Pye weed (*Eupatorium* spp.): 1.5–3 m tall; clusters of pink flowers from July to September

- *Tradescantia* spp. 'Blue and Gold': a new and striking variety; 46–60 cm tall; chartreuse leaves with gentian-blue triangular-shaped flowers

Many more plants will tolerate the conditions you describe. Don't be afraid to stop at your favourite garden centre and ask the staff for help.

Tradescantia 'Blue and Gold.'

Q. We are planning to install ground-cover perennials instead of grass in our front yard. We were hoping you could give us a list of such perennials that would work.

A. Groundcovers can serve several functions in addition to helping conserve moisture. They can act as a lawn replacement and they can add an aesthetic look to any bed or garden. The texture and colour of the groundcover can make for a very interesting look. Here are some examples of deciduous, perennial groundcovers:

Joe Pye weed in a perennial bed.

- *Ajuga reptans* (bugleweed): aggressive, mat-forming perennial; foliage is bronze-purple and is usually variegated; grows very dense and thick to keep weeds out; needs to be contained

- *Arctostaphylos uva-ursi* (bearberry or kinnikinnick): forms dense mats of glossy green leaves; light pink flowers in spring

- *Bergenia cordifolia* (bergenia or elephant ears): makes an interesting low-maintenance groundcover; deep green leathery leaves; great for shady spots

- *Aegopodium podgraria* (goutweed or snow-on-the-mountain): very aggressive groundcover; pale green leaves variegated with white/cream; attractive but make sure you contain it; will rapidly spread into areas you don't want it if not controlled; I use commercial-grade landscape edging buried at least 20 cm deep to control mine—you can also use cedar shakes

- *Galium odoratum* (sweet woodruff): borderline hardy (zone 4) can sometimes grow in cooler zones; grows very well under trees in a sheltered spot; prefers partial to full shade; bright green whorled leaves; tiny white flowers in profusion in spring; leaves, when crushed, smell like hay;

cover with lots of snow and it will come back every year

Q. I know that you have spoken in the past on daylilies and that they are one of your favourite perennials. Do you have any other favourite perennials that might like to grow in the shade on my condo balcony? I always find it interesting to hear what the experts like in their own garden. I'm having a heck of a time finding plants that look good in the shade.

A. I am always on the lookout for plants that grow well in the shade and that look great. Finding plants that tolerate the shade is getting easier with the recent introduction of the

Coral bells (bottom) with hosta (top).

Proven Winners Dolce varieties of *Heucheras. Heucheras*, or coral bells, are one of the most versatile perennials on the market today. They love the shade and look great as well, which is good news for the many condo gardeners with balconies or decks that have a north-facing exposure. *Heucheras* also love growing in containers and traditional beds, and they bloom as well. Granted, they are perennials and may cost a bit more than an annual, but the performance and look is worth the small additional cost. Plus, for me at least, I am more than willing to pay a little more to have some variety in my shade areas.

The Dolce series of *Heucheras* incorporates all the benefits of heucheras with a stunning variety of colours. *Heucheras* not only excel in shade; they are also drought tolerant, they bloom for weeks on end with flowers that are carried well above the foliage and don't need to be deadheaded, and they are hardy to −32° C. The Dolce series are the aristocrats of the *Heuchera* family. Here are a few examples of the Dolce series:

- Dolce 'Key Lime Pie': plants form 20–40 cm compact mounds of scalloped, heart-shaped leaves that are veined and mottled in shades of bright lime green. This variety takes on an almost electric glow in a shady spot. The colours of this *Heuchera* deepen and intensify in cooler weather. This excellent plant actually looks even better as fall approaches. In spring and summer, long, erect spikes of tiny bell-shaped pink flowers rise as much as 25 cm above the foliage. The blooms last for many weeks.

- Dolce 'Black Currant': bold purple leaves with silver accents make this plant a real conversation piece. As with the other varieties in this series, you will not have to deadhead the flowers. However, removing the flower stems after they have finished blooming will keep them looking neat and tidy.

- Dolce 'Crème Brûlée': this *Heuchera* has a bronze leaf form with brown-sugar highlights that transform the leaves with colder temperatures.

- Dolce 'Crème de Menthe': handles summer heat better than others. The foliage is dark green silver with striking veins.

- Dolce 'Licorice': black to purple foliage make this plant a standout. Consider planting this variety in a light-coloured container for added contrast.

- Dolce 'Mocha Mint': vivid silver foliage with an abundance of pink flowers. This pink and silver combination looks great in a bright blue pot.

- Dolce 'Peach Melba': more cold hardy than others. Leaves are peach in colour with black and red markings. This variety also tolerates full sun to deep shade.

Caring for these plants is fairly straightforward. They like to have the soil moist but not wet. They do not like to dry out between watering. That is not a huge problem, since they prefer a shaded setting and should not dry out as quickly in spots in the sun. I recommend adding a slow-release, pelleted fertilizer when you plant. I also like to add some compost to the container soil mix when planting containerized *Heucheras*.

The nice thing about these *Heucheras* is that they look great with other plants or when planted together as a mix. A container with 'Key Lime Pie,' 'Licorice,' 'Peach Melba' and 'Mocha Mint' looks amazing. The contrast of the bright yellow-green of 'Key Lime Pie' and 'Licorice' is eye catching, to say the least. Add in the contrast of the black of 'Licorice' with the silver of 'Mocha Mint' and the balance of the 'Peach Melba,' and you may have the perfect shade container. They look great whether they are blooming or not.

I am a huge fan of these new *Heucheras*. They are so easy to care for and look so great that no garden, balcony or deck that has shade issues should be without them.

Q. We are looking at adding some hostas. How do you feel about hostas?

Do they work well in the shade? What plants do they look good with?

A. One question that pops up regularly is what type of plant is best for a shady spot. Invariably, the questioner goes on to ask for examples and especially ones that are low maintenance. The answer to these questions is easy. *Heucheras* are my new love, but my old love is still hostas.

Hostas have been used for years on their own to fill in a shady place where little else will grow. With the colours and textures available today, hostas can make dramatic statements. Using tall large-leafed hostas such as *Sieboldiana elegans* (75 cm high and 1.5 m wide, with heavily corrugated blue-green leaves) as background plants with brightly coloured border hostas such as 'Sweet Sunshine' (36 cm high and 60 cm wide, with cupped, round, gold leaves held upright) can make a powerful statement in any garden.

While wonderful when used on their own, the true beauty of hostas comes out when used in combination with other plants. Too many gardeners think of hostas as exclusively shade plants, when in fact most hostas will do best when planted in a location that is only one-third shade during the day. Some of the most spectacular displays can be achieved by using hostas as background plants in a shadier area of the border with other, more colourful perennials front and centre in the sunnier portion of the bed. An example of this type of border would be using 'Big Angel' hostas (75 cm high and 1.5 m wide, with huge, 41 cm long and 28 cm wide, heavily corrugated blue-green leaves) as background plants with bright yellow *Coreopsis* 'Zagreb' and a border of 'Blue Mirror' dwarf delphiniums. This will create a bed of contrasts. The bright yellow *Coreopsis* shows against the blue-green hosta with the blue delphinium acting as an anchor. The thread-leaf texture of the *Coreopsis* also contrasts very well with the huge, heavily textured leaves of the hosta.

Another example of hostas to use in this type of bed is 'Honeybells' (60 cm high and wide, with large, undulating light green leaves that turn yellow green in the sun; can be grown in full sun). 'Honeybells' in the background with coral bells (*Heuchera*) 'Vesuvius' (dark burgundy leaves with bright hot orange-pink flowers) mixed with orange-flowered geum make a truly spectacular bed.

If your bed is more shady, you are still not restricted from mixing hostas with other plants. Large-leafed, heavily textured hostas can be used in the background effectively with astilbes in front. The airy flower spikes of astilbe contrast perfectly with the hosta leaves, and the astilbe colours are stunning against the dark background. Astilbes come in whites, pinks, reds and peach colours and are well suited to growing in shady spots. An interesting shade bed would be 'Big Daddy' hostas (30 cm high and 1.2 m wide, with large, nearly round, heavily corrugated, slightly cupped, blue-green leaves with heavy substance) as a background planting, along with ligularia 'The Rocket,' with its tall spikes of bright yellow flowers. In front of this background, a planting of bright red or raspberry astilbes would complete a very visually appealing bed.

Hostas require little in the way of care, which makes them very appealing to today's busy gardener. Hostas also come in a wide range of sizes, from dwarf types that may reach only 15 cm in height to 90 cm tall giants. This versatility in size is also applicable to today's smaller gardens. Hostas prefer a rich, well-drained soil, so proper preparation before planting will go a long way to ensuring a happy plant later. They also like to be kept moist but not soggy. There are many hostas that have been in their same location for over 30 years with no problems; dividing them every four or five years is a good idea to keep them growing vigorously. Insert a sharp spade into the crown, or centre, of the plant. If you are planning on transplanting the division, make sure that when dividing you remove an "eye," or sprout, with each section removed.

Hostas do not require a lot of fertilizing to be kept happy. A single application of a well-balanced fertilizer such as 20-20-20 once during the growing season should be sufficient.

If your bed gets a bit more sun, you may want to consider using mulch around the hostas to keep them moist. If you find that slugs are a problem, try using mulch such as pine needles around the base of the plants to discourage the slugs.

Plant breeders are constantly developing new varieties to add to the

Hosta 'Sum and Substance.'

thousands of choices available in hostas today. Hostas make interesting groupings with other plants because they offer a variety of contrasts. Colour, texture and form of the hostas can be used effectively to contrast other plants. Perhaps the most versatile perennial for shade and semi-shade is the hosta, which is bound only by the imagination of the gardener.

Q. I truly appreciate your column in winter when I am desperately looking for anything about gardening. I am planning a shade garden and was hoping you might be able to recommend a good hosta I can use. I would like it to be as large as possible, as I would like to fill in the back of this bed all with the same type of hosta. Colour is not important but a vibrant one would help.

A. I am writing this column on a day when the temperature is –32° C, and yet, gardening is never far from my mind. I'm happy to fill that gardening void even if it is only through words right now.

I have the perfect hosta for you. It is a new introduction available from Heritage perennials and was one of their top 10 perennials for 2002. It is called 'Sum and Substance.' It may be the largest hosta yet. It produces huge, rounded leaves in a glowing chartreuse yellow shade. The thick texture and waxy finish help to make the

Gaillardia 'Arizona Sun.'

leaves more resistant to damage by slugs than many of the more common selections of hosta. In time, clumps can easily reach 2 m across.

These plants will develop their best colour with some morning sun, plenty of moisture and a rich soil. Pale lavender flowers are produced in July.

Q. I would like to plant a few perennials that tend to bloom for most of summer. In this region do such perennials exist?

A. They do exist and there are a few of them as well. Here is a list of just a few examples of long blooming perennials that are hardy to zone 3:

- *Liatris* (gayfeather or blazing star): three-month bloom periods. Very attractive, rosy-purple flower spikes bloom from the top down. Foliage is dark green, grass-like and spiky.

- *Gaillardia* (blanket flower): three to four month bloom periods.

Echinacea purpurea (coneflower).

Plants form low mounds of light green leaves that bear upright stems of daisy-like flowers in red and yellow.

- *Echinacea purpurea* (coneflower): two to three month bloom periods; large, daisy-like flowers with a striking dark-coloured button eye; flowers come in variety of colours.

- *Achillea* (yarrow): three-plus month bloom periods but can vary according to species. Flat-topped flowers are borne on tall erect stems in a wide variety of colours. Plants also have varying leaf forms such as fern leaf.

Astilbe.

- *Coreopsis* (tickseed): three-plus month bloom periods. Daisy-like flowers come in shades of pink, yellow and white; many varieties.

- *Hemerocallis* (daylily): three-plus month bloom periods. Many varieties of these lilies and in myriad colours, forms and sizes. Blooms last only one day—hence the name—but are followed each day by more blooms.

Q. I am getting really bored with some of the perennials in my garden and am looking for a makeover. Are there any new varieties out there this year (2003) that I can look for?

A. I have chosen the following list based on their hardiness rating as well as their functionality in solving specific gardening problems such as shade gardens. Without further ado, here is the top perennials for the 2003 list:

1. *Astilbe chinensis* 'Visions' (Chinese astilbe): plumes of bright magenta rose; medium-sized mound of dark green leaves with lacy appearance. Blooms appear later, extending the astilbe season into late summer. Flowers are held well above the leaves. Tolerates direct sun. Fern-like leaves contrast nicely with hostas or bergenia. Zones 3–9.

2. *Campanula poscharskyana* 'Blue Waterfall' (Serbian bellflower): low-spreading form of bellflower. 'Blue Waterfall' offers a splash of

star-shaped violet-blue flowers for many weeks. An ideal height for edging perennial beds or cascading out of tubs and window boxes. Blooms in late spring and well into summer. Deadheading will encourage more buds and a fall bloom. Excellent groundcover over small areas. Good companion plant for shrub roses since bloom time is similar. Good for pastel colour schemes. Zones 3–9.

3. *Dicentra* 'King of Hearts' (fernleaf bleedingheart): long bloom time makes this an unusual shade plant. Mounding, grey-green foliage. Clusters of dangling, heart-shaped blooms in bright rose-red shade, borne well above leaves. Blooms in late spring, through mid-summer and may continue into fall with cool nights. Excellent plant for edging and contrasts well with variegated leaf hostas. Disease resistant. Zones 2–9.

4. *Hosta* 'Patriot' (plantain lily): the crisp and clean-white edges set against a dark-green centre make this white-edged hosta stand out. Wide leaf margins start the season in a creamy yellow shade, later aging to white. Bell-shaped lavender flowers in mid-summer. Medium-sized hosta good for massing or groundcover. Fairly resistant to slug damage. Zones 2–9.

5. *Papaver orientale* 'Patty's Plum' (Oriental poppy): mid-sized plant with very unique colour in poppies.

Mulberry to wine-red petals with darker spots or eyes. Flowers have a crepe-like texture; blooms for only a short time in early summer but dazzles during bloom time. Blooms held on stems above a clump of coarse and hairy, green leaves. Plant this variety at the front of a border to appreciate its show. Since Oriental poppies go dormant and disappear by mid-summer, plant next to or behind larger plants such as Russian sage. Zones 2–9.

6. *Polemonium caeruleum* 'Snow and Sapphires' (variegated Jacob's ladder): one of my favourite perennials for the fragrance of the violet-blue flowers. This variegated variety is more vigorous and reliable than older forms. Lacy, green foliage nearly fernlike, with each leaf edged in creamy white. Flowers in early summer. Protect from afternoon sun. Cut back hard after blooming to discourage self-sowing and rejuvenate attractive leaves. Site should be moist but not soggy. Attractive edging plant. Zones 3–9.

7. *Echinacea purpurea* 'Razzmatazz' (double purple coneflower): another personal favourite. Stunning. Features fully double blooms with central pom-pom of rose pink, surrounded by magenta purple daisy petals. Flowers mid-summer through fall. Remove faded blooms. Excellent as a cut flower. Combines well with *Coreopsis*. Zone 3.

If you need more information, please visit the Heritage Perennials website: www.perennials.com.

This excellent website has many tips and photos. One interesting section is on growing your own perennials from seed.

Q. I really love reading your spring columns where you talk about the new plants for the upcoming year. Are you planning on doing one for this year (2006)?

A. I pick and choose the years I do these columns because the plants have to be truly outstanding for me to pass along the best perennials list. Spring 2006 brings with it some new and exciting introductions in perennials. Plant breeders continue to do their magic with both colour and form and some of these new plants for this year are truly stunning.

Top 10 perennials:

1. *Delphinium* 'New Millennium Pagan Purples': remember the Pacific Giants series of delphiniums? They were the standard for delphiniums for 50 years. Unfortunately, they came with disadvantages such as weak stems and disease and pest problems. Plant breeder Terry Dowdeswell has hybridized a remarkable new group of tall strains called New Millennium hybrids. The series features colours ranging from white through blue and pink. My favourites, without

a doubt, are the Pagan Purples. The spectacular colours range from dark blue, deep purple to mauve. They can be found in single or double forms and on much stronger stems. Staking might still be a good idea to protect against summer storms. Hardy to Zone 3.

2. *Dianthus* 'Firewitch': selected as the plant of the year for 2006 by the Perennial Plant Association. This low-growing alpine perennial has upright stems to 20 cm that bear single magenta pink blooms about 2.5 cm across. The flowers are very fragrant, smelling sweetly of cloves. They appear in late spring. Clipping or trimming off spent blooms will encourage another bloom in summer or fall. Hardy to Zone 3.

3. *Echinacea purpurea* 'Hope': dedicated to breast cancer survivors and to the memories of those who have succumbed to breast cancer. Donations will be made for each plant sold to the Susan G. Komen Foundation. The plants feature large, fragrant flowerheads with soft, pink petals surrounding a rusty orange centre cone. Long-lasting flowers bloom in late summer and fall. Hardy to Zone 3.

4. *Echinacea purpurea* 'Razzmatazz': until recently there was a worldwide shortage of this plant. The reason for the shortage is that everyone wanted some of these, as they are

a real showpiece in any garden. Instead of the typical brown cone found on *Echinacea*, these varieties have a centre made up of layer upon layer of small, fringed magenta pink petals forming a central pompom surrounded by a circle of matching daisy petals. This variety should be front and centre in a sunny border. Hardy to Zone 3.

5. *Euphorbia polychroma* 'Lacy' (cushion spurge 'Lacy'): a variegated form of cushion spurge. The leaves are white-and-green variegated with a frilled type of edge. Combined with the bright yellow bloom, it is a very striking plant. Hardy to Zone 3.

6. *Baptisia* 'Purple Smoke' (purple smoke false indigo): forms a tall, bushy clump of grey-green foliage, with long spikes of smoky violet-blue and purple flowers, held on black stems. Very airy appearance to the blooms. After blooming, black pods form that add interest to the garden right through winter. Hardy to Zone 3.

7. *Ligularia dentata* 'Britt-Marie Crawford': new choice if you love big, bold-leaved plants. Has large leaves in a rich maroon-purple shade with an interesting, glossy finish. This plant mounds up to form a substantial clump, then bears even taller stems of golden-yellow daisies in mid-summer. The nice thing about this plant is that it easily creates its own contrast and makes a great focal specimen in a bed. It also adds a bold statement in a container or tub. Hardy to Zone 3.

8. *Lynchnis viscaria* 'Splendens Plena' (passion campion): forms low tuft of grassy-looking leaves, bearing upright stems of fluffy double magenta-pink flowers in early summer. The wiry stems are excellent for cutting. Deadheading will encourage repeat blooms. Fairly drought tolerant. Hardy to Zone 3.

9. *Heuchera* 'Peach Flambe' (coral bells 'Peach Flambe'): bright orange-red leaves turn to peach plum tones in fall. Produces tiny flowers in early summer on slender stems that rise above the foliage mound. Can be an effective edging plant or a ground cover. Hardy to Zone 3.

10. *Chrysanthemum* 'Firestorm': produces fully double blooms in bright red with a yellow centre. Blooms from early fall until freeze-up and is a very hardy choice for a sunny perennial border. Zones 3–9.

I can see it now. 'Pagan Purple' delphiniums in the back of a bed with baptisia 'Purple Smoke' in front and cushion spurge 'Lacy' for a little contrast at the front of the bed. Wow! Looks like I need to dig another perennial bed.

Q. I rely on your spring columns that feature the new perennials for the coming year. Are you going to have one this year (2007)?

A. While earlier lists concentrated on new introductions, 2007 features proven performers. According to John Schroeder, president of Valleybrook International, "Many gardeners are not interested in spending all their time gardening. Rather than planting fussy plants that require extra pampering or attention, they are looking for 'bullet-proof plants' that simply perform beautifully year after year."

Heritage's top perennials for 2007:

1. *Campanula poscharskyana* 'Blue Waterfall' ('Camgood'; Serbian bellflower): blooms in early summer with long sprays of starry, violet-blue bells. This cascading bellflower looks great in a rockery setting or tumbling over a low wall or window box or container. It makes an excellent edging plant along walkways and paths. Prefers to have full to half-day sun to perform at its blooming best. One suggested use would be as a massed groundcover planting around shrub roses. The flowering times of both would coincide, and the mauve of the bellflower complements many rose blooms. Hardy to Zone 3.

2. *Paenoia lactiflora* 'Bowl of Beauty' (single peony): peonies seem to be finding their way back into today's gardens after years of popularity in older gardens. 'Bowl of Beauty' stands out because of its unique shape, which is so different from the old double varieties. The problem with many of the older varieties is that they fall over in the first rainstorm in June. 'Bowl of Beauty,' according to Heritage Perennials, is classed as a Japanese style of flower. It has an outer row of rose-pink petals and a creamy yellow, ruffled centre. The look is very much like a carnation. The lighter weight of these flowers makes them less likely to fall over. This variety is listed as fragrant and enjoys a sunny border. It is fairly tall at 90 cm, which makes it suitable for a specimen plant or among shrubs. Zones 4–8.

3. *Rudbeckia fulgida* 'Goldsturm' (Goldstorm coneflower): introduced in the 1930s by renowned nurseryman Karl Foerster, this perennial has become a classic. The plant forms a bushy, upright clump with a profuse display of brown-eyed, golden-orange daisy blooms from mid-summer through fall. Great for cutting. In my garden, I like the combination of *Calamagrostis* 'Karl Foerster' (feather reed grass) and *Perovskia atriplicifolia* (Russian sage). The reed grass, with its changing bloom colour, and the Russian sage, with its sage green stems and leaves and purple blooms, look great with the coneflowers. This combination looks great from

mid-summer on. Plant in full sun or partial shade. Hardy to Zone 3.

4. *Salvia nemorosa* 'Caradonna' (perennial sage): tolerates almost any soil condition from moist to dry. 'Caradonna' differs from other perennial sages in that the dark, violet-blue flowers are held on jet-black stems that pop out visually when planted against a backdrop. This height of this variety (51–75 cm) allows gardeners to make use of their rich colour in the middle of the border. The plants prefer a sunny location, and deadheading is recommended. They look great planted with Shasta daisies and daylilies of any colour. Hardy to Zone 3.

The list of top performers was chosen from over 1500 perennials. It's interesting that Heritage Perennials has chosen to go with a proven performer list rather than their previous "what's new" lists. Personally, I think it's a great idea. Often we seem to be preoccupied with lining up to buy the new plants. Many gardeners ignore plants that were award winners in the past and would make a terrific addition to any garden. For new gardeners, getting to know these plants for the first time is a must, while experienced gardeners need to become reacquainted with these must-have plants.

Q. My husband and I built our house in 1998 on a completely treed lot.

Since that time, we have cleared away some trees but have left quite a few. We have large groupings of very tall poplars in our small front yard but have cleaned out the undergrowth between the trees to grow plants. We are trying to do some reworking to make the area look better. I am contemplating removing the plants I have between the trees altogether and just mulching because it gets very frustrating not knowing what would grow well in this area.

We have added a good garden mix, peat moss and compost and have covered the garden with cedar mulch to retain moisture. It is still very difficult to plant in this bed because of the remaining undergrowth roots and the hard soil. The bed is approximately 12 m by 3 m. Half of it gets the hot afternoon sun, while the other half gets partial shade. I have planted sun-loving perennials and shrubs on one side, only to find that the poplars shade the plants throughout the season. Similarly, when planting perennials and shrubs that will tolerate shade, the sun shines through the leaves and burns them.

Although some of the plants do grow nicely, the shrubs have not grown well. They live but do not grow much throughout the season. Is that because of the tree roots or because the trees suck up much of the moisture the bed may get?

A. The first thing that comes to mind with your situation is that you should be looking for perennials that are suited for both sun and shade. Below are some examples of perennials that will tolerate both growing conditions:

- *Bergenia* (Siberian tea)
- Daylilies (tons of varieties)
- *Dodecatheon* (shooting stars)
- Hostas
- Some varieties of bleeding heart
- *Tradescantia* (spiderwort)

If this bed was in my yard, I think I would plant it all in daylilies. Daylilies are extremely tolerant of sun or semi-shade. They will bloom profusely, giving great colour throughout the growing season if you mix in some early, mid- and late-season flowering types.

The daylilies will also tolerate the poplar roots, which are sucking moisture from the other plants in a big way. An added bonus is that even when the daylilies are not in bloom, their long arching leaves look great on their own.

If you want some variety, planting daylilies with bergenias is a good-looking combination, and bergenias are also very tolerant of the growing conditions you describe. An alternative is to plant tall daylilies as the background plants, bergenias

Bergenia cordifolia 'Red Bloom.'

as the intermediate plants, and some spiderworts and shooting stars as border plants.

Hostas will also do very well in these conditions, and an entire bed of hostas (mixed varieties), with tall in the back, intermediate and then short plants in front, would look great. Hostas and daylilies mixed together would also create a striking bed.

Q. We have a property we would like to landscape with low-maintenance plants. We go out to the property every second week, so plants that don't need a lot of water are a must. What perennials will get us started?

A. There is now an extensive list of plants that will grow well with less or practically no water other than that offered by Mother Nature. Here are only a few common examples:

- Russian sage (*Perovskia atri-plicifolia*): 1.6 m tall and 1 m wide. Shrubby, sage green plant that grows in a spike form. Great as a background plant. Violet, purple blooms along the spikes from mid-summer to fall. Very drought tolerant. Prefers well-drained soil and full sun.

- Daylily (*Hemerocallis* spp.): to 1.5 m high and wide, but some dwarf varieties are 30 cm high. Spiky leaves add interest even when not in bloom. Tremendous colour selection and bloom types. Blooms early, mid or late, double and single flowers with ruffled and non-ruffled forms. Very tolerant of most soils and water conditions. Fairly pest resistant.

- Yarrow (*Achillea* spp.): 1 m high and wide. Very drought-tolerant perennial. Once established, it can survive on rainwater alone. Prefers full sun. Great colour selection, including white, yellow and a myriad of pastel colours.

- Golden Marguerite (*Anthemis tinctoria*): 1 m high and 60 cm wide. Golden, daisy-like flowers. Blooms throughout summer. Great splash of bright yellow colour.

Q. I have an area about 1.8 m wide and 9 m long between my house and the neighbour's house that faces north and south. The south end is shaded by a bur oak, so it only gets sun for a few hours. However, that light and heat is reflected off the stucco of my home. Is there a low-maintenance perennial that would work there? In the past I've had limited success with zucchini and potatoes.

A. I assume that you are looking for a plant that will act as a ground-cover over this area. My first choice would be creeping lamium, a rapidly spreading perennial. There are several varieties, but the one I like is *Lamium maculatum* 'Pink Pewter.' It has silver leaves with green edges. The blooms are soft pink and flower in spring and again off and on throughout the growing season. The plant is tolerant of dry shade, which I have a hunch is the type of area you are describing.

The second choice would be *Aegopodium podograria*, also known by the lovely name of goutweed or bishop's weed. The plant has green-and-cream-coloured variegated leaves and grows like its name; namely, a weed. It is tolerant of most conditions and can be extremely invasive if not contained and controlled. An ideal location for this plant is between a house and sidewalk where it is surrounded by barriers to its spreading. If it is not contained in this way, you will need to use a plastic barrier buried in the ground to keep the plant in its intended spot. The barrier should go down at least 15 cm into the ground. This plant spreads by underground rhizomes and it can rapidly enter a lawn. Having said all this, it really is an attractive groundcover and grows well under conditions that very few other plants would tolerate.

Q. I have a chance to get some free perennials from a friend who is thinning out her perennial bed. When is the best time to move these perennials, and is there anything I need to do to help them through winter? Can I do it now if they have finished blooming?

A. You can transplant the perennials either in fall or spring. It really does not matter. If you do it in fall, make sure you do it far enough ahead of the ground freezing so the plants have a chance to establish. Water them in very well and add some mulch. Something like dried leaves piled on top of the transplants will help them during their first winter in their new location. When they have finished blooming is a great time to move them.

You can divide many perennials every three or four years. Division is easy—use a sharp spade and insert it into the middle of the plant. (I cannot stress enough the importance of using sharp tools when dividing or gardening in general. Taking a few minutes with a file to sharpen your garden tools will make the work much easier.) Having effectively cut the plant in half, dig out half of the plant. Fill in the hole with soil and tamp it in place. If the plant is large, you can cut the root into many smaller pieces. Division helps the original plant by increasing its vigour, and the bonus is you get free plants.

Q. 1. What does a "good soaking" mean? I was told at a local garden centre to give my evergreens a good soaking in fall. Do I count so many minutes per plant, like five minutes for small plants, or 10 for large ones? How much for a big spruce or mature fruit trees?

2. Where can one purchase straw?
I keep hearing that covering sensitive
plants such as perennials with straw is
a good way to help them get through
winters.

3. My husband accidentally spread
weed and feed fertilizer on a flowerbed planted with peonies and irises.
As expected, neither of the plants
recovered nor flowered this summer.
Is it possible these perennials will
bloom next year and if not, has it
caused enough damage to the soil
that it needs to be replaced?

A. Let's deal with your questions one
at a time:

1. Sometimes gardening is far
from a precise science. To a new
gardener a "good soaking" must be
confusing. I am guilty of using such
terms as well. One of my favourites is
"water the tree in well in fall." What
does that mean exactly? To me, the
definition of a good soaking or watering well is to water to the point of
runoff. That means applying water
slowly. A trickle of water will soak in
more deeply than a sharp stream of
water. The sharp stream will begin to
runoff almost immediately, whereas
the trickle will slowly penetrate
much deeper. A soaker hose is great
for watering things such as perennial beds because it waters deeply
and does not compact the soil like
a sharp stream of water would. Leave
the soaker hose on a perennial bed

for at least an hour to get maximum
penetration.

For large trees such as spruce,
I recommend using a root feeder for
watering. Doing so is especially good
in fall when you want to get the water
as deep into the roots as possible.
A root feeder is simply a metal spike
that you can attach to a hose. The
spike is around 90 cm long, and you
insert this spike into the ground
around the dripline of the tree every
few feet and let the water run until it
begins to flow out of the hole created
by the spike. There is no set time to
leave the water on. It is something
you will have to observe on your own.
This same technique can be used for
watering other trees.

For plants with surface roots such
as birch, junipers and cedars, a slow
trickle from a hose placed at the base
of the plant will work well. It is absolutely critical to water all plants very
well in fall. I like to create a depression by mounding the soil in a circle
around the base of the plant. For
smaller plants, a circle 2.5 cm in
diameter is enough. For larger plants
and trees, a 90 cm to 1.2 m diameter circle is fine. Put the hose into
the circle and leave it on a slow trickle
until the water has filled the depression and is not being absorbed by the
soil any longer. The length of time
needed will depend on how absor-
bent your soil is, how much organic
matter it has, and so on.

2. Look in your local community paper for ads for straw in fall. Sometimes, on a drive through the country, you will see signs advertising straw for sale as well. There is no easy answer as to where to find straw. You can also inquire in some of the garden centres. Some have contacts for the sale of straw.

3. It is highly unlikely that the plants will come back in spring if they have been damaged severely by the herbicide. Time will tell, but I would not bet on them coming back. The herbicide should have broken down by the following spring, so I don't think you will need to worry about the soil being damaged.

Q. My brother has a problem with what he calls "spit" bug. A small, foamy "gob" appears at the stem in a leaf axil. Inside is a small yellowish-green worm-like creature that moves in your hand. I have never seen this creature before and wondered if you could enlighten us.

A. The critter is called a spittle bug. Spittle bugs suck juices from the plant in the same way as aphids do, but they remove so much fluid and carbohydrates that excess fluid is produced. The bug covers itself with this fluid and and then adds air bubbles to create the spittle appearance. Spittle bugs usually are never present in numbers large enough to cause severe damage and are easily removed with a sharp stream of water.

Q. Along our back fence we have several large columnar aspens. They look nice, but we don't have any luck with the other things planted there. It has a north exposure, and I've got hostas, ferns, lily of the valley, goutweed (which of course is fine) and potentillas. Nothing else I've tried thrives in this location, including lamium and other supposedly hardy low-light perennials. Lily of the valleys don't bloom much, the hostas look rather sickly and the ferns aren't spreading —they're small and not sturdy at all. I wanted the area filled with groundcovers, but these are the only survivors out of many different plants I've put in. I haven't done too much with the soil there, as the roots from the trees are near the surface and I can't dig anything into the ground. I just add peat moss.

Could it be that the large trees are just sapping too many nutrients from the soil for any plants to do well with them? If so, how do I amend the soil in there with the roots? Just pile up the stuff on top of the soil and let it work its own way down? I considered manure but thought it would burn the existing plants. Perhaps it's just not a good idea to expect perennials to grow in this spot with the trees.

A. I think the problem with the bed is that the poplars are not only leaching nutrients but also every last drop of water as well. These trees are shallow rooted and have a very well-developed root system close to the surface. As you mentioned, you have trouble incorporating soil amendments because of the roots. I agree that the potentillas are probably not getting enough light, but the other plants such as the hostas and ferns are not getting enough water or nutrients.

You will have a very difficult time growing plants under the trees. I count seven poplars in the picture you sent, and all are planted fairly closely together. The roots from these trees literally are filling the bed. The goutweed actually looks quite nice in this area and looks very healthy. This plant will grow on concrete, I swear. Perhaps letting the goutweed fill in the bed would be the way to go. If you want to add organic matter to the bed, you can add a few centimetres of compost to the top of the soil, but I would not add more than 5–8 cm at a time so as not to suffocate the roots that are so close to the surface.

Q. My lily-of-the-valley is spreading in my perennial garden quite happily. However, for the past two years there have hardly been any flowers. I fertilize the area using 20-20-20 because there are junipers as well. I alternately fertilize, using a specialized fertilizer for them, once a month from May to July. It can get quite dry in the area.

Goutweed.

Can you please provide some suggestions on how to encourage flowering?

A. First, I would back off on the fertilizer. Fertilize the plants once in spring with the 20-20-20. I would also increase the watering: lily-of-the-valley does best in a moist soil.

Q. I have a shady area that I have planted with goutweed. It makes an area of my yard quite lovely where nothing else will grow. For the past few years, however, in mid-July or so, the leaves start turning brown. I can't see any insects on or under the leaves. My beautiful green and white carpet is soon so unsightly that I must cut it down close to ground level. It grows back again, but it's never as lush later in the season. What can cause the leaves to turn brown like that? Is it a blight of some sort? What products might help?

A. I had the same thing happen to mine during a very hot July. My goutweed was growing under a large spruce tree, and because of the heat and low humidity, the goutweed suffered from a lack of moisture. I was amazed to see this happen—goutweed has to be the cast-iron plant of all perennials, and, normally, nothing seems to affect it. A dry winter may have exacerbated the problem of lack of moisture. Try giving it a drink if it is very hot and dry and see if that helps.

For more on perennials, see also:

p. 44 My petunia leaves are yellowing; what can I do?

p. 178 Can I move my houseplants outside during the summer?

p. 193–197 for questions about roses

p. 218 What is the Explorer series of roses?

Container Gardening

Container gardening continues to grow in popularity. This versatile method of gardening may be on its way to becoming one of, if not *the* most popular forms of growing things.

When one looks at the advantages of container gardening, it is easy to see why more people are drawn to this type of garden:

- Gardening can be done in almost any space. From the smallest deck or balcony to the largest rural setting, container gardening will work.

- Ease of use. Really, all that is needed is some sort of container, some potting soil and the seeds and/or plants.

- Containers can be used to grow almost anything, from annuals, perennials, vegetables, shrubs and trees. They can also be used to grow combinations of plants. A one-pot garden might have lettuce, tomatoes, herbs and some type of flower for fun.

- Containers are portable and can be moved to follow the sun if needed. They can also be used to add a punch of colour to a dull space. I like to use containers to add flowers to a space that normally would not allow them to grow, like under a spruce tree for example.

- The containers themselves can be focal points adding to the visual appeal of a setting.

- Containers let anyone grow healthy produce anywhere there is sun.

Even a single container can offer a great gardening space. Using a single container does not restrict your choices in what and how you plant. An excellent system for small spaces, or for a single pot or container, is a three-tiered system. With this system, tall or climbing plants are placed at the back of the container up against a wall or trellis. Medium height, bushy plants fill in most of the container, and cascading plants fill the front of the container, thus softening the composition of the container.

This one pot works with all three dimensions of gardening, namely, vertical height, vertical drop and horizontal. Adding a trellis to a wall can be as simple as stringing some nylon garden netting on the wall or as ornate as adding one of the popular obelisk-style trellises if you have the space. Several fast-growing annual vines such as morning glory or canary vine will rapidly fill in the background of the planting without overcrowding the other plants in the pot.

If flowers are not your choice, consider a small salad garden in one container. You can have cucumbers climbing up the trellis, cherry tomato plants in the centre and a variety of lettuces growing on the border of the container. The beauty of this example is that the arrangement would be very aesthetically appealing in addition to being very functional. Vegetables can be quite attractive plants in their own right. The textures and leaf colours are pleasing to the eye. One of my favourite looks is a container full of colourful kale. For more information on growing vegetables in containers, see p. 51.

The number of plants to fit into a container can vary. If you are prepared to do the extra work, you can cram the container chock full of plants. The extra work comes in the form of consistent watering and fertilizing. With a container full of plants, the requirements for water increase dramatically. If the location is a south-facing one, you may need to water twice a day during hot months. Fertilizing should be done with each watering. A good balanced fertilizer such as 20-20-20 should be applied at ¼ the recommended strength with each watering, or use a slow-release fertilizer such as 14-14-14.

The recommendations for spacing of plants can often be adjusted to your needs. The square foot gardening system developed by Mel Bartholemew is one example of high-density planting that works extremely well.

If the plants have ample water and nutrients, high-density planting will optimize a container's usefulness. You can read more about Mel's system on http://www.squarefoot gardening.com.

There are many ideas on how to maximize the use of space in a pot or a container. One of the better systems is the garden spire. You will need some chicken wire and a small length of PVC pipe to make this system work. Begin by constructing the spire out of 2.5 cm chicken wire. Roll the wire into a tube 42 cm in diameter. Line the spire with ordinary cardboard. Stand the column on end and insert a 10 cm wide PVC pipe in the middle. Fill this pipe with rocks and sand. Fill the rest of the column around the pipe with good soil, packed down enough to prevent it sinking too much later (but not too tightly—don't compact it). Carefully remove the pipe. The stone and sand core allows the water to travel evenly throughout.

Cut slits 5–7.5 cm long through the cardboard in a spiral going round the spire from top to bottom. The spiral should go round the column six or seven times, with 15–20 cm between the slits, making about 50 slits or more.

Plant flowers, herbs, lettuce or other plants in the slits. Water and fertilize regularly. In one small pot, you now have 1.5 sq m (roughly 16 sq ft) of gardening space. This column will produce enough veggies for many salads or, if planted with something such as 'Crystal Palace' and 'White Lady' lobelia, can look spectacular.

Some ideas for a 40 cm wide pot:

Example 1

- two canary vines in the back (bright yellow flowers against a dark green foliage)
- six 'Celebrity' petunias in the centre
- two wave petunias trailing over the front

Example 2

- one morning glory vine in the back
- six dwarf marigolds in mixed colours of yellow and orange
- six 'Crystal Palace' lobelia trailing

Example 3

- one 'Spacemaster' or 'Bushmaster' cucumber trellised
- two 'Tumbler' cherry tomatoes in the centre
- 10 lettuce plants such as 'Red Sails' lettuce mixed with green leaf for a beautiful yet functional veggie container

Urban gardeners and people living with small gardening spaces need to readjust their thinking. We have all been raised with the idea that a garden or flowerbed needs to be planted on a large scale. The sprawling garden is becoming a thing of the past—yards are getting smaller, such as those in townhomes.

With baby boomers seeking out more condos, this trend toward small space gardening will continue. You can grow a container garden in as little as one square foot of space, and the choice of containers is limited only by your imagination.

One question I am asked regularly is what plants to grow in containers in north-facing or shaded areas. A number of plants will grow well in a shady spot. Hostas are an example that offers foliage as their main feature, but they are not very colourful. The plants we will look at serve a twofold function. They can be grown indoors or out or both. I really like plants that are so versatile that they add colour to the indoor setting in winter and in spring they just keep right on looking good outdoors.

Coleus is a plant that will not only do well in shade but also will excel in providing a splash of bright colour to any shady spot. Coleus are grown for their foliage colour. The flowers are insignificant. Although there are coleus varieties that are sun tolerant, most are shade-loving plants. A wide variety of colours and forms of these versatile plants are available to suit any purpose and colour scheme. The nice thing about coleus is that when fall approaches, you can bring them indoors as a houseplant that can easily be grown through winter. The bonus with bringing the plant indoors is that it will continue to grow in size. When spring comes, all you need do is set the plant out on the deck or balcony and you will have an instant focal point. Coleus ranges from 30 cm to 90 cm in height. Some varieties are quite bushy, while others are more upright.

Some tips for growing coleus both indoors and out:

- Pinch off any flower spikes that form. A coleus that is allowed to flower has completed its life-cycle, so pinching the flowers will extend its life as well as encourage it to bush out. Also pinch out the centre growth on the plant to encourage bushiness.

- Keep the plant well watered in the container. The soil should be moist but never wet. Consider using a mulch around the plants to help keep the soil moist and from drying out. Even containers that are in the shade can dry out quickly on hot, windy days.

- Feed the plants monthly with an all-purpose fertilizer such as 10-10-10 or with a slow-release fertilizer intended for container use.

Another great plant for adding some colour to any shady location is impatiens. These little gems come in colours ranging from white and red and orange to lavender, among others. Double varieties and bicoloured types are available. These bright little flowers are guaranteed to light up any dark balcony or deck, and they are among the easiest annuals to grow. Here are some tips for growing the best impatiens:

• Keep the soil moist at all times. Never allow these plants to dry out, but be careful not to keep the soil too wet. The container should be well drained.

• Pinch back the impatiens, especially indoors to keep them from getting too lanky.

• Supplement with fluorescent lighting in winter for optimum performance.

• Fertilize with a slow-release container fertilizer.

Consider grouping the two types of plants when planning your landscape next spring. Try 'Dipt in Wine' coleus with its wine-red foliage and bright green centres grouped with 'Fiesta Ole Stardust Pink' impatiens with its double rose blossoms for an absolutely striking combination. The coleus provides a brilliant background plant or is strong enough to stand on its own as the focus. These two plants will transform any shady

deck or balcony with their brilliant colours.

Another excellent plant for the shade container are begonias. Tuberous begonias are no longer only your grandma's plants. These beauties begin blooming in June and continue well into fall. The flowers are abundant throughout the season and are fully double with a diameter of 8 cm. The plants themselves are a nice compact form growing to only 20–30 cm. Another great thing about these plants that makes them ideal for high-rise condos or apartments is that they are wind resistant. They come in a wide variety of eye-catching, vibrant colours, including apple blossom pink, apricot, bright red, deep red, golden orange, deep orange, orange, scarlet, white, yellow, pink, rose, rose pink and salmon. The colourful flowers look especially good against the dark green leaves.

I have had mine sitting on my front steps. This area gets only two to three hours of morning sun a day and the rest of the time is in fairly deep shade. I have grown 'Non-Stop Orange' for two years, and the plants are truly stunning. The orange colour is almost electric and just lights up the shady spot with all the bright blossoms. Care is so simple. I use a slow-release, pelleted container fertilizer in spring and then make sure the plants are kept moist. The plants, in addition to loving the shade, are also heat tolerant. Last year, in the record heat we had during the summer, the plants never missed a beat or a bloom.

You can buy begonias in full flower at your greenhouse or garden centre, or you can save a bundle and buy the tubers and start them indoors yourself. When choosing the tubers, look for ones that are firm and that have small sprouts showing on the concave side of the tuber. Use a commercial potting mix, but mix in one part compost to three parts potting mix. Plant the tuber just below the soil level with the hollow side up. The tuber should be no more than 1 cm below the surface of the soil. Cover the pot with plastic and place in a room that is bright and warm. Do not place in direct sunlight. Give the tuber a good drink of water—the water will awaken the tuber—but don't water again until you see signs of growth or until the soil dries out. Roots are needed to absorb the water, and they need to grow first.

As soon as you see signs of growth, remove the plastic. Once the shoots are growing, water regularly, and when the shoots are 8 cm tall, feed with a liquid, balanced fertilizer at one-half strength. After two weeks, start a regular fertilizer schedule. When the plants are approximately 15 cm high, they are ready to be transplanted into containers or into beds. Remember, when planting begonias in containers, they really

do need to have well-drained soil. Make sure your container has drainage holes. I leave mine in a plain, inexpensive plastic pot and set that pot into a nicer container. Make sure the plastic pot drains freely and that the plant never sits with its "feet" in water as it will rot. Tuberous begonias love partial to full shade, and they do not like being allowed to dry out, especially during hot periods. Evenly moist but not wet is the ticket to success. When watering, try to water from below the plant, and do not get any water on the plants themselves to help avoid powdery mildew, which can be a problem with these plants. It is easily treated with garden sulphur spray, however. The only other thing you need to do is deadhead the plants regularly to keep them blooming and looking their best.

Colour and containers just seems to be a natural fit. Making your small-scale or container garden into a special retreat can be as easy as employing one of the special effects we are about to examine. What type of colour you use in your particular space is very important in achieving the desired result. We often use the words "warm" and "cool" when talking about the colours of the landscape. What do these terms really mean, and when can you use warm colours as opposed to cool ones? It is not as complicated as you may think.

Begonias in hanging baskets.

If you have a sunny balcony or deck, you can make the most of the strong colours. These are the colours at the "hot" end of the spectrum. You know the ones I mean, the bright yellows and oranges, the hot pinks and fire engine reds and maybe even the purples that have a hint of red in them. Warm colours can be used to create a true focal point with some dramatic combinations. For example, certain shades of blue combine extremely well with oranges and purples to create a colour scheme that cannot help but stand out. The thing to be careful about is that such bright planting schemes can sometimes look brash. Using planters or containers to

redress the issue can tone down this brashness.

In other words, an oversized terra-cotta pot or an urn will stabilize the planting and add "weight" to the design. Silver or grey foliage makes a great companion to the bright colours. Silver mound and dusty miller are some examples of these plants.

Cool colours offer a sense of tranquillity and include colours such as pale blues, lemon yellows, lime greens, very pale pinks, pale mauves and whites. The cool colours look best in a shady spot. These colours also look best with a background of dark evergreen foliage or an apple green colour scheme. One of the best examples of this combination I have seen was a planting of pansies in a hanging basket. The brilliant blue faces of the pansies stood out dramatically because of the curly-leaved parsley that was the companion plant in the container.

White is one of the best choices for shady balconies or decks because it becomes a focal point in the cool shade. The beauty of using white in a planting is that it also stands out during the hours of dusk and into the evening. There is also something very special about a planting scheme of white and green—the colours just seem so natural together. One of the best plants with this combination is the white moonflower. This plant features white, morning glory–like flowers with foliage that offers a perfect backdrop to the blooms. In the evening, the white flowers seem to have their own glow and have an added benefit of a lovely scent.

The final colours we will look at are the vibrant colours, the fully saturated oranges, purples and scarlets. These colours are among the strongest in the garden and can make a dramatic impact on their own without being included in a planting or colour scheme. You probably should avoid using these colours as focal points in your plantings—they do have a tendency to jump out, making

the rest of the display somewhat unbalanced.

Some examples of plants with these colours are the verbena hybrids that come in vermilions, purples and shocking pinks. Marigolds and the Ranunculus flowers in pure orange and yellow also fit into this category. These plants look great planted up in terracotta pots, or for a really dramatic look try planting them in a deep-blue glazed pot.

The right use of colour can brighten the dullest deck or balcony or make that sunny spot even more attractive and eye-catching. The wrong use of colours, such as using cool colours in a sunny location, can make the colours seem lost and faded. As always, a little research goes a long way to making the perfect planting.

Now that we have talked about what to grow in containers and how to use colour effectively, it's time to address the issues of how to plant the containers. Some advance planning and preparation can head off any future problems when planting in containers.

Take a little time when planning your containers to decide which variety would work best for you. A little homework goes a long way toward avoiding problems down the road, such as growing a tall plant in a spot that needs a short variety. Take some time to choose the colours you prefer as well. Some good references are seed catalogues or online searches.

Here is a list of tips on how to plant in containers:

- The best soil for container plantings is commercial potting mix sold by the bag at most hardware stores, home centres and garden centres. This soil is generally richer, cleaner, more insect- and disease-free, and lighter in consistency than soil found in the ground. Potting mixes are even available that contain moisture-retaining crystals. These crystals absorb water and turn into a jelly-like consistency. The water is drawn from these crystals by the surrounding soil, thereby reducing the number of waterings required, considerably. Schulz is one company that makes a potting soil with these crystals, called Moisture Plus Potting Soil.

- Plants must have good drainage to keep their roots healthy. All containers must have drainage holes in the bottom. Use pot saucers to avoid any runoff staining your deck or balcony.

- Choose containers deep enough for the plants you wish to feature (check planting instructions on the plant label). If the requirements are for a large, deep pot, then consider using a plastic, lightweight container if weight is

a concern. Using a lightweight pot also makes for easy relocation of the container.

- Fill the pot one-quarter to one-third deep with soil, and position plants at the proper depth (see the planting instructions that come with the plants). Fill in additional soil up to 2.5 cm below the pot top. This extra space at the top allows room for watering.

- Group pots together for greater visual effect and to minimize watering labour. Groupings of tropical plants create a lush, full, tropical effect. Group tropicals with annuals for added colour. Place the large tropical plants in the background and put smaller containers with coleus, sweet potato vine, purple basil, for example, in front for added colour and interest.

- Don't be afraid to bring out some of your indoor plants. They will love you for it. Use that hibiscus tree as a foundation plant surrounded by smaller potted annuals, group it with some of the large-leafed tropical varieties for an interesting look, or try a Dieffenbachia in a grouping with annuals or other large-leafed tropicals. Let your imagination be your guide in creating your own corner of paradise.

Another issue to consider when planning your container garden is water. Because plants in containers will dry out faster than those in the ground, how much, when and how to water are important considerations.

How much to water can depend a great deal on what exposure the pot has to the elements. Plants in south-facing locations have completely different watering requirements than those that face north or even east. The south-facing pot needs to be watered much more frequently. Think also about the prevailing winds: many high-rise condos or apartments have very strong winds that can batter the foliage and dry out containers in a hurry.

The solution to the problem of adverse exposure may be to use larger containers that have a larger reservoir for moisture, or use the moisture-absorbing crystals that are available in garden centres today. These crystals help in reducing the watering frequency. Some manufacturers of these crystals claim that the watering frequency is reduced by more than 50 percent, which is not only a time- and money-saving advantage but also helps the plants by having consistent moisture available. Self-watering containers are now on the market and are excellent choices for windy balconies. The added weight of the water in the reservoir also helps to keep the container secure.

Because plants in containers have a limited amount of soil to draw moisture from, they require more frequent watering. Generally, lighter soils or soil-less mixes are used in containers; they will dry out much more quickly than regular garden soils. During a hot summer day, it may be necessary to water as many as two or three times a day depending on the exposure. Plants in terracotta pots will have to be watered much more frequently than those in plastic or ceramic pots—terracotta, because of its porosity, loses moisture much more quickly.

One of my favourite ways to keep moisture levels more even in containers is to use a mulch, in particular shredded cedar bark. I like this mulch because it is very effective at keeping the soil from drying out, looks great and smells wonderful, especially when wet. The mulch can be something as simple as grass clippings. If you think I have lost it and are wondering where you are going to get lawn clippings from when you live on the 29th floor of your condo, consider the lawn service that cuts the grass at your building. Ask them or a friend who has a lawn if you can have some grass clippings. This grass mulch is very good at keeping the soil moist.

Watering plants in containers requires a slightly different technique than watering plants in garden beds. Water should be applied at a slower rate to allow the water to penetrate more deeply. If you apply it in one fell swoop, most of the water will run off the top of the container or, if the container is dry, the water will pour out of the bottom of the pot. I have seen many gardeners dump a watering can full of water onto a pot, only to have it all come pouring out of the bottom. What happens in a container that has been allowed to dry out is that the potting mix in the container actually shrinks away from the walls of the container. You end up with this lump of very dry potting mix in the centre of the pot and spaces between the soil and the walls of the container. Water poured on the pot quickly cannot penetrate the lump in the middle and spills over the sides, down and out the bottom. Very little water actually gets to the plant roots themselves.

This illustrates how important it is never to allow your containers dry out completely. If you are ever faced with this situation, the best way to solve the problem is to put the container in a bathtub or pail of water. Let it sit in the tub or pail until the water has a chance to be drawn up into the potting mix. By doing so, the soil has a chance to absorb the water and swells back to its normal size.

If your container has a saucer, be sure to drain the saucer after watering. Allowing the pot to sit in the water will keep the soil too soggy, and many plants hate having their "feet" wet.

The other solution to the problem of lack of water is to use plants that are drought tolerant. There are annuals that are able to survive with little extra water. Annuals are different from perennials when it comes to drought tolerance. Perennials can become drought tolerant or resistant after they become well established. With annuals, the growing season is short. Some annuals will tolerate drier conditions, but you will need to give them a decent start and maintain that with good gardening practices throughout the relatively short annual growing season.

Some examples of annuals that are drought tolerant:

- angel's trumpet (*Datura* spp.): 1–1.2 m tall; large white to yellow fragrant trumpet-like blooms; **poisonous**, so exercise care

- bachelor's buttons (*Centaurea cyanus*): 30–60 cm tall; blooms range from blues to pinks and purples

- blanket flower (*Gaillardia pulchella*): 30–60 cm tall; orange, red and yellow blooms

- calendula (*Calendula officinalis*): 30–60 cm tall; flowers in shades of yellows and oranges

- cosmos (*Cosmos bipinnatus*): 30 cm–1.2 m tall; in a variety of colours

- dusty miller (*Senecio cineraria*): 30–60 cm tall; grown for silvery foliage that contrasts well with many colours

- gazania (*Gazania ringens*): 30–60 cm tall; white, orange, yellow and pink blooms

- ice plant (*Mesembryanthemum crytallinum*): under 30 cm tall; variegated foliage and yellow flowers

- marigold (*Tagetes*): 30–60 cm tall; in shades of yellow and orange and bicolours

- petunia (*Petunia × hybrida*): 30–60 cm tall; in myriad bloom colours

- portulaca (*Portulaca grandiflora*): under 30 cm tall; well suited for hot and dry areas; jewel-like colours range from white to fuchsia to red and orange

- strawflower (*Helichrysum bracteatum*): 30–60 cm tall; in yellows and oranges; tough flower dries very well

- sunflower (*Helianthus annuus*): 30 cm–3 m tall; large-flowered plants in yellows, oranges and reds

- tickseed (*Coreopsis* spp.): 30 cm–1 m tall; airy flowers in yellow, pink and red

The aforementioned plant examples are tolerant of low water regimes. However, these plants will still require some moisture. They are not drought hardy—only drought tolerant. How little water they will tolerate depends on individual growing conditions such as the number of hours of direct sunlight, wind and use of mulch.

I have grown some of the examples on this list in the hottest and driest of locations with great success.

Questions and Answers: Fruits and Vegetables

Q. I want to grow vegetables in containers on my deck. I am particular about my deck and want to avoid damage to it caused by pot moisture and excess water. I have used saucers but have been told of a better device called the pottery trainer. I found it discussed on a bulletin board. I then found it on the web as well. Can you tell me anything about it?

A. I am familiar with this product, and although I have not tried it myself, it sounds like a great solution to a problem that has been around since container growing first started: decks and balconies becoming stained from water overflowing from saucers of pots and containers.

This new system installs quickly. All you do is put a bead of caulking around the existing drainage hole, then apply a phalange with a hole in it over the caulking. You then insert a tube into the small hole and thread the tubing down below the deck through the natural crack between deck boards or down the side of a solid deck or balcony. Any excess water simply runs away without ever contacting the deck or balcony surface. There is never any standing water.

You can order the product directly off the website at www.potterytrainer.com or call 1-888-626-POTS. No one in Canada is selling this product yet, but I'm sure it won't be long because the system is inexpensive.

Q. I would love to try growing some of my own vegetables in containers but am concerned about the lack of space that I have. Do you have any suggestions?

A. Plant breeders continue to develop new dwarf varieties of vegetables suited for growing in small spaces or containers. The breeders are responding to the call from gardeners for varieties of vegetables that can be grown in today's smaller gardens or in containers on condo or apartment decks and balconies. The number of

new varieties available over the past few years has exploded.

Some of the newer varieties are dwarf in size and yet retain the flavour of the older and larger varieties. Among the varieties that are worthy of trial are:

Beans

- 'Dwarf Bees'—a scarlet-runner type that grows 46–60 cm
- 'Dwarf Runner Hestia'— developed for container growing or small spaces; 25 cm tall

Cabbage

- 'Baby Head'—an amazing variety with 6 cm heads
- 'Modern Dwarf'—slightly larger variety with 10 cm heads

Carrots

- 'Bunny Bite'—with a 4 cm root, this carrot can be grown in the shallowest of containers or in soil with a high clay content
- 'Short 'n' Sweet'—another dwarf variety with 10 cm tapered roots; the taste is very sweet and the carrot is very tender

Corn

- 'Golden Midget'—60–90 cm stalks with 10 cm cobs

Cucumbers

- 'Bush Whopper'—a bush-type cucumber with no runners,

making it an excellent variety for containers or small garden beds

- 'Patio Pickles'—small plants with an abundance of fruits

Eggplant

- 'Easter Egg'—5–8 cm long fruit
- 'Early Black Egg'—13 cm fruit, very tender

Lettuce

- 'Dwarf Midget Cos'—this cos or Romaine type of lettuce grows only 13 cm tall but has excellent flavour and texture
- 'Tom Thumb'—tennis ball–size Buttercrunch variety

Peas

- 'American Wonder'—30 cm tall plants with 9 cm pods containing 6 or 7 peas
- 'Greater Progress'—46 cm vines

Tomatoes

- These have long been a favourite of breeders so there are many dwarf varieties; some of the better ones include 'Early Salad' (15–20 cm), 'Patio' (38–75 cm) and 'Tiny Tim' (38 cm).

Q. I would love to have my own fresh cucumbers. The problem is that I live in a condo high rise with a very small (1.5 m × 1 m) balcony. Is there any way I can grow cucumbers?

A. Cucumbers can be easily grown in pots and containers. There are a couple of ways to approach growing cukes. Your choices are to use the newer varieties that have been developed by plant breeders to not spread and are often called patio cucumbers, or the older varieties that spread but change their direction. Instead of growing them horizontally, introduce your cucumber plant to the vertical realm and watch it go straight up. The introduction of a trellis or garden obelisk can increase your gardening space by taking advantage of the vertical.

Vertical gardening has sometimes been called the hidden dimension in gardening. Being able to take advantage of this unused space is an effective way to grow cucumbers. Cucumbers will take very well to growing up instead of along the ground. I recommend growing at least two plants for good pollination. A pot 60 cm wide and deep is plenty for two cucumber plants. Use a good quality potting soil to which you add compost (two parts of potting soil mixed with one part compost makes a good mix for cucumbers). Plant the seeds directly outdoors, as cucumbers do not take well to transplanting when grown from seed. Wait until the evenings are warm enough and all danger of frost has passed. Planting too soon may result in poor or no germination, and if the conditions are too cool, even if the plants do germinate, they may stop growing and remain stunted.

When planting seeds pay close attention to the spacing requirements of the plants. Try not to jam too many plants into a single container. Cucumbers prefer space, and for some varieties that may mean only having one plant in a container depending on the size of the pot, of course. Cucumbers are very heavy feeders and will need to be fertilized regularly. I have found the easiest way is to use slow-release fertilizer pellets that are designed for use in containers. One application can be enough to last two to three months. For plants that you have seeded, apply the fertilizer after the plants have emerged and have their second set of leaves. Place the container in full sun. Cucumbers will not grow in shade. Water the plants regularly and do not allow the soil to completely dry out. Cucumbers will not tolerate dry conditions.

If the variety is a spreading type and once the plants are growing well with 2–3 sets of leaves you may consider adding the vertical support of your choice. Use a trellis that is approximately 1–1.5 m high or a garden obelisk of the same height. You will need a sunny location for your cukes as they do not grow well in a shady spot. Keep the container moist but not wet. You will need to train the vines to grow up the support. Initially,

tying the vines to the support will help the plant "learn" that it is growing up. Soon the vines will begin to twine onto the support and you will not need to tie them. Cucumbers grow at a very fast rate in ideal conditions. You may find that the plant is overgrowing the support. If that occurs, simply cut back the actively growing tip of the vine to encourage the plant to bush out rather than grow higher.

The easier method is to grow the patio cucumbers that have been bred to be container plants or grow to a certain height and shape. 'Salad Bush' and 'Bushcrop' are slicing varieties that are suitable for fresh eating or slicing. 'Patio Pik' and 'Bushmaster' can be used to eat fresh but can also be used for pickling. These are all good examples of cucumbers that grow with very short vines and are very well suited to growing in pots or containers. Follow the same cultural instructions when planting the patio varieties of cukes.

Q. When I lived in a house, I put 8 or 10 five-gallon pails on the south side of the house and grew the most lovely tomatoes. For five years I have lived on the third floor of a condo and cannot seem to grow tomatoes any more. I face south-southwest and the balcony is very hot. I usually have to water twice a day in hot weather, and there is no shortage of flowers, but almost no tomatoes. I've noticed there are very few bees up here, and suspect that is the problem. Last summer I took a paintbrush and swirled it in the flowers but didn't think to do so until about July. Is there a trick to doing this or did I just not start early enough? By the way, I had the same problem with cucumbers last year—lots of flowers but no cukes.

A. The problem is definitely one of pollination. You are quite correct in your observation about the lack of bees. They are far too busy doing their work on the ground, not three floors up. Fortunately, there is a simple but incredibly effective solution called Tomato Fruit Set. This spray is a hormone that takes the place of the bees and their pollination. Spray the Tomato Fruit Set directly on the open flowers, and each one will be pollinated and produce fruit. The spray is readily available in most garden centres.

As for the cucumbers, the problem is the same; the solution is not. You will have to hand pollinate the cucumbers as soon as the plants are in bloom. Take a male flower and touch its anther to the stigma of the female flowers. You can pollinate many female flowers with one male flower. It may also help to make a buzzing sound as you pollinate—just kidding!

Varieties such as 'Sweet Success' and 'Diva' are self-pollinating, but if you don't have a self-pollinating type a small artist brush can also help. Simply use the brush to transfer the pollen from the male to female flowers. There are far more female flowers on a vine than there are male, so you will have to look for the male flowers. To help tell the difference, male flowers have a single stamen and appear first.

Q. We have decided that this year we will grow our own vegetables on our balcony. I am pretty confident in growing most of the veggies except for tomatoes. Whenever I talk to experienced gardeners about this topic I seem to get hundreds of opinions. I think I am getting overwhelmed and hoped you could help out with your thoughts on how to grow these plants.

A. There is an old saying in gardening that goes something like "ask 100 gardeners the same question and get 100 different answers." One of the easiest vegetables to grow in containers are tomatoes. In the past, before container gardening took off in the way it has, many condo and apartment gardeners were hesitant to try growing tomatoes on their balconies or decks. Many tomatoes were not suited to growing in small spaces. Plant breeders now offer smaller types that are ideally suited to grow in containers. Additionally, it has been proven now that tomatoes not only will grow in containers but they may actually grow better in containers than in the ground.

Tomatoes grow incredibly well in containers for several reasons:

- Containers in a south or westerly exposure help keep the tomato roots warm. Tomatoes love warm roots. As the container warms in the sun so do the tomato roots. Because the roots are above ground, they are considerably warmer than a plant whose roots are planted in a traditional garden setting.

- It is easier to control moisture and fertilizer in a container. The area is small and concentrated, allowing for easier monitoring.

- It is relatively simple to move the container and plant to the sun. In other words, the more sun you can get on your plant, the more tomatoes you will have. It can be a large advantage if you can follow the sun during the day by moving the container.

What does it take to grow a tomato in a container?

- Sunlight—the single most important factor. At least six hours of sun a day are needed to grow tomatoes successfully. If you have a spot that gets less than six hours of sun, you are wasting your time and money trying to grow tomatoes.

- A container large enough to keep the tomato happy. The pot does not have to be huge. A 40 cm diameter container is sufficient for a single tomato plant. Use plastic, cast resin or fibreglass pots. They don't dry out as quickly as terracotta ones.

- Potting soil. Nothing fancy. Regular potting soil is just fine. Adding some compost or manure is a great idea and can make the difference between an average plant and one that produces a great crop of tomatoes.

- Even moisture is another critical factor. Tomatoes love water, but they don't like to be wet. Keep the plant evenly moist so that the soil feels moist but not wet when you stick your finger deep into the pot. During the hot summer, you may have to water the plant daily or even twice a day. Placing mulch such as shredded bark at the top of the container is a good idea to conserve moisture.

- Fertilize regularly with a tomato food, Miracle-Gro or a slow-release fertilizer. My secret? Fish fertilizer. Apply it weekly at one-half the strength recommended.

- Space. Not much is needed. A very vigorous tomato plant will only need 1 sq m.

- Support. A tomato cage is a good investment. It will keep the plant from toppling over when loaded with fruit. Yes, I said loaded. Expect great production from even a single plant.

The determinate or bush varieties of tomatoes are best for container growth. Choosing a variety that matures earlier will give you tomatoes much earlier in the season. It's very much a personal preference, but I like tomatoes that are lower in acid and higher in sugar. Some that I really enjoy and grow every year are:

- 'Sub-Arctic Maxi'—lunchbox-size tomatoes, 2.5 oz size; matures in 48 days; outstanding flavour

- 'Sugar Baby'—super-sweet tomatoes on compact plants, 1–2 oz size; matures in 54 days; sweet, delicious flavour; plants are small but very productive

- 'Bush Early Girl'—huge yields on such small plants, 6–7 oz size with good flavour; compact determinate; matures in 54 days

- 'Window Box Roma'—1.5 ft tall plants; 2–3 oz size; 70 days to maturity

- 'Tumbler'—a cherry tomato–type determinate variety that has been especially developed for planting into hanging baskets or other containers. Dwarf plants are compact and attractive, especially when laden with their harvest of 2.5–3 cm bright red fruit,

which appears in clusters and is sweet. Tumbler is one of the best choices for container growing and is perfect for placing on patios, balconies, or decks. Matures in 49 days.

Q. The deck of our townhouse abuts right up against the south-facing wall of the house. I am thinking of growing some beans up that wall and was wondering if it would work.

A. Beans are extremely useful for small space gardening because they use the vertical plane and free up the lower spaces for other plants. They also can be efficient screens if you are growing runner varieties, in addition to providing you with some tasty veggies for dinner. We will focus on the runner-type beans here since they serve a multiple function.

Beans grow well in containers but do have some limitations. Although they will probably reach the same size as beans planted in the ground, they will not crop as well. It is harder to keep the moisture levels up in the container, and the beans do not have deep enough root space. Don't be discouraged; the beans will still produce a good crop.

I recommend using a pot that is at least 46 cm wide and deep. I also recommend using a mix of one part soil-less potting mix with one part compost. You can start the beans indoors three to four weeks before planting time if you want to get a head start, or sow them outdoors after all danger of frost has passed. Beans are pretty amazing when it comes to germination. They positively explode out of the ground and grow rapidly. In fact, they grow so quickly that you will need some sort of support for them as they get taller. If you use a trellis, first secure it and then place the container in front of it, and allow the beans to climb. They will attach their tendrils as they climb, making the whole arrangement secure if you have attached the trellis securely.

You can also use sticks such as tree branches and make a teepee arrangement in the pot itself and allow the beans to climb on the branches. Make the support at least 1.8 m tall. I recommend growing scarlet runner beans—they are so beautiful with their bright red flowers, and they will form a wonderful screen when mature as well as providing some very tasty beans.

These beans ask only for soil that stays moist but not wet and to be planted in full sun. They are fairly heavy feeders, so a regular fertilizer program using a well-balanced fertilizer is needed. A fertilizer such as 20-20-20 will work. Cut the strength recommended by the manufacturer by one-quarter and use this diluted fertilizer once or twice a week when you water. On

the other hand, you could simply use slow-release pellet fertilizer for containers. These pellets come in various formulations such as 14-14-14 or 16-16-16 and all work well. One application of this fertilizer will usually last three months. Every time you water, the correct amount of fertilizer is released from the pellets, making the process less labour intensive.

Because these beans grow relatively quickly, in no time at all you will have a screen that is 1.8 m tall. It can be easily moved to screen off whatever needs to be screened. Not only do the beans make an effective way of creating privacy, but they also do so in a most beautiful way. The vines will literally be full of the bright red flowers. Even if you have nothing to screen off, the vines can soften a hard surface such as a wall or railing, adding a textural element to the small-scale garden. The texture adds even more interest because of its vertical component. While the texture adds an interesting element, there is also appeal in simply placing a container of scarlet runner beans against a wall, thus transforming a blank canvas into a living thing of beauty.

Harvest the beans when they are 7.5–10 cm long. The more beans you pick, the more beans the plants will produce. What could be better than sitting on your deck or balcony enjoying the green lushness and brilliant flowers of the scarlet runner plants and picking fresh beans for dinner?

Q. I live in an east-facing condo and have been trying to grow tomatoes for several years with no luck. My husband and I love the Roma types, and we get some blooms but the fruit never develop.

A. I always keep my eye open for new varieties of plants that are suitable for problem areas. Recently, I was looking through the Vesey's catalogue and ran across a tomato that I filed for later reference. It is called 'Window Box Roma'. This plant was bred specifically to grow in pots or containers. It is nice to see the plant breeders paying attention to the rapidly growing portion of the population who live in condos or apartments.

'Window Box Roma' are dwarf and compact. The neat thing about them is that they look decorative even before the tomatoes start to form. The supplier says the fruit is excellent in taste and storability, and the plants will produce ripe fruit in 70 days. Another exciting fact is that the plant needs only a half-day of full sun to produce the fruit.

While you are at it, why not consider growing some patio cucumbers as well? Plant breeders continue to develop more dwarf varieties that are well suited to growing in containers. One variety that caught my attention is called 'Pot Luck'. The vines on this cuke get no longer than 18 cm, and the plant itself is compact in form. It is ideal for even a small pot. The fruit is ready in just 55 days as well. I saw this variety of cuke in the Dominion Seed house catalogue.

Now if you plant the new dwarf runner beans called 'Snow White', you will have your own balcony veggie garden. This bean gets only 46 cm tall with heavy yields on the small plants. It is highly recommended for patios and balconies. I found this bean in a company in the UK, but it may be available in Canada.

Q. I read recently that it is possible to grow potatoes as well as other vegetables in containers. Can you tell me how to go about trying this?

A. There is nothing like digging up those first new potatoes to enjoy with a meal. My grandmother, who adored new potatoes, used to cheat Mother Nature a bit. You could find her kneeling in the potato patch with a soup spoon poking into the potato hills looking for tiny baby potatoes. You too can enjoy your own potato harvest in a container! The beauty of containers is that you can grow practically anything in a container that you can in the garden, including potatoes. In fact, they may be the easiest things to grow in containers. How simple is it? All you need is a container, a small bag of seed potatoes and a bag of potting soil.

When choosing a container, look for a lightweight one because of the weight of the moist soil, the potatoes and the pot, especially when planting on a balcony where weight is an issue. I recommend a polyurethane foam pot, which is not only lightweight but also can be highly decorative. They come in a variety of sizes. Choose a 60 cm wide and 30 cm deep pot. If you are not concerned about aesthetics, a plastic garbage can will serve just as well. Make sure to drill several 1 cm drainage holes in the bottom of the pot if it has no existing holes.

Place 15 cm of potting soil in the bottom of the pot. You can add compost to your potting soil to increase the nutrient value. Also add a sprinkling of slow-release 14-14-14 fertilizer. Place your seed potatoes on top of the layer of soil. Space the potatoes 12.5 cm apart. Cover the potatoes with another layer of 15 cm of potting soil/compost. The key to growing potatoes in containers is to plant the spuds at the bottom of the pot, leaving lots of room in the top of the pot.

In two to three weeks, you will start to see the leaves. When the plants are 10 cm tall, add more soil until only 2.5 cm of the foliage shows. Adding soil allows the underground stems to grow, and in the process they will produce more potatoes. Keep adding soil as the plants continue to grow. Every time the plants grow 10 cm, cover all but 2.5 cm. Soon the vines will grow up and over the sides of the pot. It is important to keep the vines from breaking. Inserting bamboo stakes and tying the vines to the stakes will help keep the vines intact. At this point, the soil should be right up to the top of the pot.

The vines will eventually bloom. Shortly after that, the underground stems will begin producing potatoes. Soon afterwards you can get your soup spoon out and start looking for new potatoes if you like, or you can wait until the tops die in fall and then harvest the full-sized spuds. An absolute must when it comes to growing container potatoes is to keep the container well watered. The soil should be moist but not wet, and it should never be allowed to fully dry out. During hot summer days or in late summer, you may have to water daily.

As for varieties, you can grow any type you want. 'Yukon Gold' is a very nice-tasting potato with a yellow flesh and, some say, a buttery taste. You can even try growing some unusual purple potatoes like 'Peruvian Blue', or even sweet potatoes. In fact, ipomoea or sweet potato vines are used in many decorative applications.

New varieties with bright, chartreuse-coloured leaves make bold statements in containers. Add a few annuals such as purple pansies to the container with chartreuse ipomoea—enjoy the colour during the summer, and savour the sweet potato harvest in the fall.

Q. I know that you are an advocate of growing your own vegetables in containers, but I don't think I have ever seen you write about lettuce in containers. Is lettuce a good candidate for growing in pots?

A. You are correct—we have never looked at lettuce as a container plant. It is one of the best plants for this purpose. You are also quite correct in that one of my favourite uses of containers is for growing veggies. I find that the produce available at the local grocery store has no taste, and I am forced to buy whatever the store's produce buyers tell me I have to buy. When it comes to lettuce, I can only choose from iceberg, green or red leaf, and, if I am lucky, Butter-crunch varieties. Buttercrunch lettuce is usually the type with the roots still attached. It can cost more than a good steak. Lettuce is one of the easiest and most rewarding vegetables for the container gardener to grow.

You can grow lettuce in any type of container you want. I have found that a long trough or window box-type of container is one of the best for lettuce.

The trough almost resembles a row, and the lettuce plants can be spread out along this row. The plants will not be crowded and will be easy to harvest. This type of container comes in a variety of sizes in plastic, cast resin or even ceramic. Choose a size that fits your space. If your space is very limited, a small container can still provide you with enough lettuce for a few salads every week.

Depending on the variety of lettuce you choose, you may not have to replant the lettuce after you harvest in order to grow more lettuce. With some varieties, such as 'Grand Rapids' or other varieties of leaf lettuce, you cut the leaves down to just above the soil level only to have them regrow and be ready for further harvest in a few weeks. You can also just pick the outer leaves of the lettuce, leaving the centre leaves to continue to grow.

My favourite variety of lettuce is 'Buttercrunch'. It is very flavourful and easy to grow. Although it is a head lettuce, I harvest it as if it were a leaf lettuce. I cut it down to approximately 5 cm above the soil level and find that it regrows nicely. As with the leaf lettuce, you can also just pick off the outer leaves of this type of lettuce.

If you prefer head lettuce, wait until the head forms and then cut it off at ground level. If you are going to grow head lettuce and want to wait until heads are formed, consider having several containers so that you have a continuous harvest. When you harvest one head, replant that space immediately. You should thus have a steady supply of fresh lettuce.

The soil you need for the container can be a good quality potting mix. I recommend adding compost to the potting mix to provide optimum nutrition for your plants. A good ratio is two parts potting mix to two parts compost. Ensure that the container is well drained and that any drainage holes are not plugged with soil. A good way to keep the holes from getting plugged is to place a coffee filter over each hole. The filter allows the water to drain away while keeping the soil in. Lettuce prefers to grow in a sunny location but will tolerate a spot that has partial shade. Keep the container well watered, and in a short few weeks, you will be enjoying your own lettuce harvest.

New varieties of lettuce are being introduced every year specifically suited to small-space gardens. One such variety is dwarf midget cos. This cos or Romaine type of lettuce grows only 13 cm tall but has excellent flavour and texture. Another example is 'Tom Thumb', which is a tennis ball-size Buttercrunch variety. Of course, any type of lettuce will grow quite happily in a container.

Q. I would like to know if I can grow strawberries on my condo balcony? I live on the sixth floor and have a south exposure.

A. Strawberries are pretty fussy about the amount of light they get. They need to receive six to eight hours of light per day. Move the container to follow the sun during the day if you can. The reward is really worth the effort.

When choosing the container, the main consideration is to ensure that it will have proper drainage. Strawberries do not like to have their roots wet. In fact, they will not tolerate wet conditions at all. You will need a saucer under the container to catch the water so as not to stain your balcony or deck, but the container should not sit in direct contact with the saucer. Use some pebbles or the commercially available ceramic pedestals to raise the container out of the water in the saucer. You can use any type of container you like: a hanging basket type, ordinary pots, barrels or tubs. The containers designed as strawberry planters are simply large pots with planting holes regularly spaced all over the sides of the pot. These are available in both terracotta and plastic. I always recommend using plastic pots because they do not allow the soil to dry out as quickly as terracotta does. If you are going to use the strawberry planters, I have a tip.

171

Watering these strawberry planters can be a bit of a challenge because the water may not penetrate all the way to the bottom of the container. Fix this problem easily by purchasing a length of 5 cm wide PVC pipe in any hardware store. Ask the staff to cut it to the same length as the depth of the container. Then you will need to drill holes evenly spaced all over the pipe. The holes should be approximately 3 mm wide. Space the holes 5–7.5 cm apart. Place the pipe in the centre of the planter and then fill the planter with soil, but do not allow soil to enter the pipe. When watering, direct the water into the centre of the pipe, filling it to the top. The water will seep out of the holes right to the bottom of the pot. Water is an important factor when growing strawberries. They do not like to dry out completely. Stick your finger into the soil. If the soil feels dry 1 cm down, give the strawberries a drink.

The soil you use should be one that drains well. Regular potting soil will work fine, but add compost to the mix. Two parts potting soil and one part compost works great. Strawberries are fairly heavy feeders, so also add some slow-release fertilizer pellets to the top of the container.

Choosing a variety is all about personal choice. The two basic types of strawberries are June bearing or everbearing. June-bearing types produce one crop over the course of a few weeks in spring or summer. They are the highest producers, but they generate lots of runners, so they may not be the right choice for you if your space is limited. The everbearing types have two subsets. One is the double-cropping types that produce one crop in spring and another in fall. The day-neutral types produce one crop in early summer. Take a trip down to your local greenhouse or garden centre to check out which varieties they carry. The type of strawberry you choose will also determine the spacing needed when planting.

Q. Is it possible to grow grapes in a pot? I just think it would look so cool to have some grapes growing up a wall in our townhouse.

A. While grapes will grow in a container, the unknown issue is whether they will flower and fruit the first season. I have had grapes flower and bear fruit the first season, but I have also had some that did not bear fruit for two seasons. A number of grapes are hardy and may even overwinter in a container. Be warned, however, that getting even the hardy grapes to overwinter in a container comes with its own set of challenges. You must be prepared to do one of two things. You can bring the containers into a garage (unheated) and wrap the pot and all with R20 home insulation, or if you are trying to get them to overwinter outdoors, you will need to add even more insulation in an effort to keep the roots from freezing totally. Because grapes usually take two to three years before they will bear fruit, getting the plants through the winter is critical if you want to have grapes. While growing grapes in a pot is challenging, it certainly can be done if enough protection is afforded to the roots.

'Alpha', 'Beta', 'King of the North', 'Valiant' and 'Dakota' are varieties that are suited to our growing conditions. 'Beta', 'Valiant' and 'King of the North' are the most hardy. All of these grapes taste similar to the Concord grape but are generally smaller, except for the 'King of the North'. This variety produces larger fruit that is good for eating from hand or for jams and jellies, whereas 'Beta' and 'Valiant' are better suited for jams and jellies only. 'King of the North' is also more vigorous than the other two and will fruit at an earlier age; as well, it produces five to six times more growth in a single season.

Because grapes tend to have larger root systems you will need to choose the correct container to allow for the root growth—a container at least 60 cm wide and tall will work. I recommend a container that is plastic or a cast resin as opposed to terracotta. Terracotta tends to dry out much more quickly. A well-draining potting soil is the best choice as grapes like to be well drained.

Grapes prefer full sun. A south exposure works best, but other sunny exposures may work. They also need protection from prevailing winds. Planting the grapes up against a wall may be the best way to avoid exposure to the winds.

Grapes are very heavy feeders and will need to be on a regular fertilizing schedule if in containers. Every time you water, you should fertilize the container with a dilute solution (one-quarter of the recommended strength) of a well-balanced fertilizer such as 20-20-20 or Miracle-Gro. The soil should be kept moist but not wet. Adding a mulch such as shredded bark to the top of the container will help with moisture retention. Grapes require some type of support, and a trellis of any type will do the job quite nicely as long as it is at least 1.5–1.8 m tall.

Questions and Answers: Herbs

Q. I watch a lot of cooking shows, and some of them talk about growing your own herbs indoors. I live in a walk-up condo complex and would love to try growing my own herbs, but I really don't know where to start.

A. Growing herbs is useful, rewarding and quite easy to do. Most herbs require between four to six hours of direct sunlight to perform to their best. An unobstructed south, west or east exposure will provide the best light for your plants. Some herbs such as mint, watercress and chervil require a bright north-facing window. If your windows do not receive full sun, consider an artificial light source such as a gro-light. Regardless of your light source, you should turn your plants frequently to make sure all sides get good light exposure. Be careful during cold days that your herbs are not too close to the glass. They can be easily damaged by getting too cold or even freeze from touching the window.

You will need to pay attention to water and humidity requirements. Different herbs require different levels of moisture. For example, basil, parsley, mint, chervil and arugula do best if kept moist but not wet. Let Mediterranean plants such as rosemary and lavender dry out slightly before you water again. As a general rule for most herbs, water when the top of the soil feels dry, and then allow the soil to dry out again before watering. The choice of pots will affect the amount of water the plant requires. Plastic or ceramic pots will retain water better, and you will need to water less. Terracotta, on the other hand, tends to dry out the soil more quickly, and plants need water more frequently.

Humidity during winter is often a problem for herbs, as it is with many houseplants. An excellent way of adding humidity to a plant or grouping of plants is to put the pots on trays of pebbles. Add water to the tray and pebbles until the water reaches a height just below the top of the pebbles. It is important that the water never touch the pot itself. Misting the plants frequently will also help.

While humidity needs to be optimized, it is just as important to ensure that there is proper air circulation around the plants. Plants grouped too closely together with poor air movement can experience fungal problems. Air movement in and around plants is often neglected, and yet is very important to the health of the plants.

Many herbs grow quickly and will need to be harvested frequently to keep their shape. You can dry the harvested herbs for later use. You may also consider replanting herbs you harvest often so you'll always have a fresh, young plant to take the place of an older one. Buying fresh-cut herbs in the grocery store can be expensive, and buying a new plant every few weeks is still the less expensive alternative.

Be careful not to over fertilize your herbs. Use a well-balanced fertilizer such as 20-20-20 at one-quarter the recommended rate. Apply this diluted fertilizer every two weeks.

Herbs that grow well indoors include basil, bay, chives, marjoram, mint, oregano, parsley, rosemary, tarragon and thyme. Herbs that require special care include chamomile (extra light), chervil (extra light), coriander (sparse watering), lemon verbena (sparse watering), sage (sparse watering) and tansy (sparse watering).

Questions and Answers: Houseplants

Q. My friend and I share a condo and have been looking for an unusual plant to be a conversation piece. We read that you can grow your own ginger by buying the roots at the store and starting them indoors at home. I have been unable to find any information on this. Can you please help? We have seen ginger growing and love the way it looks.

A. You can grow your own ginger plant quite easily. The plant itself is not only attractive but is also functional: it will provide you with your own fresh ginger roots to use. Here are some tips for growing ginger successfully:

- Buy fresh ginger roots from the grocery store. Pick ones that are plump, have many buds and are not wrinkled. If you can find ones that are starting to show green growth, then all the better.

- Plant the roots indoors in spring, when it is easier to supply warm temperatures to the tubers. The

dormant tubers will sprout only when the mercury hits 24–29° C.

- Use a container that is about 35 cm across and 30 cm deep and has excellent drainage. This size will hold three average-size tubers comfortably.

- Fill the container with a good quality potting soil that has been enriched with compost. Fill the pot, leaving 5 cm at the top.

- Soak the tubers overnight in warm water and then plant them with the buds facing up. Cover with 2.5 cm of soil and water lightly at first, increasing the amount of water as the plant begins to grow. Keep them on the dry side during winter when they are dormant.

- Set the pot in a warm spot in a bright room out of direct sunlight.

- Set the pot outside after temperatures are above 10° C, but protect the plants from strong winds.

- Expect plants to reach maturity, and a height of 1 m, in 10–12 months.

- Dig up new, young sprouts that appear in front of the main plants (they form their own tubers), use what you need, and freeze or replant the rest.

- Cut tender, young shoots at anytime.

Q. I have heard that it is possible to grow clivias indoors as a houseplant. Is that true? If so, can you tell me what growing conditions and special needs it requires? I'm looking for a unique houseplant that will bloom. Is this plant a good choice?

A. Clivia, also known as the Kaffir lily, is a striking tuberous-rooted evergreen herbaceous plant in the Amaryllis family. While there are many different species, *Clivia miniata* is the most common species grown as a cultivar. Its broad, strap-like, dark green leaves grow in an arching fashion up to 30 cm long and 7.5–10 cm wide. Brilliant clusters of flowers emerge from the centre of the dense leaf clumps. Often, between 10 and 20 of these large lily-like flowers bloom on each umbel during their blooming season.

Their blooming period is from mid-winter through early spring, with most blooming from March to April. After their blooms are spent, ornamental red berries often appear, which offer an additional cheerful display.

Clivia is not undemanding in its requirements. It will not bloom if left in a heated room during winter or if the watering rules are not followed closely. It needs winter rest, an unheated room (4–10° C), no fertilizer and just enough water to keep it from wilting. Clivia will also not tolerate being moved when in bud or in flower; never repot unless the plant is pushing its way out of the container. This plant prefers bright light, but avoid direct sunlight during summer.

Clivia is truly a beautiful plant, but as can be seen in its requirements, can be rather demanding. If you are prepared to do the work needed and follow the rules, you will be rewarded with spectacular bloom.

Q. I just moved into a new town-home and am tired of my silk plants. I would like to grow my own houseplants. I have a brown thumb, so can you give me some tips so I don't kill them all again? I really want to keep them happy this time. I recently read that houseplants can clean the air we breathe.

A. Plants do actually clean the air we breathe. In 1984, NASA senior research scientist Dr. Bill Wolverton tested houseplants for their ability to maintain clean air for future habitable lunar bases. Testing in sealed chambers, Wolverton found that philodendrons and golden pothos were excellent formaldehyde controllers. Health Canada says formaldehyde is released from a number of sources such as wood products, some latex paints and many other sources. Gerbera daisies and chrysanthemums were great at purging benzene from the air, while pot mums and peace lilies were highly rated for trichloroethylene control. Benzene and trichloroethylene sources are paints and waxes, among other things.

Wolverton suggested that one to three mature plants were enough to improve the air in a 100 cubic foot area. Another NASA study concluded that the houseplants they tested removed up to 87 percent of toxic indoor air within 24 hours. A German study (1994) found that a single spider plant could clean the air in a 100-cubic-foot room contaminated with formaldehyde. Further tests found that bamboo palms eliminated carpet odours, and the snake plant cleared household cleaner contaminates.

So how do you keep your plants healthy and happy? Here are the tips:

- Lighting. Do the research into how much light your plants need. Light is absolutely critical to the health of your plant. Far too many people try to force a high-light plant into a medium- or low-light area with very poor results. If you provide the right light conditions, you will be rewarded with a plant that performs to its optimum. As a rule, flowering plants and those with coloured leaves will need higher light levels than those grown just for their foliage.

- Watering. One of the most common mistakes made with indoor plants is overwatering. While some plants do prefer conditions that are evenly moist (Norfolk Island pine, crotons, ficus, palms and others), many houseplants prefer the soil to dry out between waterings. Use the "finger test" to check for water content in the soil. Stick your finger into the soil up to the first knuckle, and if the soil feels dry, it's time to water. When watering, make sure you give enough water for it to run out of the drainage holes. Again, do your homework when buying a plant to know its watering requirements.

- Fertilizing. Many indoor plants undergo a period of dormancy during winter. Fertilize these plants sparingly during winter and start fertilizing again in February, following manufacturer's directions for concentration. You can't go wrong with a balanced fertilizer such as 20-20-20.

- Humidity. Many indoor plants benefit from having humidity levels increased during winter. Place the plant on a tray filled with pebbles and add water to just below the top of the pebbles; mist regularly. Grouping your plants together helps to increase the humidity and makes a dramatic decorating statement. Having single plants is fine, but having a grouping of plants is always more dramatic.

- Cleaning. Wiping the leaves with a damp cloth to remove dust and debris will help the plant to "breathe."

- Bugs. Being vigilant is key to heading off any problems with insects. At the first sign of a problem, try knocking off the invader with a sharp stream of water such as from your shower. You can also use an insecticidal soap. Using a natural insecticide such as Doktor Doom Botanics will also work.

Q. I live in a condo with a south-facing balcony. I would like to add some greenery to the balcony but don't want to spend a lot of money on plants that will not survive winter outdoors. I have many houseplants. Do you think it is a good idea to move some of those plants outdoors in spring and summer?

A. One piece of advice I find myself constantly telling people with houseplants is to take them outdoors in spring. Indoor plants love being outdoors. They enjoy the humidity, the thorough waterings they get and the added benefits of being directly in the sun without any glass. There is enormous potential in the use of indoor plants in your balcony or deck gardenscapes.

Some of the most spectacular foliage and flowering plants are grown as indoor plants in our climate because of our winters. Summers, however, are in most cases every bit as warm and humid as other parts of the world. Take advantage of the summer by moving your indoor plants outdoors—it will benefit your plants and will enhance the beauty of your surroundings. In many cases, where the plant is an older specimen, you are adding a larger specimen that would be very costly to buy new and one that will create a very dramatic impact to the space you place it in.

The benefits of moving the plant outdoors are enormous. The plants will always grow better and will be healthier if grown in an outdoor environment. Certainly the increased humidity has a lot to do with this increase in vigour. At times, during the Canadian winter, the interior of your home can be drier than the Kalahari Desert. Even with a humidifier, it is difficult to maintain adequate levels of humidity to keep your plants happy. Many indoor plants will also appreciate the change in temperature in the evenings outdoors. In the home, the temperature is mostly constant owing to our heating systems. Many plants prefer the difference in temperatures and

Houseplants can be brought outside and mixed with annuals.

will respond with increased vigour and growth.

The indoor plants will also enjoy the increased frequency of waterings and the quantity of water. For some reason, and I am guilty of this myself, we are willing to water more frequently outdoors than indoors. I'm not sure if we do this purposefully or if it is simply a case of being forgetful. It may be in my case that I enjoy playing with the hose and sprayer outdoors. Whatever the reason, your indoor plants will love being outdoors. You will also find it easier to fertilize, prune and treat them with insecticides outdoors.

Be vigilant for any infestations that may occur while the plant is enjoying its outdoor vacation. Treat any pest problems quickly. Spray the plant with a sharp stream of water to knock off the culprits. Sometimes that is all that is needed. If the pests persist, use an insecticidal soap or an organic pesticide such as Doktor Doom Botanics before bringing your plant back indoors. Then check the plant very carefully for any pests you may have missed.

Another consideration to bear in mind is to ensure that the exposure you are offering your plant outdoors is the correct one. A plant that has been kept out of direct sun in the house cannot be plunged into full sun without causing some problems. Even a plant that is used to being in full sun indoors should never be placed in full sun outdoors. In a home, the full sun exposure usually means that the sun is coming in through a window and not from above. Outdoors, of course, the sun is not only coming in laterally but also swings overhead. The overall exposure to sun is far greater outdoors, and this is why plants do so well outdoors. Even a plant that is used to being shaded in the house should have some extra shade outdoors until it gets acclimated.

Plan out your new balcony or deck garden carefully to take advantage of your new plants. For example, a semi-shaded spot in a corner would be a great place to feature a parlour palm (*Chamaedora elegans*). A Boston fern (*Nephrolepis exaltata* 'Bostoniensis') would look great combined with the parlour palm, instantly creating a Victorian look to your balcony or deck. Since your new outdoor garden will mostly be in semi-shaded or shaded areas, expect to have that cool look of the tropics with the placing of your indoor plants. An ideal complement to this setting would be some colourful annuals to add that splash of colour. Some orange and yellow nasturtiums would make a colourful statement. Don't be afraid to mix in as many annuals as you see fit. The extra colour will set off the foliage plants very nicely.

In fall, make sure you start bringing your indoor plants inside over time and acclimatizing them to the indoors well in advance of freeze-up.

For more on container gardening, see also:

p. 130 What are some flowers that would look good together in a container in the shade?

Trees and Shrubs

In landscaping circles, trees and shrubs are thought of as the foundations of any landscape. The placement of these landscape features can be critical to having a yard that offers eye appeal.

Deciding on the style of landscape for your landscaping plan can be confusing. We can simplify the factors influencing your choice of landscape down to four basic ones:

1. Cost: How much expense are you willing to put into your landscape?

2. Look: What look are you really after, and what will make you happy?

3. Maintenance: How much time and effort do you really want to put into the garden?

4. Function: Will the landscape serve a purpose, such as providing sitting areas and shady spots to relax in, or will your garden be your entertainment centre?

Landscape style is one of those questions where there are no right or wrong answers. The type of landscape you choose will depend on the aforementioned factors as well as your personal preferences and tastes. It is not unlike some of those decorating shows on the tube where so-called expert designers pooh-pooh someone's choice in home décor. The same holds true for the home landscape. Some experts are constantly spouting about choosing a style and sticking with it. I'm of the opinion that if you like it, that's really all that matters.

Apart from certain rules of landscaping, such as never planting trees too close to a house or never planting so much plant material that you can't see the house, there really are no hard and fast rules about which style to use. What I can offer here are some tips that may make your choice of landscape and planning it easier:

- Make an outline drawing of your house and yard. It can be simple, but a scale drawing is very helpful when planning your landscape design.

- Gentle curves add interest to a landscape. Use a garden hose to outline a pleasing shape before breaking ground. Straight lines are not as appealing but, having said that, some formal gardens in the world have all straight lines and are stunning. It's an excellent example of there being no rules in landscaping.

- Use some restraint in the selection of plants. A good rule is to limit yourself to three kinds of shrubs in the front yard. Consider colour, texture, growth habits and so on.

- Add interest with an accent plant and colourful bedding plants near the front door.

- Pay close attention to the information about the mature width and height of the plants, and don't plant too close to the house.

- Using plants in odd-numbered groupings (3, 5, 7 and so on) is more interesting than even numbers. It is better not to arrange the shrubs in straight lines like toy soldiers. When one plant dies or is stunted, it becomes very obvious in a straight-line setting. Again, having said that, I have an area in my yard where I have single plants of every type because I collect plants. I have yet to walk away from a garden centre without making a purchase. If I like a plant a lot, I buy it, and it goes into my collection bed where I can enjoy it for what it is and its attributes, not because it fits into some landscape plan.

- Use trees to frame and shade the house, not to hide it. Choose trees with a mature size that will be in good proportion to the size of the house. If you are in a new subdivision with a narrower yard, keep that in mind as well when choosing a feature tree. Putting a tree that gets 9 m wide when mature on a lot that is 10 m wide is a poor choice.

- Spend time in preparing beds using good organic matter and fertilize regularly—it will pay off. If you put this step off until after you plant, adding organic matter or soil conditioners becomes difficult.

My old landscape design instructor taught me a principle that I still use to this day. The idea of landscape design in a yard, especially a backyard, is to create a series of "outdoor rooms." Doing so breaks up the expanse of the entire yard and creates areas and pockets of interest throughout the area.

These "rooms" can be created by using low hedging as borders, defining plants or through the use of a shrub bed or even something as simple as an edging material to break up the run of one area and define another.

Don't be afraid to use your own likes and dislikes in the plan. Decide early in the plan if you are following a formal idea such as an English garden or if you are going totally informal. It will help you in your planning.

Have a budget in mind when designing and planning your yard. Far too many gardeners have "Cadillac plans" and a "Volkswagen budget." Before you begin a project that will be an investment, take the time to carefully price out the plants, trees, shrubs and accessories to see if your plan is a reasonable one.

Remember that the entire yard need not be done in one fell swoop either. Many gardeners construct their yards over a period of several years to accommodate financial considerations and work load. Trying to do too much all at once can make the task a drudge and a chore rather than an enjoyable one.

I have chosen to place the chapter on trees and shrubs last because without a doubt it is an area in which I receive the most questions. This fact never surprises me because trees and shrubs truly are the basics of any landscape. In many cases, they can also be the largest single investment in the landscape, depending on how mature they are when purchased. Homeowners are also very interested in dealing with any problems these plants have at an early stage so as to preserve their investment. A tree that is diseased, dying or dead can not only ruin a landscape, but the removal of that tree can also be expensive and messy. Replacing a mature tree can be expensive, so it is easy to see why homeowners ask so many questions about trees and shrubs.

Questions and Answers: Tree Diseases and Pests

Q. I have had problems with spruce sawfly in the past. Is there anything I can do to prevent this problem from happening again?

A. Spruce sawfly larvae are what you need to be vigilant for. These larvae are caterpillar-like at this stage. When first hatched, they are 3–4 mm long and have yellowish bodies and yellow-brown heads. When mature, they are 16–20 mm long and are dark glossy green with lighter stripes down the side. The heads are reddish brown. The adult females lay eggs in June by making a slit in the bark of a spruce branch just at the base of a needle. They deposit a single egg. After hatching, the larvae feed for 30–40 days until mature. At this point, they drop to the ground and form a cocoon in which they overwinter. In spring (end of May, beginning of June) the adults emerge, and the cycle starts over again.

You should treat trees that were affected last year as soon as you see any eggs or larvae. Start by spraying from the top of the tree on down. New growth needs special attention, because that is what the critters like to feast on most. If you treat the soil under the trees in the following few weeks, you will be able to control some of the emerging insects. Anyone who had the problem in the past year should be doing the soil treatments and tree application before the end of May. Sawflies normally survive for three years, so treating the soil of an infected tree in fall will also help eliminate the sawfly from overwintering under the infected trees. For these applications, I recommend using Doktor Doom Residual under the tree and spraying Doktor Doom House & Garden on the tree itself.

Q. Our majestic poplar (I don't know the exact type; it's not a cottonwood or aspen, and it's as wide as it is tall) in the backyard has been trimmed by a professional company over the last few years. Last fall, we discovered some sawdust at the back of the trunk, and a small part of the trunk seemed "gone" (like an open wound, not a defined hole). The arborist looked at it, and his verdict was that a burying insect was in the tree, and that he could do nothing but cut it down in two to three years. We are stunned, and not quite ready to throw in the towel. This tree is over 40 years old. It is the largest tree on the street, and you can see it from afar. Other than the "hole" in the trunk, it is completely healthy and beautiful. Would you have a recommendation for us?

A. The problem you describe is most likely a poplar wood borer. You can read all about these voracious little guys at the Agriculture and Agri-Food Canada website: http://www4.agr.gc.ca/AAFC-AAC/display-afficher.do?id=1199732202622&lang=eng.

You can actually insert a wire into the hole and keep poking it and moving it along in an in-and-out fashion not unlike a plumber's snake. You will eventually reach the borer if you have enough patience and can spear him with the wire, ending his munching days forever. I would certainly try this method, as you likely can save the tree on your own.

Q & A. During a recent appearance at a garden centre, I had a gentleman stop by to ask about a problem he had with his bur oak tree. When he showed me the photo of his tree, I initially could not see the issue. To me, it looked like acorn clusters, but upon closer examination, I could see that the bumps were not acorns but some type of gall.

One of my best resources is the Alberta Bugs mailing list I belong to. This emailing list contains some of the province's premiere insect experts. I simply entered the symptoms and information I had and sent it off to the list. Within an hour, I had replies with ideas as to what this problem was. The first to reply was Mike Jenkins, the Biological Sciences technician with the City of Edmonton Environmental Services. Here is Mike's reply:

"Yes, it sounds like rough oak bullet gall wasp. They are caused by a Cynipid wasp (*Disholcaspis quercusmamma*), and the galls cause considerable cosmetic damage to bur oak trees. In the first year or so, the gall also exudes a sticky, honeydew-like substance that can be very attractive to ants and yellow jacket wasps. Many (if not most) bur oaks have at least some galls, and some trees have almost every branch end covered in the galls.

"Unfortunately, by the time the galls are visible, there is very little to do for control. The wasp larva is well protected inside the gall, so any sort of spray is ineffective. A systemic pesticide might work to kill the larva, but it wouldn't get rid of the galls that have already formed. The galls will fall off on their own after several years. Galls can be removed from the tree without serious injury to the tree but it is time-consuming, and may be very difficult on large trees with tall branches.

"One study in Colorado found that galls under 9 mm in diameter were often host to a wasp parasitoid that had killed the Cynipid larva in the gall, while galls over 11 mm had rarely been parasitized. They recommend that if you are removing galls, only remove those that are 11 mm or larger, to leave the parasitic wasps capable of attacking another generation.

"The City of Edmonton Environmental Services Lab has collected a variety of galls from oak trees in the city, and are rearing them to see whether or not we have any similar parasitoids in this region."

The next reply was from Scott Digweed with the Canadian Forest Service. He has been studying this problem since 2003. Here is Scott's reply in part:

"...last year, many of the populations of *D. quercusmamma* that I was monitoring were absolutely hammered by birds (not sure which species). The birds have no problems getting past the wasps and ants on the honeydew, and apparently can become very adept at opening the galls (before they harden) to extract the tasty Cynipid larvae. They are probably our best bet to check *D. quercusmamma* populations."

Scott also mentioned that treatment for existing galls is, "to clip off the affected branch tips (or just break off the galls) in late September once they've gone brown and hard, but before the adult females emerge to oviposit in October."

Q. I am hoping you might have some information regarding bronze birch borers. I have two paper birch clumps that are dying—can I do anything to save them this spring? They are beautiful trees and it saddens me to have to tear them out and replace them.

A. According to the University of Saskatchewan, the bronze birch borer has developed into the most important pest of ornamental birch trees. This insect will usually attack older trees that are stressed. They bore under the bark and then feed on the sap. They commonly attack the top of the tree and work their way down. One of the symptoms of a tree with bronze birch borer is a tree with no leaves on the top. (Note that the dead tops can also be a symptom of dieback as a result of a lack of moisture during winter.) Look for signs of the adults boring into the bark to confirm the infestation. If you see signs of holes in the shape of the letter "D," these are their entry points. The holes would be the same size as this "D."

Control is best achieved by keeping the tree as healthy as possible. One of the most important factors is moisture. Birch trees are native to areas with high water availability. In spring, birches will take up literally hundreds of gallons of water. The tree becomes stressed if this water is not available. It also reinforces the need to water birches very well in the fall. Once trees have been infested, controls are not very successful, I'm afraid.

Q. My linden tree has leaves that are covered with protuberances. I have been told they are galls and that I need to spray the tree with horticultural oil in the fall. Can you please tell me what gall is, and will it spread to other trees and shrubs?

A. The gall—or protuberance—is caused by, in your case, a mite that is attacking a single plant cell in the leaves. The attack causes injury to the cell, and it responds by creating the gall. The galls may be caused by eriophyid mites, which are host specific—meaning that each type of mite attacks only one type of plant.

Q. I noticed leaf rollers in our columnar aspens last year. Several garden centre experts have told me they won't hurt the trees; however, if they are infested on a yearly basis, I can't help but feel that it will weaken them. Spraying is useless because of the nature of the "roll," but I wonder about early treatment before the larva rolls up to feed.

A. Aspen leaf rollers seem to be more prevalent this year. While out walking with our dog in the creek area near our home, I noticed many of the poplars and aspen have been affected by the rollers. The people you spoke with are quite right in that the insects do not have an adverse effect on the vigour of the tree because the loss of foliage is relatively low. The larger problem is one of aesthetics. You can help the appearance of your tree by picking off the rolled leaves and/or pruning out heavily infested areas.

Control is difficult, as you noted, because once rolled, the insects are basically immune to any insecticide applications. There are some things you can try before they roll. In early spring and before bud break, apply dormant oil to help eliminate the egg masses that were laid the previous summer. Be sure to read the directions, as dormant oil can be harmful to certain plants such as maple or

walnut. An application of carbaryl (Sevin) may be effective if applied in late May or June while the larvae are still exposed. *Bacillus thuringiensis*, which is a biological insecticide, may also be effective if applied when the larvae are exposed.

Q. I have a 30-year-old laurel leaf willow in my backyard. It was planted too close to my fence and overhangs my neighbour's yard. Over the years, I have cut off the branches overhanging his yard so that has not been a problem.

The small branches are covered with black aphids, and the wasps are having a real banquet on the aphids. I should probably take the tree down as it is too old. My neighbour and I are concerned about the number of aphids and that they will spread throughout the neighbourhood. This tree is very large and spraying would be difficult. I assume these are aphids—black, very small, some have wings and appeared within a short period while I was away. The aphids are not on double flowering plum, apple or Russian olive trees that are real close.

Is it necessary to spray the tree to protect the neighbourhood? I could cut the tree down within a couple of weeks.

A. The problem does sound like aphids with the wasps being attracted to the honeydew that is produced by the aphids. It is also true that the aphids can spread to other trees in the area. My best suggestion would be to call a certified arborist who is qualified and able to spray a tree as large as the one you have described. The arborist can also tell you if the tree is worth the effort of spraying or if it is getting on in age and would be best cut down.

Q. I have a crab apple tree that is six years old. This year it has wonderful apples, more than it ever has had before. The branches are heavily loaded, which is great. The apples are now ripened, and we usually slice them up for baking and just plain good eating. The sad part is that almost every apple has a small white worm in it and lots of brown spots—it's basically ruining the fruit. I have never seen this problem in this fruit—what could have caused it and when? It seems like the bug must have entered the knot on the stem side but where the blossom was. Have you any answers?

A. Although I addressed this problem this past spring, it is time to revisit it again since apple harvest is beginning. The problem is apple maggot. I contacted Gerald Hilchie, an entomologist at the University of Alberta, to ask if there was any progress in a control for the insect. Here is what Gerald said:

"The Agriculture Canada information sheet states that the maggot was first detected in Edmonton in 2005. That is wrong. It has been in the city for quite a while. I first became aware of it in the late 80s. I doubt there will ever be an effective control of the pest in Edmonton because we are not an 'apple growing area.'

"Native hawthorns in the river valley, people's backyard crab apple trees and other similar trees will provide a large reservoir for re-infestation. Unless there is total community involvement, trying to control the thing is all but a lost cause. I have noticed over the years that some apple cultivars are more resistant to the maggot than others even when planted nearby. Some apples show oviposition scars, and look quite blemished early on (mid-August) and others do not show much, but are just riddled with maggots later in August. Infested fruit may be aborted by the tree (early fall) but that may not be the case for some apple varieties (especially crab apples).

"I do not advocate pesticide use, because it would require multiple treatments in mid- to late summer for control, and then only partial control. Anything that had entered the fruit would be out of reach for most domestic pesticides. And you do not want to use systemics on a food-producing plant owing to residue problems. I guess we will have to live with the problem and use sanitation to try and limit the success of the fly."

By "sanitation," Gerald means ensuring that any infested fruit that falls from apple and crab apple trees is disposed of by placing it in a plastic trash bag and setting it out with the other trash for pick up. Do not compost these fruits. Removing the fruit from the ground will keep the maggots from burrowing into the soil and pupating.

You can also try using traps that can be found in some garden centres. They look like large red apples and you paint on a coating of a sticky trap material such as Tanglefoot. The adults lay their eggs directly into the apples so they will become trapped when trying to lay eggs on the trap.

Q. We have an oak tree that is 30 years old. It is a healthy tree except for blisters that have started appearing on the tops of the leaves. I have looked and see no sign of any kind of bugs. Should we be concerned, and what can we do about this problem?

A. I believe the problem is oak leaf blister, which is a fungal problem. The initial symptom is a slight yellowing of infected leaf tissue. This yellowing is usually followed by raised, circular blisters. The blisters are formed when the infected cells are forced to enlarge by the infection while the cells surrounding the infected cells remain rigid. The

leaves may even drop prematurely in the fall.

The disease is a pain aesthetically more than it affects the vigour of the tree. If you want to treat it, spray on a lime-sulphur solution at the rate of 10 Tbsp to 1 gallon of water. The application must be done as a dormant spray, which means applying before the leaves emerge. Collecting and disposing of the infected leaves does not help prevent the disease.

Q. I have two apple trees and they are different types. I have fireblight on one of the trees and have been cutting off and disposing of the infected branches. It does not seem to be helping, as the fireblight seems to keep spreading to more branches on the tree. Is there anything I can do to prevent the fireblight from spreading any further?

A. You are correct in trying to remove the infected branches. You should be cutting the branch at least 10 cm below the dead wood. If you make the cut any closer you could not be getting all of the diseased branch. You should also be disinfecting your cutting tools after each cut. Reusing the same tool can spread the disease itself. Disinfect in a 1:5 solution of household bleach.

You can apply a Bordeaux spray in early spring before the tree has budded out. A Bordeaux spray is copper sulphate and hydrated lime mixed in water. You can find the spray in some garden centres. The spray is a fungicide that works to protect the tree.

Q. We have a hawthorn tree that has been planted over a pair of spreading juniper shrubs and an apple tree in a slightly removed area, also planted over a spreading juniper. A couple of years ago in the spring, we thought that some of the unpicked apples had fallen into the juniper as they were soft and brown. Later, the hawthorn tree had similar growths under the tree in the juniper. We have since had to remove one of the junipers as it was severely affected. The leaves of the hawthorn are now pitted with orange bumps, and the apple tree also appears to be affected, but not very severely.

I believe that the trees and junipers are suffering from apple-cedar rust. Can you confirm that, and can you suggest a treatment program? In his book, Roger Vick suggests "that if you ensure that the plants of the primary host are not planted anywhere near the secondary host, this rust is not likely to pose a problem." The distance mentioned was "a few hundred metres," which may be possible at Devonian Gardens, but hardly reasonable in residential neighbourhoods.

A. Your diagnosis is correct. The problem is one of either cedar-apple rust or cedar-hawthorn rust. Both are related and the treatment is the same. The difference is that cedar-hawthorn rust will not cause the death of the branch it is infecting, while cedar-apple rust will. On evergreen hosts such as the junipers, you will see the formation of galls, which you described as resembling apples in a very good analogy. They look like brown apples. When mature, they send out bizarre-looking, gelatinous, orange fingers. On deciduous hosts such as your hawthorn and apple, the leaves will begin to show yellow spots. Over time, these spots will turn orange and eventually develop black spots. By mid-summer, you can see tiny tubes forming on the under surface of the leaves.

This question sent me off on one of my patented research forays. I know that there were several fungicides on the market for treating the problem, but those have been removed from the market at least for public use. I called on my friends at Apache Seeds, and Greg told me that they have been recommending the use of sulphur for treating rusts. I wasn't convinced that sulphur would be strong enough to work on something like cedar-apple rust. As I did more research, I kept finding that many experts are recommending the use of sulphur as a means of treating cedar-hawthorn and cedar-apple rusts. Your local garden centre will carry a sulphur spray. Start spraying in the spring when the flower buds are turning pink. Spray again when the petal fall is at 75 percent and once again 10 days later.

Q. I have a tree with dark purple leaves and small black berries at this time of the year. I've no idea what tree it is. It could be a sandcherry or chokecherry. It's about 3 m tall. Three years ago, a dark brown, bulky patch appeared on the bark of the tree. The problem gets worse as time goes by. Now, the top end is a big blackish brown patch, and the lower part is rectangular, about 18 cm long (vertical), 4 cm wide and 8 mm bulging out from the bark, like a rectangular tumour! There is no bark on the problem area, just wood. I've never seen anything like this before. I need help. Please tell me how to treat this disease.

A. Firstly, the tree is most likely a Schubert chokecherry. The problem sounds like black knot. This fungal disease causes the cells of the plant to go into a rapid cell production mode, which causes irregular swellings on some branches. These knots start off as corky, olive-green in colour and are firm. In time, they will turn black, hard and brittle. They persist from year to year and expand lengthwise each year. They can swell from 1.5 cm to 30 cm in length and up to 8 cm in width. The knots will rarely totally encircle a limb, but if there are numerous infections on several branches the tree's health will decline and eventually it will die.

The disease is spread by spores, and it can spread rapidly if the conditions are right. The fungus needs moisture to survive and spread. Rain helps to spread the spores, as does overwatering the plant or watering at night. Using sprinklers or irrigation systems on the tree will also compound the problem.

The disease can be controlled through pruning. Cut off the knot 10 cm below the swelling if possible. Burn or bag and dispose of any cuttings.

Q. I have had a Pembina plum for four seasons. For the second year in a row it has been having problems with its maturing fruit. About halfway through the growing season the fruit turns yellowish and expands like a balloon (sort of looks like a small nerf ball including the porous texture). If the fruit is left on the tree, it will expand to about triple in size then turn brown and fall off. Do you have any idea what's causing this problem and what can I try to prevent it from recurring?

A. I had heard of this problem before but never really knew the cause. I found the answer on the Agriculture and Agri-Food Canada website. The problem is called plum pockets.

Agriculture Canada says the disease is caused by a fungus and it can affect the leaves, shoots and fruits. It goes on to say, "Symptoms on fruit are visible soon after fruit set. The fruit becomes very large, sometimes 10 times normal plum size, hollow (without pits) and bladder like. They are yellow at the start but soon turn red and later powdery grey. Affected twigs are swollen and distorted, and affected leaves are malformed and curled."

The fungus overwinters on the infected twigs and branches and spreads via spores. Cool, wet weather is needed for the fungus to spread. The recommended control, according to the website, is to prune back infected branches and to burn or dispose of them. In addition to the pruning, a dormant spray with a fungicide is recommended. Agriculture Canada recommends 2 tbsp per gallon of thiram or a Bordeaux mixture. Bordeaux mixtures can be found in garden centres. Follow application directions carefully.

Q. We live on an acreage surrounded by natural trees including white and black poplar, willows and a variety of birch. With the dry summers we have had, many of the birch have died off. The last two summers, the trees seem to be "bleeding." They are losing sap from their leaves, enough so that the plants underneath look shiny. Over time, everything is very sticky, and the sap collects enough to turn black on the leaves below. It is happening everywhere in the yard, not just underneath the willows. We do not water our large yard, and we used a natural fertilizer on the grass in the early summer. Is there anything we can do, or is it just part of what happens after repeated dry weather?

A. Have you had a close look at the trees? Do you see any signs of aphids or spider mite webbing? When a birch or other trees have an aphid infestation the trees appear to be dripping sap from their leaves. This "sap" is actually an excretion from the insect and is called honeydew. It will drip onto other leaves or plants under the affected tree, creating the shiny look you describe. Treating a number of large trees is something best left to an arborist.

Questions and Answers: Shrub Diseases and Pests

Q. I have several lilacs, and my problem is that on some of the plants and only on some of the branches the leaves will curl up, turn brown and drop off. I have not lost any bushes from this disease yet. I think it must be a systemic disease because I have never been able to find any insects.

A. Several things may be causing your problem. Firstly, bacterial blight can cause the symptoms you described. This disease is more common on the white-flowered varieties. The disease is worse when the weather is wet and young shoots are just developing. Thin the plant to encourage air circulation and remove and destroy any diseased shoots and leaves. Avoid excessive use of nitrogen fertilizers in and around the lilacs.

Verticillium wilt can cause wilting and premature leaf drop. The disease is indiscriminate and may kill only one or several branches. There is no chemical control. Remove affected branches and destroy.

Lilac leaf miners are insects that are not easily seen in the beginning of their invasion. They burrow within the leaves, causing the leaves to turn brown. Eventually they will curl the leaves up, feeding within the curled portion. You can control even moderate infestations by simply picking off the infested leaves.

Q. I have juniper bushes along the sidewalk in my backyard, and several of them are turning brown. It has never happened before; they have always been healthy and nice and green.

A. Without having more detail, the problem might be spider mites. Take a look at the plants and see if you can see any signs of fine webbing or any sign of the spider mites themselves. They are very small, about the size of a pin head, so you will have to look closely. Take a sheet of white paper and hold it under a branch you suspect is infested and give the branch a shake. You should be able to easily see the critters on the paper if they are there. If this is the problem, sometimes just knocking them off with a sharp stream from your garden hose will work.

Q. I have a Kesselring dogwood, with nice purple bark and bronze-green foliage. My problem is aphids; they have taken over the tree. I have used insecticidal soap once a week but it doesn't get rid of them. What harm are the aphids capable of doing? The leaves are crumbled and do not fully open, and the aphids are underneath. Also, I notice ants climbing on the shrub. Are the ants doing any harm?

A. The aphids are capable of doing severe damage to the shrub if allowed to continue unabated. I suggest using an insecticide such as Doktor Doom House and Garden. I have found this product very effective in dealing with aphids. The ants you mention are not causing any problems. They are attracted to the honeydew produced by the aphids.

Q. I have a beautiful new Morden Sunrise rose that I planted over a month ago. Just this week, I noticed what I guess must be blackspot (leaves are yellowing and there are black spots on them). Can you tell me what product to use to treat this problem, and if I should remove all

Morden Sunrise rose.

of the affected leaves? I have a Persian Yellow and a Cuthbert Grant in the same bed, and they look healthy. Should I pre-treat them with anything to prevent the disease?

A. Blackspot on roses is caused by a fungus. You can help prevent blackspot by watering your roses from below and never watering on their leaves. Keep your roses away from crowded conditions because poor air circulation also contributes to the problem.

I like using Defender, which is a fungicide from Safer's. It is a sulphur-based product that actually coats the leaves and protects the plant from the fungus. It can be used as a preventative measure as well. Apply before the buds open in the spring.

Q. I am having problems with my rose bushes. They are hardy roses (Morden, etc.) and in the last few days are having two problems. White "stuff" on the leaves (possibly powdery mildew?) is making the leaves curl up and look bad. Also, there are many holes in the leaves (decimating the plants very quickly). Any ideas?

A. The white stuff is most likely powdery mildew. It can be treated with a garden sulphur spray. The holes in the leaves may be slugs, which is especially true if you cannot see any insects when checking the plants. Use slug traps or brewed coffee poured around the base of the roses.

Q. We have a cotoneaster hedge that has scurfy scale. Last year I cut it out (or thought I did). Is there another remedy other than cutting it to the ground?

A. Scale is an insect that really does not look like an insect. In fact, most times it does not look like an animal but rather a fungus. The appearance is that of many whitish spots dotting a branch or trunk. If you pick off one of the white spots, you will see a critter hiding inside the armoured shell. It is this shell that makes the insect almost impossible to control with conventional insecticides. The insecticides cannot penetrate the protective covering.

It is the adults that you find in the armour. The young "crawlers" can be treated with insecticide, but you have to apply it at just the right time to get them—it is almost impossible. The only thing you can do is to apply a product called dormant oil in the winter well before spring. The oil will suffocate the insects in their shells. You may need to reapply. Make sure you follow the manufacturer's directions carefully because this product can damage your shrubs if not used correctly.

Q. Last week I had a beautiful bed of lavatera in full bloom. This week the unopened blossoms are falling off, and the plants are looking pathetic. There seems to be an army of tiny ants all over the blossoms. I think they're getting drunk on the nectar! I've never had this problem before. Is there anything I can do other than destroy the whole mess?

A. I doubt that the ants are the problem. More likely there are aphids on the plants and the ants are "milking" them for their honeydew. I think if you were to check your plants, you'd find the aphids. Spray the plants with Doktor Doom House and Garden, making sure you get under the leaves and on the stems.

Q. I have a small bed of several varieties of hardy Explorer roses. They initially bloomed, but now the new buds seem to have been eaten by an insect of some kind that makes small brown holes all over the bud, which eventually dries up and never fully blooms. Can you tell me what this might be and how it is treated?

A. A few insects could be responsible for the damage you describe. First, it could be thrip damage. They are notorious for loving to attack the buds. Thrips are flattened insects with four long, strap-like wings fringed with long hairs. Colours vary from yellow to orange to tan, dark brown and black. The young resemble the adults except they are smaller, lack wings and are paler in colour.

Controlling thrips can be difficult because they can actually hide in the buds, making it difficult for the pesticides to reach them. Diazinon is a chemical that is effective on thrips. Repeated sprayings may be necessary to eliminate the problem.

The other insect that could be the cause is the rose weevil or rose curculio. The adult weevils are about 8 mm long, bright red in colour with a black under surface, black head and a long snout. There are no registered chemicals known to control these critters, so you will have to pick them off by hand. Removing and destroying damaged buds is another good control method with these insects. Look for the insects at the first sign of the buds forming in the spring.

Q. I have approximately 25 tender roses in my garden. Some are getting older (five to seven years), but they have thrived with some careful overwintering each year. Last year's big hail storm stripped my roses completely bare except for roses in bud. They grew more leaves, and some bloomed but most struggled. I overwintered them in the fall, and this year they came back but in a somewhat weakened state and did not bloom vigorously (some just sent up spindly long shoots). They are also struggling with powdery mildew and blackspot. I have not overwintered them yet as they have not produced any rose hips; they are still trying to bloom. It is almost as if their internal clock is broken. I gave them both liquid and the slow-release pellet rose food over the summer, and they are all situated in a sunny spot in my garden. They are a lot of work, but I absolutely love them. I would appreciate any suggestions you may have as to how to get them back on track, or should I just start over with new plants next year?

A. It never ceases to amaze me the dedication of so many gardeners to the plants they love. This email is an excellent example and reminds me of a gardener I once knew who had 200 hybrid tea roses. When I asked the gardener why she had so many roses and how much work they must be to keep them happy and to overwinter them, she looked at me in a way as if to indicate she really did not understand my question and simply said, "Because I love them all."

Without question, your roses have gone through some trauma. What they are "telling you" is that they are still recovering from the shock. Your analogy describing their internal clock as being broken is right on the money. They will take some time to recover.

First, deal with the disease problems. A spray with garden sulphur will control the powdery mildew. Use a sulphur powder on the blackspot. Do it now to keep the diseases from cropping up next season. I would also help them along by pruning them back in the spring. Plants that have been shocked appreciate being pruned back. In this way they can concentrate on recovering rather than maintaining a larger plant body. Be careful not to overfertilize. The slow-release rose food is a good choice. I would not give up on them yet.

Questions and Answers:
Tree Problems

Q. I have a bed with globe cedar, ninebark, birch and a double flowering plum in it. I have had these plants for over 20 years with no problems until recently. There are suckers of some type appearing in my lawn near this bed. How do I get rid of these suckers and what is causing this?

A. I was puzzled by this question because none of the trees or shrubs that you mentioned should cause this suckering problem. I called the gentleman who had left the question to ask if there was a mayday tree close to this suckering area. He said there was indeed a mayday very close to the problem.

The problem, most likely, are suckers coming from surface roots of the mayday. Maydays are notorious for suckering from their surface roots. However, the problem may also be as a result of young maydays springing

Mayday tree.

forth from seeds that dropped from the previous season's fruit. I have seen literally thousands of plants germinating under the parent mayday right in the middle of a lawn. There is little you can do about this, other than setting your lawn mower a little lower in the area where this is happening and cutting all the suckers or sprouts down.

Q. We planted an Amur cherry four years ago. It now stands approx 4.5–6 m high and has a 8 cm trunk. It has grown very well until this summer. It had been leaning slightly to the left, owing to slope and prevailing winds. However, a wind storm in July pulled it down until it was almost lying on our driveway although no roots were exposed. We staked it on the right side. One month later, another windstorm pulled it down, but this time to the right side, with a bit of the roots showing. We then staked it as well on the left side. I'm not sure why this tree's roots are so unstable and what will become of it as it grows bigger? We cannot stake it for the rest of its life can we? What can be done to help the tree support itself? By the way, it receives a fair amount of runoff from our neighbours on the right.

A. Your problem may be just more than the tree not being staked properly. It may be planted on a site that has compacted clay soil and/or shallow topsoil. It does sound like the planting site does not drain properly if a four-year-old tree is toppling over

so frequently. I would relocate the tree if possible. If that is not possible, then your tree needs to be staked properly. Secure it on three sides of the tree either with metal stakes and tree wires or with ropes tied to the tree and then to smaller stakes in the ground. This tree needs to be stabilized quickly. It has gone through a lot of trauma already. Ensure that the tree wires or ropes are not sitting directly on the tree. Slip a piece of old garden hose over the wire or rope to prevent it from rubbing directly on the trunk.

Once you have staked the tree, take the time to tamp down the soil around the base of the tree. Do a thorough job of this tamping to ensure you have removed any air pockets that may have formed around the roots. Form a dam with soil around the base of the tree to divert the water that is coming from the neighbour. You will not have to keep this tree staked forever. It just needs enough time being stabilized to allow its roots to grow and secure the tree. If you properly stabilize the tree now and do the tamping, it should be just fine. If it is properly staked and tamped, you should need to leave it staked for only one or two growing seasons. —

Q. We purchased a large caliper (10–15 cm) Dropmore Linden tree in the summer of 2003 prior to it leafing out. When it arrived to be planted, about 30–40 percent of the branches were dead or had died back. We planted it on a small hill in the grass with the root ball mounding out of the grass; we intended to bring more dirt up to the ball. However, we liked the look of the "hill" it created and left it.

For two years in a row, it has leafed out to the top of about five to seven branches and leafed out halfway up other branches. The leaves are about 1–2.5 cm big with some larger ones at the bottom of the tree (clearly not the size they should be). We've also noticed that some sort of caterpillar/worm has been eating whatever leaves it has. The caterpillar is two-toned striped brown/cream. My questions are:

1. Should we spray the tree for the caterpillars and with what product?

2. Should we trim the branches back or give it a few more years to see if the branches come back? Is it bad to leave dead branches on a tree? If we should prune, when is the best time?

3. Would a general fertilizer or a root fertilizer be best?

4. Should we just yank the tree out and start over? I'd rather not, but if it's going to take years and years— around 10 years—for it to recover it might be the best option.

This tree is very important to us as it is supposed to provide us with some shade in a west-facing backyard. We

did contact the company that sold us the tree about its condition. Their arborist said it should be fine as it had leafed out to the top and the dieback was over the entire tree, not just on one side.

A. You should have contacted the firm that sold you the tree when it arrived with 30–40 percent of the branches dead. You may have compounded the problem with a tree that sounds like it was already in some difficulty by not planting it at the correct depth. It is critical when planting trees or shrubs to plant them at the same depth they were planted in at the nursery. By leaving a large portion of the roots above the ground, you have exposed the roots to air and drying out. That is what is causing the tree to die back. Below is a plan for what I think you should do.

Either bring in extra soil to cover the rootball properly or dig up the tree, dig the original hole deeper and replant the tree. Do that as soon as possible. I fear that the tree will not survive much longer if it is not done immediately. The decreased leaf size is a definite sign that this tree is under stress.

Spray the tree with an insecticide such as Doktor Doom to eliminate the caterpillar infestation.

Trim off all dead or damaged branches on the tree. It does nothing for the aesthetics of the tree to leave on the dead branches. Also, the dead branches could pull off in a strong wind and rip or tear the bark causing further damage.

This tree can be saved if planted at the right depth. It will take some time for it to recover, but it should recover.

Q. I am hoping you can settle an argument I am having with my son. He says that dew worms are not found as far north as Edmonton, and I say they are.

A. I hope you bet lunch on this question. Dew worms are found in Edmonton.

Q. Can you advise whether I should cut off lower branches of spruce trees when only the ends have needles and the inside of the tree is all dead and dried out, or should I not cut these branches? The trees are otherwise very healthy.

A. This issue is one where, if you have 10 gardeners discussing it, you will have 10 different answers. It is very much a personal choice. You will not harm the tree by removing a few lower limbs, but some purists believe that you will ruin the appearance of the spruce. If the tree looks ugly with the dead areas showing through, then I would cut off the lower branches.

Many gardeners comment on how removing the lower branches opens up the yard to the light. I have seen some trees whose lower branches have been removed to a height of 1.8 m or more. I think those trees look a little silly, but that's my opinion.

Q. We have a Schubert chokecherry in our front yard outside the east kitchen window. The house is 32 years old, and the tree may have been planted fairly early in the life of the house. It offers us speckled shade and privacy, as well as berries and a resting place for birds. We love it.

On the other hand, each year since we moved in four years ago, the tree sends up more and more suckers into the lawn and garden at its base. Two years ago, after the drought years, someone suggested the tree might need fertilizing, so I buried some fruit tree fertilizer spikes into its drip line. Perhaps there were fewer suckers last year, but this year there seem to be twice as many. We usually cut the suckers off at ground level, but in my more mean-spirited moments, I spray them with Round-Up. It makes no apparent difference. What next? How can I minimize the suckers and enjoy the tree?

A. I'm afraid that nothing will work on controlling the suckers other than cutting them down as soon as you see them. There is a product in the U.S. called Sucker Stopper, but after checking, I don't think it is available yet in Canada. You could try laying down heavy duty landscape fabric in the area where the suckers are coming up, but sometimes that will just force them to come up elsewhere. It is one of the major disadvantages to the Schubert chokecherry.

I do not recommend using Round-Up. It works by finding its way down into the root system and killing the plant. If you use too much of the chemical you could kill—or at least damage—your tree.

Q. Our Thunderchild flowering crab apple tree has not bloomed for the past two springs. The tree is about 15 years old. We really miss the beautiful pink blossoms. Otherwise it seems quite healthy.

A. There are several reasons for a flowering tree or shrub to not bloom. The most common relating to your case are:

1. A late-spring frost injury at the time of budding.

2. Cultural practices: the tree may be too close to a lawn and is getting too much nitrogen from the lawn fertilizer. This excess nitrogen will inhibit flower production.

3. The tree may not be getting enough sun. Sometimes the environment around a tree changes as it ages. Surrounding trees get larger and screen the sun.

Q. We recently planted a Toba Hawthorn tree in our front yard and it is not doing very well. A year ago we removed a Colorado spruce from the same spot and had the stump and most roots removed. We shovelled away all the needles and kept working in new soil over the course of the past year.

On July 29, we purchased the hawthorn from a local nursery. We planted it the next day, following very carefully the planting instructions we were given. We watered the plant in very well and used root booster as well. That week, the weather was not very hot, and it rained several times as well, so we did not water more. We were away for two days at the end of the week, and when I looked at the tree Saturday (six days after planting), the leaves were curling up and turning brown. We watered it twice a day for the next three days, even though the ground was moist when we noticed the brown leaves. The leaves have continued to brown and fall off, but I am worried we are drowning the tree.

My question now is what to do—should we dig the tree back up and amend the soil more?

A. I am a big believer in watering the heck out of newly planted trees. In your case, I don't think water is the problem. What may have happened is that there may be an air pocket trapped around the roots.

A very large Russian olive tree.

Air pockets have been known to cause all of the symptoms you have and can kill the tree if not corrected. Try stepping down hard all the way around the tree. If you find yourself sinking in too easily, there may be an air pocket. Take a garden hose and turn it on slightly. Then push the tip of the hose down into the soil around the tree with the water running. Push it in as far as you can and then pull up slowly. Do it all the way around the roots, going up and down many times. That should collapse any air bubbles.

Q. Our once-beautiful Russian olive was planted at least 20 years ago. This year, it was very late in leafing out and

somehow the upper part of the tree looks dead. Are we being too anxious (we've had a late spring); should we wait a while longer or can we prune now, or is it wise to wait until late winter or early spring? When we do prune, it will have a drastic effect on the cosmetics. How much of the live portion of the tree can we prune at once?

A. Russian olives do not tolerate heavy clay soils that drain poorly. We have so much clay in this area that sometimes it is difficult to avoid planting in it unless you remove a large amount of clay in the planting hole and replace it with well-draining soil. Even then it may not help;

eventually the tree roots will grow into the clay.

Although the tree will grow in most soils, mature Russian olives do not always adapt well to changing soil conditions. If the area was dry at the time of planting but owing to changing conditions becomes a wet area, or if we have a wet summer and the soil does not drain sufficiently where the tree is planted, the tree will not do well.

All you can do is hope that this tree will recover, but it might not. If the pruning needed is extensive, I recommend calling an arborist to do the job and to advise on how much of the tree can be removed safely.

Q. I have a columnar pine that I've had for eight years. It's about 46 cm wide and 3.5 m tall. I'm not sure if it's *Pinus mugo* 'Fastigiata' or *Pinus strobus* 'Fastigiata.' It's only supposed to get 60–90 cm wide and 6 m tall. During the winter of 2006–07, we had a wet snowfall and the branches were flopped right over, some almost touching the ground. I was afraid they were going to break off so I shook the snow off and then loosely wrapped chicken wire around the branches. I thought it would help strengthen the branches (like training bonsai) so I left it on probably for about 15 months. When I removed the chicken wire, the branches splayed again. Did I mistakenly think

my efforts would strengthen the branches? Should I put the chicken wire back on? Is there anything I can do to correct this problem?

A. I have to admit that I am surprised that your solution did not work. It was an excellent method to correct the splaying, and 15 months should have been enough time for the branches to find their way into being upright again. It may be worth the effort to put back the chicken wire and try it again. You are quite right in that bonsai hobbyists often manipulate branches by wiring them into place. After a time the wire is removed and the branches remain in the desired position. The principle behind the bonsai method is not unlike what you did to your pine. You might want to try making the wire "cage" a little tighter. That is the only thing I might do differently.

Q. My crab apple tree trunk cracked last spring in the middle section of the trunk. The wood normally covered by bark is exposed. The area is dry and otherwise the tree is healthy. What is the cause of this cracking? Should I apply anything before winter to protect the tree?

A. Don't seal the wound. You could just trap the problem under the sealant. If the problem is a disease, sealing it would be the worst thing to do. If the wound is dry and there are no other symptoms, it may simply be bark cracking from excess moisture or it even may be from frost damage last winter or early spring. I would just keep an eye on it until spring and see what it is doing then. There is little you can do now anyway.

Q. I have several different types of pines in my backyard. I noticed in fall that a lot of the needles yellowed and then fell to the ground. What causes this to happen?

A. It is a normal occurrence in pine trees that is simply called fall needle drop. The needles that are turning yellow or brown are actually the older needles on the inside of the tree and it is not a problem.

Some years the needles will turn yellow quickly, while in other years they turn much more slowly and not nearly as noticeably. Pines normally shed their needles in fall. This natural needle discoloration may be more noticeable on trees that have experienced root stress that can be caused by poor growing conditions, such as drought during summer. These dry conditions, coupled with heavy clay soils, compound the stress to the roots and make the needle drop more dramatic.

The newest growth—this year's needles—is still green and healthy. You can help the trees by watering them very well during the growing season and ensuring they are watered in well for fall.

Q. We have a number of Colorado spruce trees over 9 m tall that I water in every fall. I assume there is no point in watering at the base of the trees, so I have been watering at the drip line. However, the roots must go halfway across the neighbours' lots. Should I be watering a much larger area than the drip line?

A. I'm glad to hear you are watering in your evergreens in the fall. It is one of the most important tasks on the fall gardening "to-do" list. Everyone should take the time to keep watering all evergreens very well right up until freeze-up. Since evergreens do not go completely dormant in winter, this source of moisture is extremely important to help them survive winter. While true for all evergreens no matter where they are located in the landscape, it is even more important for those that are foundation plantings and are close to houses or other outbuildings. For these evergreens you may even have to give the plants a drink during warm times of the winter months, especially if there is little snow cover in these foundation planting areas.

As for your question, watering up to the drip line is fine, but you can also set a lawn sprinkler to provide moisture to all areas of the roots. I would not be too concerned about the roots that enter into neighbouring properties as long as you are getting lots of moisture on your side. Deep watering is important as well. I like to use a root feeder to do the deep watering for my evergreens. I insert the root feeder every few feet and allow the water to run to the point of runoff. When inserting the feeder, insert it to a depth of 60–90 cm.

Q. I have some winter damage on two of my evergreens. One is a dwarf Alberta spruce and the other is a cedar. The spruce is on the south side and is planted in a bed right next to the house. It is showing a lot of browning on the side that faces the house. The cedar appears to be turning brown from the inside. What is the cause of both of these problems and what can I do about it?

Dwarf Alberta spruce.

A. Dwarf Alberta spruce is a plant that is very prone to winter burn. The browning can occur from being burned by the winter sun or from the drying winter winds. The likely cause in your case is sun damage. Your house reflects the sun directly onto the spruce that is planted next to it and that burns the sensitive Alberta spruce. I see so many examples of this plant having this type of damage. Dwarf Alberta spruce definitely needs to have protection from the winter elements. It should be watered in very, very well in the fall. I also recommend erecting a burlap screen to keep the sun and prevailing winds off the plant.

The cedar is likely still suffering from last year's hot summer and lack of moisture. Cedars will often begin to brown from the inside out if there has been a lack of moisture. Make sure you keep watering it throughout the summer. Next fall make sure you water it in well right up until freeze-up.

Q. Could you tell me how I should handle the soil in my backyard in preparation for planting a maple tree hardy to zone 3? I have just cut down a 6 m spruce tree and have a 1.2 m stump leftover. Once I have the stump removed, how should I handle the spruce tree roots and subsequently the soil in preparation for planting another tree? We are thinking of a maple tree because it grows quickly and will provide us with privacy. The grass in our backyard is a mess from the acidity of the spruce tree needles.

A. I assume you are going to have the stump ground out. If so, the grinding will remove most roots in the immediate proximity of the stump. You might ask the company doing the grinding to pay extra attention to removing as many of the roots in the area as they can. Once that has been done, I would remove a lot of the soil that remains in the area. This soil is likely poor in quality and has been depleted of much of its nutrients. I would dig down at least 20–25 cm and replace the soil with a good quality topsoil. Mix compost or manure into the topsoil, one part organic matter to three parts topsoil.

When digging the hole to plant the maple, ensure the planting hole is at least twice as large as the rootball of the maple. Use the same topsoil compost mix to fill in the hole around the rootball. I would also use some Myke for trees and shrubs in the bottom of the planting hole.

Q. I have two dwarf balsam firs that took a terrible beating over the winter and so had lots of brown needles in the spring. They have recovered nicely with lots of new green growth but the brown needles are still very noticeable, and I would like to get rid of them. Are the branches with the brown needles ever going to produce new growth again, or can I just remove the branches?

I have written to you several times in the past about the Swedish columnar aspen that was literally taking over my yard. It seems to get worse every year and now is starting to affect other well-established plants, and we are regretfully now considering removing it. It is about 9–10.5 m high and is very healthy (obviously). Other than having a professional come in and remove the tree, can you think of any way we can do it ourselves and still have it survive? My son has an acreage and would love to have the tree. If we can't move it without killing it, do you have some general suggestions about removing it?

Last year I did manage to start several small trees from the shoots the columnar aspen was spreading throughout the yard. They survived the winter and now are 90 cm–1.5 m tall and growing rapidly. It is definitely time to move these to their permanent home at my son's acreage. What is the best way to do so? What is the best time of year to take them out of the ground and move them? Can I do it now? Should I transplant them into pots for a period of time, or can I simply take them directly from my yard to his yard?

A. The brown on the branches will not come back, so pruning it off is your best option.

Moving a 9–10.5 m tree on your own is almost impossible. I would not recommend attempting it. The likelihood of the tree surviving is very poor indeed if not done professionally. A tree-moving service might be able to do it for you if they can have access to the tree with their tree spade.

Spring is the best time to move these trees before they leaf. There is no need to pot them up prior to the move. When you are ready to move them, wrap the rootball in some burlap to keep it intact during the transport and go right from your yard to your son's.

Q. I have two 10-year-old bristlecone pines, some distance from each other, and one is not as happy as the other one. Its new candles are consistently fewer and shorter. Also, its colour is slightly paler, and the needles tend to have a touch of brown just at the tips. I have ruled out lack of nutrients, since these trees normally grow in very poor conditions. The only problem I can think of is excessive wetness. Would you say the symptoms I have described are consistent with such a situation?

A. You are quite correct in suspecting that the problem is moisture related. Bristlecone pines will not tolerate wet

conditions at all. Yes, the symptoms you describe could be a result of too much moisture.

Q. I have a sour cherry sucker growing from a root that is more than 8 cm in diameter. I cannot cut the root to pot the sucker, so what can I do to induce the sucker to root? The sucker is now about 30 cm tall, and I intend to use it as a rootstock for grafting.

A. Normally, I would tell you to root prune the tree by cutting through the root at the base of the sucker, but an 8 cm root is a problem. Instead, cut off the sucker from the root and dip the sucker's cut end in rooting hormone powder, which can be found in most garden centres. Stick the hormone-dipped end into a container of moist sand. Keep the sucker moist, and mist the top occasionally. Keep it out of direct sun. It should root in a few weeks.

Q. We planted four regular aspens in our backyard 10 years ago. We like them very much, except for one thing. Whenever we have rain and high wind, they want to keel over. We've had them anchored to the fence for a few years now, but every once in a while a rope breaks and we have to do an emergency rescue. Our backyard is not lawn, but chips and fabric, and is well settled.

Our two Swedish columnar aspens are steady as a rock in the same conditions, so I don't know why the other ones don't get a better foothold. Have you any suggestions? Would cutting them down by a third force them to make stronger roots? In the wild, they're usually surrounded by underbrush, but that wouldn't be suitable in our yard.

A. Newly planted trees and especially large ones need a very secure attachment in order for the roots to get a hold. If the wind moves the tree trunk even slightly the roots will move as well. If the roots are moving they are creating air pockets and are unable to set themselves in the soil. From your email it sounds as if the rope being used is not very reliable if it keeps breaking. It also sounds as if you are attaching the tree to the fence in only one spot. Use a good quality nylon rope tied very securely to stakes that are driven into the ground securely as well. You should have at least three ropes and three stakes spaced around the tree. Leave the ropes in place for at least two to three months and check them from time to time to make sure they are still tight.

To keep the rope from chafing the trunk of the tree, I like to use old garden hose cut into lengths around 30 cm long. Thread the rope through the hose and wrap the hose around the trunk before tying the rope to the stakes.

There is no need to cut the trees back in order to stimulate root growth; just provide a good solid support for the trees.

Q. We have a birch in our backyard that appears to be dead. It has no leaves. It was healthy for the first six years and over the last two it just went downhill fast. Why?

A. I get many, many questions about birch trees. Over the past few winters and growing seasons, we have experienced what some are referring to as drought conditions. Even though we have had some moisture, it has not been enough nor has it been the same as in the past. Now I can hear some of you saying that the weather office has been saying our levels were normal. What we are lacking are those nice three-day gentle rains that give everything a good soaking. We get similar amounts of rain but all delivered in a few downpours that end up running off rather than soaking in. Couple this situation with a few winters with relatively low snowfall totals.

Birch trees are very shallow-rooted trees: most of their roots are very close to the surface of the soil. They are therefore prone to dry conditions or lack of moisture. If nature does not provide the necessary moisture and there is not supplemental moisture coming, these trees will begin to stress. This stress will continue over time, and if the moisture levels are not increased, the stress will lead to the death of the trees.

The answer to this problem is simple. Water. Get the hose out. Place the end at the base of the tree and turn the water on so it is trickling out, not pouring out. The slower the trickle the better because this slow application of moisture will allow the water to soak into the ground deeply rather than running off if applied with pressure. Let the water run slowly for two hours or more. Once you notice the water starting to run off instead of being absorbed, turn off the hose. Do this type of watering at least once a month. If your tree is stressed now, do it once a week.

The key, without a doubt, is to continue this watering right into fall. The time before freeze-up is critical not only for birch trees but also for cedars and many other trees and shrubs. Water them in very well in fall.

Q. I want to plant trees in our backyard along two fence lines to act as a screen from the alley and neighbours. The fences (1.8 m high solid wood) are on the south and east sides of my yard. What would be a suitable tree for this purpose? I prefer conifers so they act as a screen all year. I don't want them to get too high or too wide but want a hedge that would get fairly dense and is hardy for this area.

Also, what is the best way to prepare the beds for planting the trees? The area is currently in lawn. I prefer not to just strip off the sod and take it to the landfill. Can I compost or recycle the sod?

A. I suggest planting spruce as a hedge. In the past, gardeners were restricted in the size of the spruce available, and ones that were used for hedging had to be pruned on a regular basis. Some newer varieties on the market now are a perfect size for hedging. One that comes to mind is the columnar spruce (*Picea pungens* 'Fastigata'). This tree grows to 3 m tall and 1 m wide. The narrow, upright habit is perfect for your application. The bonus with these trees is that they have a brilliant blue colour. If you are looking for something a little taller, you could try the Bakeri spruce. This tree grows to 4 m tall and 2 m wide. It too has a conical shape and has long, dark blue needles.

The planting bed preparation is very important. A little extra effort in preparing the bed properly will reap benefits for years to come. Once you have determined the planting scheme, mark each hole with a stick. Take some care in ensuring that the holes are evenly spaced from each other. Dig each hole twice as wide and deep as the rootball of the tree you will be planting. If the soil you have removed from each hole is of good quality, you can work with that. If it is not, get some good topsoil. Remove any clay that comes out of the hole and discard it. Use the soil/organic additive mix to refill the hole.

I like to mix a good compost or manure such as mushroom manure with the topsoil. The ratio should be two parts soil to one part compost or manure. Break down any lumps you find in the soil and mix in the organic matter well. I no longer advocate adding bone meal to the planting hole. Not only does bone meal take a very long time to break down, but today's bone meal is not the same as the one used by our grandparents. Bone meal today has had many of the desirable components removed for other purposes. Gardening expert Art Drysdale convinced me of this fact. If you want to read more, visit www.artdrysdale.com/april2001.html.

I now recommend adding Myke to each planting hole. Myke is an all-natural soil supplement that is normally added at the time of planting. Several Myke products contain a biological growth supplement, which is a mycorrhizal fungus. This fungus establishes a beneficial relationship with the roots of the plant. Growing in association with the roots of plants, the mycorrhizal fungus increases the ability for the roots to take up water and nutrients. This totally beneficial fungus offers some amazing results. It has proven so effective that some of the garden centres and nurseries are adding a stipulation to their plant warranties saying that Myke should be used at the time of planting of the tree or shrub. Make sure you use the Myke designed for use with evergreens and follow the directions on the container.

Make sure the tree is planted at the same height as it was in the pot it came in or if balled and burlapped at the same level it was in the nursery. It is very important to tamp the soil down well around the roots when planting. That will remove any air pockets that may have formed in the soil, which can damage the tree. I like to insert a hose into the soil after planting and work it in an up and down fashion with the water running slowly. That also helps collapse air pockets.

Your sod can certainly be composted. Cut it into smaller pieces and add it to the compost pile or composter. It will break down quite nicely.

Q. My spruce trees are literally showering down large volumes of a yellow powder. I cannot ever recall seeing this before. Is this normal? There is so much that it is even accumulating in my pond and along the edges of my sidewalks. I park my truck behind my garage, and after leaving it out overnight, it is covered in this powder. I would appreciate any information you can pass on.

A. The yellow powder is actually pollen being produced by male conifers. Conifers are trees such as pine and spruce. My speculation was that the drought conditions of the past few years had caused a stress condition in the trees, and now that environmental conditions had improved, the amount of pollen production was a result of the improved conditions.

After several phone calls to Alberta Sustainable Resource Development (ASRD), I found my hypothesis to be only partially correct. Leonard Barnhardt, a plant geneticist with ASRD, referred me to some literature that stated that the conditions of the previous year are very much responsible for the production of either vegetative (growth) or reproductive buds. Hot, dry conditions tend to produce more reproductive buds, which means that there would be more pollen production.

Leonard and I also discussed how it is possible that stress caused by drought conditions can result in an increase in pollen production. The amount of pollen produced this year is a direct result of the weather last year and perhaps the stress from the last several years. There is no need for concern, as many of the conifers I have seen this year are experiencing excellent growth along with the pollen production. It also does not mean there is no longer a need to keep the trees well watered. Keeping the trees watered right up to and especially in fall before freeze-up is an excellent way of maintaining tree health.

Q. I just planted a new apple tree, and my son was playing on his bike and managed to nearly tear off a branch on my new tree. The branch was still hanging on when I got to it, and I quickly put it back in place and wrapped it with some duct tape. What should I do? Will it come back?

A. You did the right thing and may have saved your branch. Red Green would have been proud to see the use of duct tape as well! I would remove the duct tape. Do it very carefully as it will be very sticky and can easily pull the branch off as you remove it. I like to use plastic electrician's tape for such repairs. It allows me to pull it very tight to eliminate any air trapped in the repair area. Wrap several layers of tape around the break. If it is a small branch, the tape itself will hold. If it is larger, you need to wire it onto an existing branch for support. Make sure the branch is fitted well into its original position before taping and, yes, the branch should do just fine.

Q. The mountain ash tree we planted three years ago (now approximately six years old) had berries in the past, but this year it has none. Is there something wrong with it? Is there anything I can do to "fix" it for next year?

Mountain ash.

We planted several columnar aspen trees this year as well as two Manchurian ash. All were planted with Myke rooting product. The aspens (5 gallon size) were planted in spring and I watered them throughout summer and added Miracle Gro fertilizer once or twice in the summer. The ash (10 gallon size) were planted in late August. Both ash and one or two of the aspen are completely leafless—their leaves were mostly gone just prior to that recent snowfall we got and totally gone afterwards. The rest of the aspens still have plenty of leaves. My question is, is this early loss of leaves an indication that the trees will be dead by next spring and if so, is there anything that can be done to prevent the loss of these trees?

We have several spruce trees (green and blue) approximately 20 years old bordering our yard. They are currently about as tall as our house is and as tall as I would like. Is it possible or practical to have spruce trees topped so as to prevent or slow upward growth?

A. My mountain ash has the same problem, if we can call it that. Most likely just when the trees were flowering or getting ready to flower they were zapped with a late spring frost. This frost will have killed off the blossoms and any fruiting that would follow would have been lost. It is not a bad thing. The energy that a tree saves by not fruiting one year is made up for with extra growth and vigour, allowing the tree to produce even more fruit the following year. There is nothing we can do to prevent the late spring frost damage.

The loss of leaves does not necessarily mean the trees are dead. Sometimes loss of leaves is a reaction to the tree being stressed in some way. I did notice that some aspens and poplars were turning colour even before the snow you mentioned. It could be that the trees were just reacting to a frost and losing their leaves naturally. Keep a close eye on them in spring looking for signs of the buds swelling. They may not be "sleeping" but just "resting their eyes." From your description you did everything that you could have done to promote healthy growth.

Spruce can certainly be topped. It will do several things. It will slow their upward growth while encouraging the tree to fill in and become fuller. I would advise hiring a tree surgeon or qualified arborist to do this procedure. For one thing, it is dangerous getting up high enough to do the cut and secondly knowing where to make the cut is very important.

Questions and Answers: Shrub Problems

Q. We have a lake cabin that we would like to landscape with low-maintenance plants this coming spring. We go out to the property only every second week so plants that don't need a lot of water would be a must. Can you give us a list of shrubs to get us started?

A. An extensive list of plants will grow well with less or practically no water other than that offered by Mother Nature. Here are only a few common examples:

- Lilac (*Syringa* spp.): Great old standby that still works today. Fragrant blooms in spring with colours that include purples, mauves, pink, white, red and even blue. Dwarf forms 'Miss Kim' or dwarf Korean types (1–1.5 m high and wide) are available for smaller applications.

- *Potentilla* spp.: to 1.5 m high and wide. Another reliable performer in most soils and drought conditions. Blooms non-stop from early summer to fall, has great colour and is extremely low maintenance. Flower colours include white, pink, orange, red and shades of yellow.

- Juniper (*Juniperus* spp.): Great for foundation plantings, these evergreen plants are very drought tolerant. They come in myriad of shapes, sizes, colours and forms. Upright forms such as 'Skyrocket' grow 5 m tall. Low, sprawling groundcover types such as 'Blue Rug' grow 20 cm tall.

Q. I live on an acreage. At the edge of our yard along the road we have a steep incline (a ditch) that faces south. At present, the ditch is seeded in grass. The problem is that the incline is so steep that it can't be mowed, and I am tired of weed-eating it. Do you have any recommendations for what could be planted there? Our yard is an old farm site that is surrounded by lots of huge spruce trees, so I would like to go along with that theme. The soil is fairly sandy, and it gets really hot there in spring and summer.

A. One plant that comes to mind for this area would be a creeping juniper (*Juniperus horizontalis*). This plant makes an excellent woody, evergreen groundcover that is very tolerant of spots that are dry and hot. They are vigorous growers that are capable of covering a large area fairly quickly. They are an excellent plant for banks and slopes.

If you take the extra time to clip the tips of the branches for a couple of seasons, the plants will form a very dense mat that will be nearly impervious to weeds. When planting, space the plants 60–120 cm apart.

Some of the best varieties for groundcover use are:

- 'Andorra': This flat-topped variety has a compact growth habit. The foliage is a grey green and grows to a height of 45 cm. In winter, the foliage turns a purplish colour.

- 'Bar Harbor': Low grower to 20 cm high. Grey green in summer and more grey in winter.

- 'Blue Rug' or 'Wilton': flat to the ground growth habit. Foliage is a great blue colour that is retained throughout the year.

These evergreens would work nicely with the evergreen/spruce theme you mentioned. If you want to control weeds from the outset, you might think about laying down landscape fabric prior to planting. That will also help to retain a little moisture in a very dry location.

Q. I recall some advice from past columns about wrapping pyramidal cedars in garden netting to prevent the tops from splitting in heavy wet snows. Now that I have cedars, I'm ready to pay attention. Do I wrap them for winter only, or do I leave the netting in place as the cedars grow? My cedars are Holmstrops and approximately 1.2 m tall.

A. The netting should be in place for winter and removed in spring. Having said that, you can leave the netting in place if you are shaping your cedars in a topiary form. Garden netting can be used to create interesting forms but should be removed after winter if you are not shaping the plants.

Q. I see pyramid cedars growing all over, the small and the tall. I have purchased, planted and pouted at the results when spring arrived— the cedars died! I purchased three 1.2 m cedars last spring, properly planted and well watered all summer. With fall, I covered the base with grass clippings and heaped leaves all around the base. I wrapped single ply jute over them, and when spring arrived and frost was out of the air and ground, I uncovered them. They all died. My neighbour planted four, with those same results.

I'm guessing it matters to some degree where the trees were shipped from and that northern BC would be better than some northern states (Washington). Also, the exposure to the elements and a sheltered south preferred. Well, my neighbour dug his out, but I did not! I painted mine! I took a sprig sample from another neighbour who had his planted on the same northeastern exposure as mine and went to the paint store to match a green elastomeric paint.

I used a spray gun with a large orifice that is used for spray undercoating or heavy viscose material. I taped a couple or cardboard cartons together for spray protection for the brick and sprayed away. Some who examine them still do not believe they are painted. It should last three or four years before a recoat is required; in the meantime, they require no care or water.

A. It never ceases to amaze me when it comes to the ingenuity of people. This one had me laughing out loud. If you can't get the thing to grow for you, just paint it green! This philosophy is taking hold in other areas. There are companies in the U.S. that actually offer lawn painting service. An example can be seen at www. alwaysgreengrasspainting.com.

Painting lawns is popular with realtors selling homes and with businesses that do not wish to go to the cost and effort of maintaining a lawn. When I received the email on painting cedars, I had to run it. Let's have a look at how one can help cedars make it through our winters without having to resort to the paint gun.

Cedars need to be watered in very well in the fall right up to freeze-up. If they are planted close to a foundation, you may have to give them some water during winter on a warm day, especially if there is little snow cover in the area they are planted. Erecting a burlap screen rather than wrapping the cedars is also a good idea to help them through winter. The screen should face the direction of the prevailing winter winds. Pound three long sticks into the ground in front of the plant, in the shape of a "V." Staple burlap to these sticks or pieces of wood as high as the plant is tall. This technique will keep the drying winds off the plant while allowing the evergreen to breathe, which does not happen if they are wrapped completely in burlap.

If you don't want to go to the effort of erecting the burlap screen, you can use a product called Wilt-Pruf. You can buy this product as a concentrate and mix it yourself for spraying on your cedars. It is a natural product made from tree sap. Wilt-Pruf helps keep the moisture from evaporating from cedars and other evergreens. Moisture loss in the dry winter winds often causes the browning of evergreens.

Make sure you follow the instructions listed on the bottle thoroughly, especially on when to apply this anti-dessicant. If you apply it too soon, you can damage the plants, so read the directions carefully. I mix according to directions and then apply it with a hand sprayer. I have the kind that has a pump built in to the top of the sprayer. It works great for applying the anti-dessicant, and if the nozzle plugs, which it might, just rinse it under hot water and you are good to go again.

The reader who wrote in even took the time to colour match the paint—I can see it now, designer colours for all trees and shrubs.

Q. We just put cedar bark chips around our lilacs. Will it harm them? They are about four years old. They did not bloom well this year, and we wondered if the mulch may have caused this condition? Could it be caused by trimming them last year after they had finished blooming?

A. The cedar chips will not harm the lilacs. Trimming the lilacs after they had bloomed last year was the perfect time to prune them. Lilacs bloom on the previous year's wood. Check to see if the plants are too close to a lawn where they may be receiving more nitrogen than they need. Fertilizing a lawn that is close to flowering shrubs or trees will often give the plants more nitrogen and will inhibit the formation of blooms. Instead, the plant will produce more leaves. The other concern that comes to mind is a lack of sun. Lilacs need four full hours of sun each day to bloom.

Q. What can you tell me about the new re-blooming lilac? Does it really bloom all summer, and will it survive our unpredictable weather?

A. I assume you are referring to the new lilac variety named 'Josee.' According to retailers, this lilac will bloom all summer long. Note that the first spring bloom is the showiest, and then it will bloom intermittently during summer right up to the first fall frost. The pink blooms stand out against the small, green, heart-shaped leaves. The plant will grow in full sun to partial shade and will reach 1.2–1.8 m in height. It is reported to be hardy to zone 2, which means that it should do fine in our area. However, having said that, I have not grown one of these myself nor have I heard of anyone else who has, so it remains to be seen how well it does here.

Note that other lilacs will rebloom. 'Miss Kim' is one such example. However, these lilacs have a major spring bloom and another bloom in mid-late summer and do not have the intermittent bloom that the variety 'Josee' does.

Q. I have two very large (1.3 m tall) globe cedars in my backyard. I am putting in a garden pool this year, and the cedars are right where I want to put the pool. They are beautiful plants, and I would hate to lose them, so I have decided to move them to a bed in the front. I want to do the move myself because getting a bobcat into the backyard is impossible. Do you think I can make such a move without killing the cedars? If so, do you have any tips that would help me?

A. Moving shrubs, trees or any plant comes with a certain amount of risk. A plant that goes into transplant shock can be difficult to save, but I have moved many such plants successfully and I'd be happy to share some tips that work for me. It does take some effort. First, the root system of these plants is fairly shallow but spreading. That makes it easy to dig out, but you have to be careful to make the rootball as large as possible. Try to take as much of the root system as you can without making the ball too heavy to handle. I recommend watering the area under the plant a few days before you plan to move it. The water will help the soil to stick to the roots. Moving a dry rootball can cause the soil to drop off the roots, exposing the roots and subjecting them to drying.

Wrap the ball with burlap to hold it together and slide a wheelbarrow under the plant. Roll the ball onto the wheelbarrow and make the move. Since you can visualize the size of the rootball now, dig the receiving hole to be twice as large as the rootball. Fill the bottom of the hole with a good quality compost and mix it in with the existing soil. Tamp it in place. Make sure the depth of the hole is the same as the depth of the rootball. The top of the rootball should sit at the same level with the soil as it did before.

Roll the ball and plant into the hole and have someone hold the plant upright. Ensure that it is straight and begin to fill in the hole with soil and compost mix, being careful to avoid creating any air pockets. Air pockets around the roots can actually kill the tree so tamp the soil down very well. I call this tamping the "one-legged tree dance" because I like to use one foot to stomp down the soil. Once the soil has been replaced I use a technique taught to me by a mentor I had in landscaping. Get your garden hose and stick it into the freshly packed soil. With the water running move the hose slowly up and down. Move the hose to a new spot and repeat working your way all around the rootball. This up-and-down motion while the water is running is great at eliminating any air pockets as well as watering the newly planted tree.

One last thing I like to do when moving cedars is to spray them with Wilt-Pruf. This natural product keeps the plant from losing too much moisture via transpiration. A plant that goes into shock can actually dry out completely by losing too much moisture, and cedars are very prone to losing moisture. Keep the plant very well watered for the rest of the spring and into summer. No need to fertilize. You just want it to start growing some roots.

Q. I have been planning my garden for next year and have always wanted to have a rose garden. My problem is that I have had terrible luck trying to grow hybrid tea roses. It has reached a point where I won't even look at them in the garden centres anymore. They grow fine and will even bloom, but I cannot get them through the winters. I have heard that Explorer roses are much better for our area, but I really know nothing about them. Can you please help me out with some information on these roses?

A. This subject is a favourite of mine. I am a big fan of these roses. The Explorer series of roses was developed to survive Canadian winters by Agriculture and Agri-Food Canada at the Morden Research Station in Manitoba. They are hardy down to −35° C with snow. The plants are disease resistant, require minimal pruning and will bloom throughout summer. They come in a wide variety of colours, sizes and forms, and many are fragrant.

John Cabot rose.

When I first started looking into Explorer roses, it was hard to find a definitive list. While the following list is not complete, it offers a good selection of roses to choose from:

- Alexander Mackenzie: medium red; base of petals light yellow; very hardy; disease resistant; 1.5 m by 1.2 m; good as a short climber

- Champlain: bright red; ever-blooming

- Charles Albanel: medium red; hardy; disease resistant; low growing

- David Thompson: red, profuse bloomer; hardy; blackspot resistant; compact
- De Montarville: new variety; upright growth habit reaching 1.2 m; good repeat blooms and disease resistance; deep pink buds open into mottled, medium pink, semi-double blooms
- Frontenac: deep pink, double blooms in clusters of 6–8; many flowers and good repeat bloomer; disease resistant; to 1.2 m
- Henry Hudson: white semi-double blooms, occasionally blushed pink if nights cool; fragrant, continuous bloomer;

J.P. Connell rose.

90 cm–1.2 m tall, 1.2 m or more wide
- Henry Kelsey: medium red; flowers freely and repeatedly; mildew resistant; can be used as a climber with branches reaching 1.8–2.4 m
- Jens Munk: double pink; low growing 1.2 m by 1.2 m; blackspot and mildew resistant
- John Cabot: dark pink to red, disease resistant; can climb up to 2 m
- John Davis: medium pink; free-flowering; good pillar rose; disease resistant; to 1.8 m
- John Franklin: dark red, fringed blooms, in clusters; continuous bloomer
- J.P. Connell: creamy white bloom with yellow centre borne singly or in clusters; almost thornless; vigorous; 90 cm–1.5 m; very hardy; my personal favourite.
- Lambert Closse: light to dark pink; fairly new introduction; hybrid tea–like blooms; flowers from June to September; resistant to blackspot and mildew; 90 cm by 90 cm
- Louis Jolliet: very full blooms, medium-pink flowers, in clusters; trailing habit; can be trained as a climber; continuous bloomer; hardy and disease resistant

William Baffin rose.

- Simon Fraser: medium-pink, single flowers early in the season, followed by semi-double flowers; upright growth habit; requires little pruning

- William Baffin: deep pink; yellow centre; hardy; free-flowering; mildew resistant

- William Booth: new introduction; deep red unopened bud changes to a medium red at the blossom stage and later fades to a light red in the fully opened flower; grows 1.2–1.5 m high and 1.5–1.8 m wide; excellent resistance to blackspot and powdery mildew

- Marie Victorin: introduced in 1999; can be used as a low climber to 1.5 m high and 1.2 m wide; deep peach buds born in clusters of 7 open into pale peach fading to pink, semi-double blossoms; resistant to blackspot and mildew; repeat bloomer throughout season

- Martin Frobisher: dainty, light pink blooms; grows to 1.5 m high; very hardy

- Royal Edward: medium-pink; semi-miniature, low-spreading rose; resistant to blackspot and powdery mildew

Q. I have a very small yard and am looking at growing some roses on trellises. I don't want to grow the tender types. Can you tell me what varieties would be hardy and how to grow them?

A. One aspect of gardening that is often overlooked is the vertical plane of gardening. That maybe even more true for the second-home landscape. Second homeowners tend to concentrate on the shrubs, trees and perennials that grow on lower levels. People tend to ignore the vertical plane. Climbing roses are an excellent choice when it comes to vertical gardening. These roses can be used to soften the lines of a home while adding colour and texture. A simple wooden trellis with a climbing rose can easily transform a drab view of

Hydrangea 'Annabelle.'

plain siding into a focal point. To me there is nothing worse than approaching a home and seeing a massive expanse of wall and siding.

Today, the Explorer series of roses include some very hardy and beautiful climbing roses that deserve more use in the second-home landscape. These plants are not the climbing roses of old. They tolerate many growing conditions and do not require a great deal of maintenance. Since roses are heavy feeders, you will need to fertilize for optimum performance. Use a fertilizer with a higher second number such as 15-30-15. You may also choose to use a slow-release granular fertilizer, which will keep nutrient levels more even and will free you from having to fertilize at regular intervals. Roses do need to be in full sun for at least six hours a day and will not perform well in semi-shaded or shaded locations.

If you are not sure how to display these roses properly, all you really need is a trellis, a wall or even a fence where the roses can be supported. Once established, these roses will basically look after themselves. The occasional pruning to maintain shape and a little fertilizer and water is all they need. For a striking effect, try growing a climber such as the pink William Baffin intertwined with a purple Jackmanii clematis. The effect can transform the drabbest siding into a work of art. Growing two varieties such as William Baffin and Henry Kelsey also creates a spectacular focal point.

Q. I am interested in adding three or four hydrangeas to a semi-shaded spot in my backyard. Which varieties would you recommend, and can you offer any help in how to grow these plants?

A. Hydrangeas are among the showiest summer-flowering shrubs in our area. They have huge flower heads that can reach 30 cm in size that last for up to three months. What makes them even more desirable is that the flower heads last through periods when few other shrubs are still blooming.

These plants prefer partial shade to sun, and soil preparation is critical. They prefer a soil that is rich in nutrients, moist and, above all, well drained. Keep the plant well watered, never allowing the soil to dry out. Because of the size of the heads, you may have to offer the plant support when it is blooming. Two varieties are well suited to growing in our area:

- 'Peegee' grows 1.5–1.8 m tall and wide. It has huge, pinkish-white, cone-shaped flowers up to 46 cm long and 30 cm wide.

- 'Annabelle' grows 60–90 cm tall and wide. The large flower heads are 15–30 cm across.

The exciting news is that a new variety called 'Endless Summer' was introduced a few years ago. This hydrangea blooms on both old and new wood and blooms in colour. Blooming on new wood means that even if the plant dies back to the crown or is pruned at the wrong time of year, it will still bloom.

Soil chemistry will determine the colour of the flowers. If the soil is acidic, the blooms will be blue. If the soil is alkaline, the blooms will

Hydrangea 'Endless Summer.'

be pink. You can amend the soil and turn it acidic by adding an acidifying fertilizer such as Miracid. You can also cut the flowers to enjoy them indoors because harvesting the blooms actually encourages more flower production.

'Endless Summer' is hardy to zone 4, but I have had one growing happily in my backyard for several years now. 'Endless Summer' grows 1–1.5 m high and wide, making it a perfect size for smaller gardens as a specimen plant or in larger gardens planted in a grouping.

In cold winter areas, here are a few tips for helping 'Endless Summer' to survive:

- Stop all applications of fertilizer after August 15 to acclimate the plant for winter.

- Keep the soil moist through the fall months until the ground is frozen.

- Cover the plant with a 10 cm layer of organic mulch (wood mulch, leaves and so on). There is no need to cover all stems to the tip or to cut them back.

- Covering should be done when fully dormant (around November 30) or at the same time you would cover perennials in your garden.

- In spring, uncover when the ground is no longer frozen.

Q. We planted a row of lilacs two years ago. They did bloom the last two springs, but the tips are not growing and seem to be dying back rather than showing new growth. The stems are okay, and the leaves seemed fine—just the tips were dying—and the lilacs are not growing at all. The plants get lots of light and are not overwatered. We laid down landscape fabric and put down a layer of rock mulch when they were planted. Any ideas as to what might be wrong?

A. The problem might be the rock mulch. Rock mulches sometimes create an anaerobic situation, meaning that air is not circulating under the rock. That would certainly account for the lack of growth and dieback of the tips. I would try removing the mulch and using an organic one such as shredded bark instead. Organic mulches are safer to use than rock or stone. Adding a little mulch each year will ensure that the optimal level is maintained as the original mulch settles and breaks down naturally.

Q. I have a well-established weeping caragana in a small back garden next to the deck. During the winter, I piled snow in this garden and around this shrub. My thinking was to retain the moisture that I was shovelling off the walkway and deck. To my dismay, I seem to have hindered rather than helped. The graft at the crown of the plant is cracked, and I can only assume that it's because of the weight of the melting snow. Can I somehow tape or close over the gap in the crack? It's about 5 cm long and 1 cm deep. Or is the plant a goner?

A. While your idea of using the snow for moisture and as a mulch was a very good one, how you pile the snow is very important. Snow is one of the best ways to help insulate plants during winter, and it also provides a good drink for the plant in spring. I, too, am guilty of sometimes forgetting what is under all that snow.

It is best to pile the snow around the base of the plant and even up the trunk or main stems, but try to avoid piling too much snow on the branches themselves. I think the plant can be saved. I have had good success with using a technique that I will share with you.

The determining factor on which technique to use is based on the caliper (diameter) of the trunk. If the diameter is still relatively small, in the order of 2.5–4 cm, taping the crack together should work. The key here is to have someone hold the crack together as tightly as possible while you do the taping. You might even resort to using a clamp—but use one that has rubber on the clamping surface to cushion the clamp against the trunk. Gently apply pressure until the crack is totally together. I recommend using electrical tape owing to its ability to flex while taping; this flex will help hold the crack together. Apply several layers of tape, making sure you totally cover the crack from top to bottom.Leave the tape in place through the growing season. If you notice the crack opening and the tape letting go, slightly reapply more tape. Check the crack in the fall by removing the tape. Hopefully you should see the wound mended.

If the trunk is larger than 4 cm, you may need to use a bolt system to hold it together. This simple but very effective procedure is used for cracks in larger shrubs and trees. I have found it particularly effective when repairing cracks in the crotch of trees. You will need a machine bolt to start with. How large a bolt will depend on the trunk caliper. You want to damage the trunk as little as possible and yet you want a bolt strong enough to do the job. For trunk calipers 4–7 cm, a bolt that is 0.5 cm in diameter will do. If the trunk is larger than that, look at a 1 cm diameter bolt. You will also need four washers to fit on the bolt and one nut for the bolt.

Choose a drill bit of the same diameter as the bolt and drill a hole through the trunk right through the middle of the crack. Put two washers on the bolt and insert the bolt through the hole you have drilled. Put on the last two washers and the nut and begin tightening the bolt. Stop tightening once the first washer has entered the bark to a point where it is even with the bark. The beauty of this repair is that that is all you will ever have to do. The crack should heal and eventually the trunk will grow around the bolt and nut. Do not remove the bolt even though the crack appears to have healed. The plant will have grown around the bolt inside the trunk sealing it in place. Trying to remove it will only damage the plant.

Q. I have a Therese Bugnet rose that was planted in 2001. The main plant appears to be at least 90 percent dead. However, there are about six little bushes around the main one. I think that I would like to remove the original big bush and keep the babies. Should I move them or leave them where they are? They would kind of be in a semi-circle, or would they actually be attached to the original plant? Is this normal for roses? None of my other ones have done anything like it before. Also, I have a Polar Star that is just right out of control and since it is so thorny it is hard to deal with. If I can manage to get it out of there how long should I wait to plant another plant in that spot and can you plant a rose in a rose hole or should you plant a different type of plant there?

A. Therese Bugnet rose has its own root, meaning that it has not been grafted onto another rose rootstock. By having its own root stock, the suckers you describe will all be true to the original plant. I would dig out the suckers. They are connected to the old root but should come off easily. I would then remove the old root that has died or is dying and then choose the strongest of the "babies" to plant in the same spot that the old root occupied. Many roses sucker in the fashion that you described.

Planting another rose in the same spot is just fine, but amend the soil with lots of organic matter prior to planting the new rose. You can plant in the same spot immediately.

I have a hint about handling the thorny rose. Use newspapers to handle the stems. Wrap several thicknesses of newspaper around the stem. That will definitely help in avoiding being skewered by the thorns.

Questions and Answers: Pruning Trees

Q. I planted a Harcourt dwarf apple tree last fall. It is about 2.4 m tall. I would like it to be under 3.5 m in height after five years. It has 10 branches, with one going straight up the centre. The greenhouse suggested I cut the whole top off and leave only five branches on the tree. If I do that, the tree would be about 1.2 m tall. Is that a good thing to do to keep the apple tree short? Should I do it in April?

A. I have always kept my fruit trees under 3.5 m in height. In fact, I prefer mine to be no more than 2.4 m tall. I find it much easier to reach the fruit at harvest time and to prune the tree. So my recommendation is that, yes, keeping the apple tree small is a good choice. The advice you received at the greenhouse was good. By removing the leader (main centre branch), you will encourage the tree to remain smaller while encouraging the tree to fill out. The tree will continue to get a little taller than the 1.2 m you mentioned. Remember that the trunk will continue to grow vertically. This growth will certainly not be as rapid as it would have been with an intact leader, nor will it reach its normal height, but you may end up with a tree that is around 2.4 m tall.

Pruning fruit trees such as apples is best done in early spring, but if you need to prune for shape, you can also do so in late summer (August). I prune my apples to keep the shape I want in the summer. I also like to remove any vegetative growth in the summer (water sprouts) that may be stealing vigour from the tree.

One of the best websites I have ever seen on pruning and training apple trees is available on the Ecological Agriculture projects website at McGill University: www.eap.mcgill.ca/CPTFP_7.htm.

Q. We have a grafted apple tree in our backyard, which has been growing for the past eight or nine years. This past spring we pruned it according to instructions through your column. It is doing fine, but now there are numerous "water shoots"—small shoots 25–30 cm long—sprouting from many of the branches. Should they be cut off, trimmed back or just ignored?

A. Sometimes, when a tree is pruned back, it will respond to the pruning by sending out water sprouts. These fast-growing shoots can be identified easily as they will grow straight up and will originate from the trunk or the scaffold limbs. They are usually non-productive growths and should be removed. You can prune them off without harming the tree.

Q. Is it too late to prune an apple tree in March to get rid of some of the "interior" branches and last year's growth (i.e., long slender branch extensions)?

A. March is an excellent time to be pruning apple trees. I was out looking at mine yesterday and the buds are swelling nicely but nothing has started to open yet. Pruning to "open up" the interior of the apple tree is an excellent idea. It helps with air circulation and makes for a healthier plant. Many people don't understand that air circulation makes a huge impact on how a plant or tree grows or its health. Having good airflow eliminates many disease and insect problems as well.

Q. We have a Thunderchild tree that we planted three summers ago. We noticed that all kinds of shoots are pushing through the ground...it almost looks like a bush surrounding the base of the tree. Is there anything we should do with these shoots or do we just let them grow? By the end of the summer, some of them were 90 cm tall.

A. You should prune back the suckers growing at the base of your Thunderchild flowering crab apple. Cut them down right to ground level. Letting them grow takes energy away from the main plant. Simply take a sharp pair of pruners and cut off the suckers. There is nothing that you can do to prevent this growth.

Q. I have a question about my Amur maple. When is it a good time to be pruned? I read that it should be done in the middle of July because that's when the sap has stopped running. Then I read a gardening article that says it can be pruned in February or March before the buds appear. Could you please provide clarification? It would be great if I can do it now since I can see the branches better, and the weather we are having is nice enough to do it.

A. My first choice would to prune the maple in mid-to late summer, i.e., July. If you prune in February or March, you run the risk of having the sap start running before the pruning wound has had a chance to heal. This "bleeding" of sap could weaken the tree, and it may even cause its death.

Of all the maples, the Amur maple *(Acer ginnala)* requires the least amount of pruning. All you need to look for is any dead or injured branches. Also, remove any branches that affect the appearance of the tree, including any branches that are rubbing against each other or are at unnatural angles. With my Amur maple, I always like to remove the long branches that reach skyward. I cut them back by one-quarter to one-third to encourage the plant to become more full.

Q. Could you tell me when is the best time to prune my Evans cherry tree and Pembina plum that is now three years old? The plum tree has a few plums this year, and my cherry tree is loaded, but they both have grown branches up to 60 cm long this season. Also, on my cherry tree, some of the fruit turns half red then falls off. Is that the tree's way of culling fruit it can't handle?

A. The best time to prune the plum and cherry is early in spring before the buds start to open. However, if the branches are getting unruly, it will not hurt the trees to prune back the branches now. In fact, I like to prune my apple trees and other fruit trees in August because I can see which branches need attention when the tree has leaves. As for the dropping of the fruit, yes, if the tree has a lot of fruit, a certain amount of "culling" is done by the tree. It is nothing to be concerned about as long as you don't start losing too much fruit.

Questions and Answers: Pruning Shrubs

Q. I've heard that the pruning of lilac trees has to be done at a different time of year and the way in which it is done is also different from fruit trees, spruce trees, etc. Is that true, and if so, would you know how and when it is done?

A. Lilacs should be pruned immediately after they finish blooming in the spring. If you prune before they bloom, you will be removing the wood on which the plant will bloom. When you prune after the bloom, make sure the first thing you do is remove all of the spent blossoms. That keeps the plant from forming seeds and encourages the plant to form buds for next year. Trimming out larger stems from the centre of the plant will help to increase air circulation. While you are at it, cut off any suckers or shoots that are coming from ground level. Many gardeners "top off" their lilacs, meaning they

flatten the top by removing all the top growth. Doing this has a tendency to reduce the vigour of the plant. If you have an old lilac that is in need of reconditioning, I recommend doing this over a three-year period. Cut back one-third of the old branches to just above the soil level. Allow the new growth to survive the next year while you remove another third of the older branches and so on.

Q. I have several gold mound and gold flame spireas in my yard. I would like to know just how much they can be pruned in the fall. I generally prune them 15–23 cm but wonder if a deeper pruning might be better for them.

A. For spring blooming shrubs such as spireas, avoid removing too much growth in the fall—these shrubs will bloom on this the past year's wood. With these it is best to do any dramatic pruning in the spring following their blooming period.

Q. Our church has pink shrub roses—name unknown—growing on the east side of the building. They are up to 1.8 m tall, need staking and have only a few blooms. Can we trim them down? If so, how much, and what time of the year would be best for a more compact growth and to encourage blooming?

A. The best time to prune the roses is in the spring before they bud out. My rule of thumb when pruning back is

Mugo pine.

to cut one-quarter. So in your case, you would be cutting off 46 cm. I'm a little concerned that the roses may not be getting enough sun on the east side of the building, and that may be why they are not blooming well and going lanky. They should be getting at least six hours of sun a day to perform at their best.

Q. I have a mugo pine that in the past I have kept pruned by trimming the new candles in half as recommended. But as of late, I have been negligent, and it is growing too large. How can I prune it back to a more preferred size without completely destroying it?

A. The best way to keep this plant under control is to remove the new growth (candles) in the spring, but you can also carefully prune the plant. When you prune back each branch make sure that you do not cut into the area on the branch where there are no needles. The pine will not grow back on the inside where there are no needles.

Q. Potentilla! Not my favourite shrub, but because the deer and elk have the same attitude toward potentilla, I am beginning to like it. We live in Jasper and are attempting to xeriscape our front yard. We have several potentilla bushes, some planted last year and more this year. They are doing very well and I would like some information regarding pruning. I see bushes

229

everywhere in Jasper that are large, appear to be overgrown and do not bloom very profusely. I would appreciate any advice you could give me or could you suggest a book with information specific to potentillas?

A. Potentillas have to be one of the most maligned shrubs in the landscaping repertoire and part of the reason for the poor reputation is that many homeowners are not pruning them correctly. Potentilla should be pruned in the early spring before they show any signs of new or emerging growth. You should remove the oldest stems right to the ground every spring. Doing so will encourage the plants to send out new growth keeping the entire plant in continuous blooms as well as encouraging new growth.

The overgrown specimens you refer to are in serious need of being cut back right to the ground to allow the plant to start all over again. Once the new growth starts, it is easier to keep them pruned correctly. A potentilla that is pruned correctly can be a beautiful thing that offers continuous bloom over most of the growing season. You can't say that about many other shrubs. If you detect that I am a potentilla fan you are right. For applications such as yours where animals can be a problem or in xeriscapes they are a perfect addition to the landscape.

Q. I would appreciate knowing if I can trim back low-lying junipers and golden pfitzers without killing or damaging them. I originally planted them when they were small in our front yard (approximately 24 years ago). They primarily face south and west as they are planted in the shape of the capital letter J. The long part of the J is in front of a brick planter and the curled part in front of a bay window. The junipers are approximately 1.2–1.3 m high in places, and they are higher than the planter. I understand that these shrubs remain brown underneath and only produce green growth from the top areas. I would like to trim approximately 30–46 cm off the tops and shape them. If it is possible, is the winter the time to be doing this before spring sets in?

A. Pruning junipers takes a little time and patience. Many gardeners just take the shears to the juniper. The problem with this method is that it creates a dense growth of foliage on the plant's exterior. This growth then shades the interior growth, and the interior begins to turn brown and show dieback.

The best method is to prune each individual branch back to an upward-facing branch, thus creating a plant that has a natural look to it. With junipers, you want to create a look where the base of the shrub is wider than the top. That keeps the top from

Dwarf Korean lilac flowers.

shading the base and causing the dieback.

You are quite right that the top is only going to produce the green growth and that any areas on the base that have died back will remain so. Sometimes you can pull branches over to fill a bare spot and tie it in place with wire. It is really quite easy to do and can save a juniper that has lost its aesthetic appeal.

You can prune the shrub in winter, but I would not prune on days where the temperature is below zero. Ideally, the best time to prune is in early spring before any new growth has started.

Q. I have a dwarf Korean lilac hedge that is 16 years old. It is 1.8 m tall, 1.5 m wide and has gotten wider than I would like it to be. It is on the east side of the house and up against the property fence, which is 1.8 m tall. If I prune 25 cm or so off the side of the hedge, will it fully leaf out on the side or will it be rather barren? The present 1.8 m height is fine.

A. Because you are removing the actively growing tips of the plants when you prune, the plants will start off in the spring a little sparse. However, it will not take long for the plants to send out new growth and new leaves. You should also know that since lilacs bloom on last year's wood, the amount of bloom will be considerably reduced as well.

Q. I have two large Nanking cherry bushes, I am assuming they were planted when the house was built 30 some years ago. They do produce some berries, but they are sparse and are mainly on the new growth—extremely difficult to pick. What is the best way to prune and rejuvenate them? They are lovely when they bloom, and I would think if they were pruned and happy, they would be absolutely spectacular.

A. The shrubs can be rejuvenated with pruning, but it will take a little effort. What is happening right now is that the plant has been allowed to go "wild," which means it spends most of

Nanking cherry tree.

its energy in producing new growth rather than producing fruit. It sounds as if the shrubs are tall enough to make picking the fruit at the very top difficult at best. You need to prune the shrubs back to approximately 1.5–1.8 m tall. That should make harvesting the fruit much easier. Also, by cutting the plant back drastically, you will give it new energy.

If the shrubs are quite a bit taller than 1.5–1.8 m, you may have to prune back in stages. In other words, if you are looking at a shrub that is 2.7–3 m tall, cut the shrub back to 2 m this year and 1.5 m the following year. Doing so will help to prevent

the plant from going into shock. In addition to pruning back the height of the shrub, you may want to look at containing the width as well. The same rules apply to the width in terms of shock. Once you have cut back the plant to the desired dimension, the next step is to remove some of the branches that have grown into the centre of the plant. It is essential to have good air circulation in the plant. If it is clogged with many small branches at the centre, then air will not move well through the plant. Remove most of the branches in the centre of the plant, leaving mostly the strong stems and branches that form the framework of the plant.

Prune the shrubs this spring before they leaf out. In addition to the pruning, I would apply a well-balanced fertilizer such as 10-10-10 or 20-20-20 around the tree. You can use fruit tree spikes if you like. Keep the tree well watered this year, and you should be rewarded with a good crop of cherries the following year.

Q. My question is when and how to prune a mock orange. It is about eight years old and is really looking unruly. It has many small branches coming from the bottom.

A. Some types of mock orange can sucker quite a bit. These suckers, if left unpruned, can make a shrub look scraggly. Prune mock orange after they have finished blooming. Remove all of the suckers at the base of the plant. A good rule of thumb is that as soon as you see a sucker, cut it off. Letting it grow just means the plant sends energy to the process of growing the sucker rather than directing it toward more useful enterprises. Prune out the centre of the plant as well. Remove any dead or diseased branches or branches that are rubbing against other branches.

If the plant is getting too tall or too wide, don't be afraid to cut it back to within the parameters you have chosen. Pruning, even if dramatic, will not harm the plant, and in many cases, it is beneficial. Use your "mind's eye" to prune the shrub into the shape you want.

Ruffled flowers of a mock orange plant.

For more on trees and shrubs, see also:

p. 35 What trees will tolerate acidic conditions and grow quickly?

p. 39 How do I redo the soil around my shrubs?

p. 119 Is October too late to plant trees and shrubs?

p. 144 What does it mean to give my trees a "good soaking" in fall?

p. 146 Why won't anything grow underneath our trees?

Appendix: Botanical Names

I have heard some people in the plant industry complain about the use of botanical, or Latin, names for plants. Frankly, I am at a loss to try to understand where these people are coming from. The genus, species and variety of a botanical name helps to avoid the confusion that common names often bring. Common names not only vary from one province to another but also can vary from one greenhouse to another.

A good example is bluebells. The common name bluebell leads to nothing but confusion. Is the name referring to *Mertensia virginica* or *Mertensia ciliata* or *Scilla nonscripta* or *Campanula glomerata*, which are all types of bluebells? The use of botanical names eliminates all confusion and allows gardeners across the world or across the street to communicate on the same terms. With the plant *Heuchera* 'Frosted Violet,' *Heuchera* is the Latin genus and 'Frosted Violet' the variety. The varieties are often descriptive of the plant itself, while the Latin name allows the buyer to know exactly what plant they are buying.

I am in favour of using a combination of common names and Latin. In this book I have tried to use Latin names where appropriate, but you may see some examples such as the hosta that have lost the capitals and italics on the genus name of the plant, because hosta is used as both the Latin genus and the common name in many cases.

Index

Photo by Julie Whinn.

Jerry Filipski credits his father as his gardening inspiration, and believes that gardening is an art. His beginnings were all about gardening books, courses and design diplomas, devouring all the information he could so he could use his art form effectively. In his years as a landscape contractor he learned that there is no right and wrong in landscape design: it's all about the eye of the beholder.

With Jerry's passion for gardening and love of solving problems, he has been able to help other gardeners for nearly 20 years as the gardening columnist for the *Edmonton Journal*. Since retiring from the Biological Sciences Department at the University of Alberta, Jerry and his garden are now one.